Grant Carstairs
Knocknairn
Dunira Street
Comrie
Perthshire
PH6 2LJ

The ULTIMATE Book of
ORGANIZING
Hints & Tips

The ULTIMATE Book of
ORGANIZING
Hints & Tips

Cassandra Kent

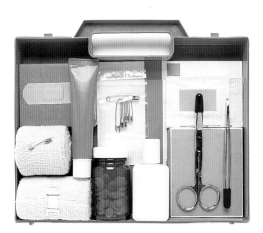

DORLING KINDERSLEY

LONDON • NEW YORK • SYDNEY • MOSCOW

A DORLING KINDERSLEY BOOK

Project Editor Katie John
Project Art Editor Ellen Woodward
Editor Samantha Gray
Designer Helen Benfield
Series Art Editor Jayne Jones
Production Controller Alison Jones
DTP Designer Jason Little

Managing Editor Stephanie Jackson
Managing Art Editor Nigel Duffield
Senior Managing Editor Krystyna Mayer
Senior Managing Art Editor Lynne Brown

First published in Great Britain in 1997
by Dorling Kindersley Limited,
9 Henrietta Street,
London WC2E 8PS

Copyright © 1997
Dorling Kindersley Limited, London

Visit us on the World Wide Web at
http://www.dk.com

A CIP catalogue record for this book is available
from the British Library

ISBN 0 7513 0450 6

Reproduced by Chroma Graphics, Singapore
Printed and bound in Italy by Lego

CONTENTS

INTRODUCTION 6

USING THIS BOOK   6
SETTING UP SYSTEMS   8

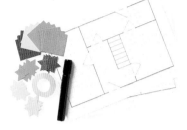

UTILIZING SPACE 10

PLANNING ROOM BY ROOM   11
USING STORAGE SPACE   18
STORING SPECIAL ITEMS   23
SORTING OUT STORAGE   26

SETTING UP ROUTINES 28

CLEANING THE HOME   29
ORGANIZING LAUNDRY   35
PLANNING FOR DECORATING   37
MAINTAINING THE HOME   43
ENSURING SECURITY AND SAFETY   46

Preparing Food 48

Maintaining a Kitchen	50
Buying Food and Other Goods	52
Organizing Food Stores	54
Preserving and Chilling Food	56
Cooking Economically	60
Entertaining Guests	62

Structuring Work 66

Setting Up a Home Office	67
Managing Work Time	71
Communicating Effectively	74
Keeping Records	76

Running a Household 78

Organizing Personal Care	79
Organizing Childcare	82
Catering for Special Needs	87
Arranging Medical Care	89
Planning Petcare	92
Maintaining Family Transport	94
Planning Special Events	96
Dealing with Crises	98

Planning Travel 100

Preparing for Travel	101
Packing Efficiently	104
Planning a Journey	108
Coping in All Situations	112

Moving Home 118

Preparing to Move	119
Sorting and Packing	120
Carrying Out a Move	125
Moving In	127
Sharing Your Home	129

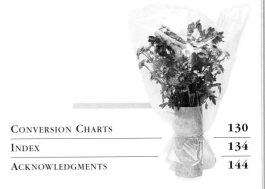

Conversion Charts	130
Index	134
Acknowledgments	144

INTRODUCTION

T*HE KEY TO SUCCESSFUL ORGANIZATION lies in a few simple, effective techniques. This book contains helpful tips and ideas for streamlining every area of your life. By following the advice in this book, you can take the stress out of everyday tasks and free yourself to make the most of your time.*

USING THIS BOOK

ORGANIZING YOUR ENVIRONMENT

Creating a well-planned environment is the first step to an organized lifestyle. *Utilizing Space* explains how to lay out rooms in your home so that you can keep items tidily and find them easily. In this chapter you will find room plans that show sample rooms and illustrate how to make the most of storage spaces. To keep your home clean and in good repair, it helps to set up easy-to-follow routines. *Setting Up Routines* describes how to plan household tasks so that you, or other members of your household, can carry them out efficiently. In *Preparing Foods*, there is also advice on shopping for foods, organizing food stores, cooking, and entertaining.

Pre-packing tablets
To learn exactly how to plan regular doses of tablets for a week in advance, turn to page 89.

Subdividing shelves
To see how to divide kitchen shelf space effectively in a shared home, turn to page 129.

MANAGING WORK AND A HOUSEHOLD

Organizing your work and home life efficiently requires initial thought and planning, but the rewards are that you will be able to manage your time effectively and be well prepared for any event or crisis. *Structuring Work* sets out simple techniques for keeping track of work, managing time effectively, and meeting deadlines. In *Running a Household* there is lots of practical information on every aspect of organizing personal and family life, such as advice on childcare, medical care, planning special events, and dealing with any crises that may arise.

Travelling and Moving Home

Potentially stressful events such as travelling and moving home can be managed with relative ease if you plan each stage carefully beforehand. *Planning Travel* describes the practical steps that you can take to ensure that you have prepared properly for the journey and packed all the items that you will need. This chapter also provides tips on how to protect your luggage and your home when you go away. In *Moving Home* there is all the information you will need on preparing to move, packing your possessions, keeping them safe when you transfer them to a new home, and moving in.

Keeping socks together
To find out how to secure pairs of socks so that you will not lose them when they are laundered, see page 35.

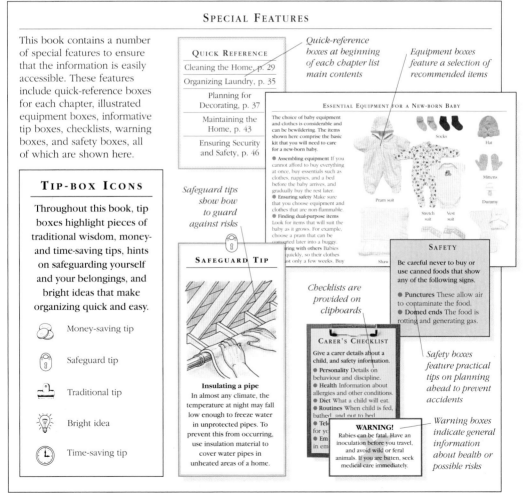

SPECIAL FEATURES

This book contains a number of special features to ensure that the information is easily accessible. These features include quick-reference boxes for each chapter, illustrated equipment boxes, informative tip boxes, checklists, warning boxes, and safety boxes, all of which are shown here.

Quick-reference boxes at beginning of each chapter list main contents

Equipment boxes feature a selection of recommended items

QUICK REFERENCE	
Cleaning the Home, p. 29	
Organizing Laundry, p. 35	
Planning for Decorating, p. 37	
Maintaining the Home, p. 43	
Ensuring Security and Safety, p. 46	

ESSENTIAL EQUIPMENT FOR A NEW-BORN BABY

The choice of baby equipment and clothes is considerable and can be bewildering. The items shown here comprise the basic kit that you will need to care for a new-born baby.

● **Assembling equipment** If you cannot afford to buy everything at once, buy essentials such as clothes, nappies, and a cot before the baby arrives, and gradually buy the rest later.
● **Ensuring safety** Make sure that you choose equipment and clothes that are non-flammable.
● **Finding dual-purpose items** Look for items that will suit the baby as it grows. For example, choose a pram that can be converted later into a buggy.
● **Purchasing with others** Babies grow quickly, so their clothes last only a few weeks. Buy . . .

Socks

Hat

Mittens

Pram suit

Dummy

Stretch suit

Vest suit

Shawl

TIP-BOX ICONS

Throughout this book, tip boxes highlight pieces of traditional wisdom, money- and time-saving tips, hints on safeguarding yourself and your belongings, and bright ideas that make organizing quick and easy.

Money-saving tip

Safeguard tip

Traditional tip

Bright idea

Time-saving tip

Safeguard tips show how to guard against risks

SAFEGUARD TIP

Insulating a pipe
In almost any climate, the temperature at night may fall low enough to freeze water in unprotected pipes. To prevent this from occurring, use insulation material to cover water pipes in unheated areas of a home.

Checklists are provided on clipboards

CARER'S CHECKLIST
Give a carer details about a child, and safety information.
● **Personality** Details on behaviour and discipline.
● **Health** Information about allergies and other conditions.
● **Diet** What a child will eat.
● **Routines** When child is fed, bathed, and put to bed.
● Tel . . . for y . . .
● Em . . . in em . . .

SAFETY
Be careful never to buy or use canned foods that show any of the following signs.

● **Punctures** These allow air to contaminate the food.
● **Domed ends** The food is rotting and generating gas.

Safety boxes feature practical tips on planning ahead to prevent accidents

WARNING!
Rabies can be fatal. Have an inoculation before you travel, and avoid wild or feral animals. If you are bitten, seek medical care immediately.

Warning boxes indicate general information about health or possible risks

MANAGING TIME EFFECTIVELY

By planning your use of time, you will be able to achieve a great deal without undue effort. For housework or routine office tasks, arrange the jobs so that you can carry out several in the same block of time. Write lists of the tasks to be done each day, so that you will remember to do all of them. For complex operations such as planning a wedding or moving house, you will need to plan a detailed schedule well in advance. You can do this easily by writing a countdown list, which gives a number of tasks to be done each day.

Using a family organizer
If you have a family, you will need to plan their time as well as your own. Make an organizer that the whole family can use.

MAKING AND ADAPTING EQUIPMENT

Many people are concerned about saving money and cutting down on waste. You can achieve both of these aims if you reuse waste materials in your home. Adapt suitable items to create useful and eye-catching equipment. For example, cut up an empty plastic bottle to hold cleaning brushes, or make an empty detergent box into a container for files. You can also transform old clothes or make equipment from inexpensive items. For example, make pockets in an old apron for holding small objects, or turn a length of net curtain into a simple mosquito net.

Making a knife roll
For storing kitchen knives, make a canvas roll, which can be just as effective as an expensive knife block or magnetic rack.

ADOPTING GOOD HABITS

Once you have planned routines for organizing time and space, you will need to keep to these routines so that your life will run smoothly. You can make this easy for yourself by arranging equipment in a logical order, and by making time each day to plan the next day's activities. These tasks will soon become habits, and you will be able to carry them out almost without effort. If you share your home with other people, teach them to follow these routines, so that they also benefit from learning good practices.

Tidying a desk drawer
To keep office stationery tidy and accessible, use a plastic cutlery holder to separate different items.

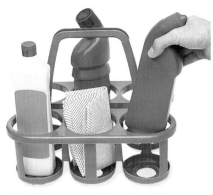

Making up a cleaning kit
Cleaning will be easy if you have the correct equipment to hand. Use a container with a handle, such as this plastic bottle carrier, so that you can carry items with you as you work.

FINDING EASY WAYS TO WORK
You will work best if you are comfortable and mentally relaxed. To make your work quick and easy, have the correct materials ready for use. Take care to renew supplies of equipment before they run out completely. When you plan a schedule of tasks, allow yourself only as much work as you know that you will do in a set time. Work at the best time of day for you, whether that is in the morning or late in the day.

CARING FOR YOUR HOUSEHOLD
As well as organizing yourself, you may have to take care of children, pets, or even houseplants. Plan your home so that it is safe for children, and involve them in household tasks in a way that will be fun for them. If you have pets, make sure that you have the time and money to care for them properly. Take special care of children and pets when you go on holiday or move home. Plants may not need a lot of attention, but be sure to leave them with adequate water when you go away, and protect them during a move.

Packing plants for travel
Cover plants completely with clear plastic so that they retain moisture during a journey.

CREATING LOGS FOR PLANNING TASKS

This book gives tips on making and using logs so that you can plan tasks easily. File copies of each type of log, and keep the files together in one place.

CLEANING LOG
On page 34 you can find out how to organize a series of tasks for a thorough cleaning session in your home.

DECORATING LOG
On page 38 you can discover how to collect samples of materials and order them so that you can plan a complete home decorating scheme.

HOME MAINTENANCE LOG
On page 45 you can learn how to plan a series of general maintenance checks that you can make on the structure and systems in your home.

WORK LOG
On page 73 you can discover how to schedule and simplify a variety of common work tasks.

FAMILY HEALTH LOG
On page 91 you can learn how to create a comprehensive medical record for yourself and all of your family.

Keep all papers together in a file

UTILIZING SPACE

QUICK REFERENCE

Planning Room by
Room, p. 11

Using Storage
Space, p. 18

Storing Special
Items, p. 23

Sorting Out
Storage, p. 26

*T*HERE ARE NO SET RULES *for organizing your own home. How you plan the layout of your home will depend on the space available, the number of people living there, their ages and states of health, and your own individual taste. Remember to allow enough space for people to move freely between different rooms or areas, and ensure that you organize all storage spaces efficiently to minimize clutter.*

MAKING THE MOST OF ROOMS IN A HOME

Make sure that the overall plan of your home includes enough space for everyone's possessions and activities. Before planning a layout for each room, consider the amount of available space and the locations of windows, doors, power points, and radiators. Organize the rooms so that any areas that are used for related purposes, such as a kitchen and a dining room, are close to each other.

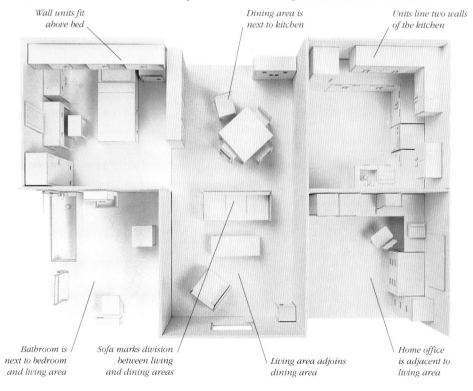

Wall units fit above bed

Dining area is next to kitchen

Units line two walls of the kitchen

Bathroom is next to bedroom and living area

Sofa marks division between living and dining areas

Living area adjoins dining area

Home office is adjacent to living area

PLANNING ROOM BY ROOM

YOU CAN REARRANGE THE FURNITURE in your home at any time, either to organize storage space more efficiently or simply for a change of surroundings. Before starting, consider the structure and function of each room, and plan what to do.

MAKING THE MOST OF STRUCTURE

While you cannot easily change the design of your home, you should be able to make the most of the rooms as they are. Check that your home utilizes energy efficiently. Plan the use of the available space by considering different layouts for the furniture in each room.

MONEY-SAVING TIP

Insulating a carpet

For an economical alternative to underfelt, clean a hard floor, then put down a thick layer of newspaper, overlapping the sheets. Lay the carpet over the newspaper.

MAXIMIZING WARMTH

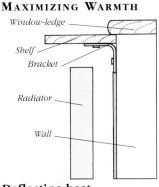

Window-ledge
Shelf
Bracket
Radiator
Wall

Deflecting heat

Where a radiator is fitted under a window, fit a shelf between it and the window, directly beneath the ledge. This will deflect heat into the room so that it does not escape through the glass.

ADDING INSULATION

● **Blocking out draughts** Seal gaps around windows and doors to save heat. Ensure that rooms are well ventilated to prevent condensation.
● **Fitting double glazing** If you cannot afford to fit double glazing in every room, then concentrate on rooms that face away from the sun.
● **Insulating a roof** Fit roof insulation to trap the heat that rises through the house.
● **Protecting a water tank** Do not lay insulation under a water tank in a roof. Allow warm air rising from the rooms below to keep the water from freezing, and insulate the tank itself.

MAKING A FURNITURE FLOOR PLAN

By making a floor plan, you can work out where to put furniture if you are reorganizing rooms. You can also make one to use if you move house (see p. 124).

● **Positioning furniture** Use a floor plan to find the best place for each item of furniture. Bear in mind practical considerations. For example, do not put wooden or upholstered furniture in direct sunlight. The light may bleach wood and fade fabrics.
● **Laying out a living room** Place all the seating within reach of low tables. If you have audio equipment or a television in the room, make sure that all the seating allows easy access to it.

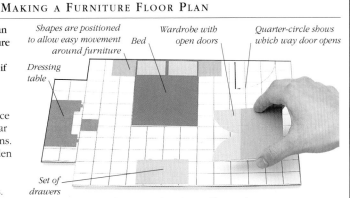

Shapes are positioned to allow easy movement around furniture
Wardrobe with open doors
Quarter-circle shows which way door opens
Bed
Dressing table
Set of drawers

Constructing and using a furniture floor plan

On squared paper, make a plan for a room or a floor, using a scale such as 1:20. Mark the positions of windows, doors, power points, and radiators. Cut shapes from thin card, to the same scale as your plan, to represent pieces of furniture. Label each one. Fix them to the plan with spray glue so that you can reposition them if you change your mind.

PLANNING A KITCHEN

Organize a kitchen for safety and ease of use. Decide on your preferred layout, and adjust this to fit in with the existing structure of your kitchen. If you are fitting a new kitchen, check safety and hygiene regulations with your local environmental health authority.

BASING A KITCHEN LAYOUT ON A TRIANGLE

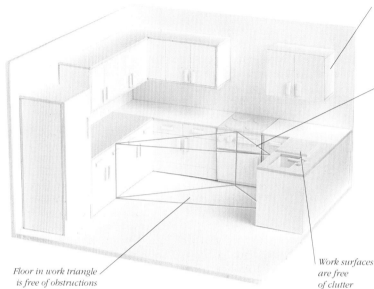

High-level units are shallow to allow easy access to back of work surface

Triangle shows clear paths between frequently used areas of kitchen

Floor in work triangle is free of obstructions

Work surfaces are free of clutter

Planning a layout
The cooker, sink, and refrigerator, and the work surfaces next to them, are the most frequently used areas in a kitchen. The paths between these areas often form a triangle. For easy access, keep this triangle clear.

SAVING SPACE IN A KITCHEN

By using space effectively you can maximize storage and leave plenty of room for work. Keep everyday items together and within easy reach of the cooker and work surfaces. Store as much as possible in the available space. Stack utensils, and hang items from a ceiling.

STACKING EQUIPMENT
● **Storing saucepans** Keep a set of saucepans on a narrow, vertical stacking rack.
● **Organizing crockery** Stack plates and saucers on plastic-coated racks with different-sized shelves. Put the racks in any corners of work surfaces that cannot be used for work.
● **Grouping bowls and tins** Store different-sized bowls and cooking tins one inside the other to take up a minimum of space. Leave room around them so that you can remove and replace them easily.
● **Arranging cleaning items** Use stackable plastic baskets to hold small cleaning items such as scourers and cloths.

HANGING POTS & PANS FROM A CEILING

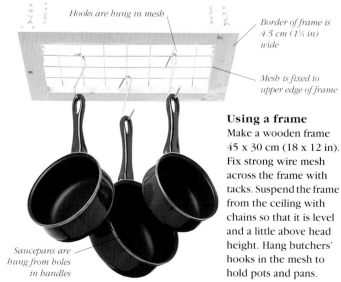

Hooks are hung in mesh

Border of frame is 4.5 cm (1¾ in) wide

Mesh is fixed to upper edge of frame

Saucepans are hung from holes in handles

Using a frame
Make a wooden frame 45 x 30 cm (18 x 12 in). Fix strong wire mesh across the frame with tacks. Suspend the frame from the ceiling with chains so that it is level and a little above head height. Hang butchers' hooks in the mesh to hold pots and pans.

ORGANIZING STORAGE IN A KITCHEN

Making the best use of storage spaces and using space-saving devices in a kitchen will allow you to keep worktops clear. You can buy specialized items that enable you to keep a lot of equipment in a particular place, or you can easily modify a kitchen area yourself.

UTILIZING DRAWERS

Adapting a drawer
To create an extra work surface, measure the depth of a chopping board, and fix wooden battens in a kitchen drawer at this depth. To use the surface, lay the board on the battens. You can keep items in the drawer even while you are using it as a work surface.

UTILIZING WALL AREAS
● **Holding rolls** Hang paper towel holders on a wall to store materials on rolls such as paper towels and clingfilm.

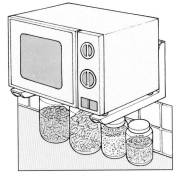

Fitting a microwave oven
Mount a microwave oven on a wall using strong metal brackets. Check that the oven is at an appropriate height for everyone who uses it. Use the work surface beneath for storing jars of food.

KEEPING AREAS CLEAR
● **Reducing clutter** Use work surfaces to store only those items that you use constantly. Group the items together. For example, put wooden spoons and spatulas in a large jar.
● **Using wall space** Fix cup hooks to walls under shelves or high-level units. Hang lightweight items such as ladles and sieves from the hooks.
● **Using a peg board** Fix a peg board to a wall, then hang small items from the pegs.
● **Holding recipe books** Fold a piece of clear polythene in half, then fix the back and edges to a wall near a cooker. Leave the top open to form a pocket. Put open recipe books in the pocket while you are using them to leave the work surface clear for cooking.

HIDING WASTE BINS

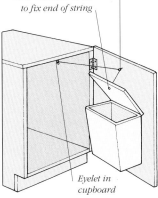

Eyelet on door is directly above hole in lid

Hole is drilled in lid to fix end of string

Eyelet in cupboard

Fixing a bin in a cupboard
Mount a plastic waste bin on brackets inside a cupboard door. Fix eyelets inside the cupboard and above the bin. Thread string through the eyelets and the lid. The lid will lift as the door opens.

BRIGHT IDEA

Fixing a shelf over a sink
Fix a small shelf over sink taps to hold washing-up items such as washing-up liquid and brushes for scrubbing. Make sure that the shelf is high enough to allow easy access to the taps. Support the shelf on lengths of thick dowelling.

FILLING CUPBOARDS
● **Fitting shelves** You do not need to keep the shelving that is already fitted in a cupboard. If you need further storage surfaces, fix small brackets at different levels to hold adjustable shelving.
● **Adding hooks** Fix a batten along the back of a cupboard. Screw hooks into the batten to hold cups, mugs, measuring jugs, and similar small items.
● **Storing flat objects** Fit plywood boards vertically in cupboards to make narrow compartments. Use the spaces to store flat items such as baking trays and cooling racks within easy reach.
● **Utilizing doors** Attach favourite recipes and other useful information to the insides of cupboard doors for quick reference.

PLANNING A BATHROOM

Organize a bathroom so that it is safe and comfortable to use. If you do not wish to refit it completely, add inexpensive storage units and decorative features. Make several plans before beginning work to find the most effective way of using the space available.

MAKING THE MOST OF A BATHROOM

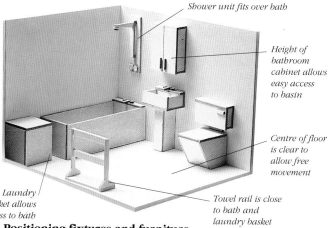

Shower unit fits over bath

Height of bathroom cabinet allows easy access to basin

Centre of floor is clear to allow free movement

Laundry basket allows access to bath

Towel rail is close to bath and laundry basket

Positioning fixtures and furniture

Whatever the size of your bathroom, leave at least 1 m (3¼ ft) of clear space in front of the bath, basin, and toilet, so that you have easy access to them. Position furniture so that it will not restrict access to these fixtures. For example, use space at the end of a bath to keep a laundry basket out of the way of people using the bathroom.

SAVING SPACE IN A BATHROOM

Bathrooms are often small, so it is important to make the most of the space. Fit shelves in empty areas such as the space above a door. Use odd-shaped areas, such as the space under a basin, to give extra storage. Group toiletries so that they are within easy reach of users.

USING BASIN AREAS

Storing under a basin

To create enclosed storage space, fix waterproof curtains around a basin. Attach the curtains to the basin with touch-and-close tape. Remove and clean the curtains every few weeks.

USING SMALL SPACES

● **Storing around a toilet** Use the space behind a toilet bowl to keep cleaning items.
● **Collecting bath toys** To prevent bath toys from cluttering a bathroom, store the toys in a plastic vegetable rack. Wash the toys and the vegetable rack once a week.
● **Fitting a seat** Instead of putting a chair in a bathroom, fit a pull-down seat to one wall to keep the floor clear.
● **Using another room** If a bathroom is very small, keep non-essential items in another room. For example, put a laundry basket in an empty corner of a bedroom.

STORING TOILETRIES

Filling a corner

If you have a corner of empty space beside a bath, fix a small set of shelves there for holding toiletries. Position the shelves so that they will not restrict access to the bath taps.

PLANNING A BEDROOM

Organize a bedroom so that it will look attractive and also accommodate clothes and other personal objects neatly. Ensure that there is sufficient storage space for the occupier's needs, so that they are able to keep surfaces clear and tidy when they are using the bedroom.

ADDING FURNISHINGS

● **Testing a new bed** Before buying a bed, the person who will use the bed should lie on it to see if it is the correct size and softness for them.

● **Adding cushions** If you read in bed, buy a triangular or armchair-shaped cushion to support your back while sitting.

● **Adapting a table** Cut down the legs of a small table to make a surface for food or hobbies when you are in bed.

● **Lighting a dressing table** Fix small light bulbs around a dressing-table mirror. Choose bulbs that emit clear light.

● **Lighting a bed area** Position bedside lights so that they can be turned off from the bed.

CREATING BED HEADS

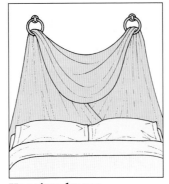

Hanging drapes
Fit two brass rings into the wall above a bed. Drape a long piece of lightweight, sheer fabric through the rings, leaving a swag between them. Hide the ends behind the pillows or mattress.

PROVIDING STORAGE

● **Choosing a bed** Increase storage space by buying a bed that is fitted with drawers in the base (see p. 18).

Keeping soft toys
To store soft toys, fix two hooks on adjoining walls at one corner of a room. Fix a hook at the point at which the walls meet. Fasten a triangular piece of netting to the hooks. Put toys in the netting.

SAVING SPACE IN A BEDROOM

Arrange furniture and storage units so that you can make the best possible use of the available space. Use all potential storage areas, such as a gap underneath a bed or the top of a wardrobe. With careful planning, you can even make room for other activities such as exercise.

MONEY-SAVING TIP

Creating a bedside table
Place a sturdy wooden box by a bed, with the open end facing forwards. Drape fabric over the box. You can then stand items on the box, and store objects inside it.

ADDING BED SPACE

● **Keeping a camp bed** Stow a camp bed under a normal bed so that it is easily accessible whenever you need it.

● **Using a mattress** Keep an old mattress to use as a spare bed. Vacuum clean it regularly, and examine it to check that the fabric has not worn out.

● **Converting a futon** Put a futon in your bedroom or living room. Keep it rolled up so that you can use it as a low-level couch when you do not need the bed space.

● **Using a sofa-bed** Keep a sofa-bed in a spare room or living room to accommodate guests. Leave space in front of it so that you can unfold it when you need to use it.

FILLING WARDROBES

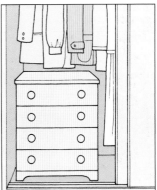

Installing drawers
Stand a small chest of drawers on the floor of a fitted wardrobe. Hang short garments such as jackets above it. Ensure that the handles of the drawers do not obstruct the wardrobe doors.

PLANNING LIVING AND DINING AREAS

These are the areas of the home that are used the most, so ensure that furniture and furnishings are robust and fairly dirt-proof. If you are working to a tight budget, you can buy second-hand furniture and use the tips below to create an attractive effect for little expense.

CREATING DINING SPACE

● **Finding an area** If you do not have a dining room, convert part of a living room. You could also use a kitchen, a spare bedroom, or a large hall.
● **Making a table** To create a dining table quickly, use a wallpaper table or trestle that folds away when not in use, and cover it with a cloth.
● **Adding a table top** If you occasionally wish to enlarge a dining table but do not have an expanding table, have a thick piece of board cut to the shape and size that you need. Rest it on the table. If you wish to store the board easily, cut it in half, and fit it with a hinge so that you can fold it.

SITUATING SPEAKERS

Make neat pile to form stable column

Making a speaker stand
Stand speakers off the floor to protect them from damage and stop sound from being muffled. Place them on piles of unwanted telephone directories or books. Cover with an attractive fabric.

BRIGHT IDEA

Preserving a carpet
Move large furniture regularly so that it does not dent a carpet permanently. To get rid of a dent, leave an ice cube to melt in it. Allow the carpet to dry naturally, then vacuum clean the spot.

SAVING SPACE IN LIVING AREAS

Make the most of living space by keeping it tidy. The less clutter you have on display, the more attractive, relaxing, and safe the area will be. Allow enough storage space for items such as cassettes and magazines, and display only those objects that you really want to see.

ORGANIZING YOUR LIVING SPACE

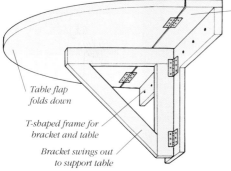

Lip of support allows room for bracket when table is folded

Table flap folds down

T-shaped frame for bracket and table

Bracket swings out to support table

Fitting a folding table
If you have no space for a dining table, fit a wall-mounted folding table in an empty space, and put up the table whenever you need it. Keep the area clear so that you can always use the table.

MAKING STORAGE SPACE

Storing drinks
Decorate an old filing cabinet by spraying with aerosol paint, and use it as a drinks cabinet. Use a lockable drawer to keep alcohol from children. Fill any other drawers with soft drinks.

CLEARING AWAY CLUTTER FROM LIVING AREAS

● **Tidying up** Clear your living areas each evening to stop clutter from building up.
● **Stowing chairs** If you eat in a living room, use stacking chairs. Put them against a wall when you do not need them.
● **Putting away toys** Keep a large, plastic laundry basket in an unobtrusive place for tidying children's toys quickly.
● **Using a magazine rack** Use a rack to store newspapers and magazines tidily.

PLANNING A HOBBY ROOM

It is best to reserve a special room or area for hobbies. This will keep leisure equipment from cluttering the rest of the home and allow enthusiasts to pursue their particular hobby uninterrupted, without having to clear away their equipment immediately after using it.

KEEPING EQUIPMENT FOR ACTIVITIES

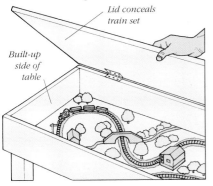

Lid conceals train set

Built-up side of table

Covering a train set
Conceal a train set or car track on a table by making sides and a lid for the table. Build high sides on to the edges of the table. Cut a large board to form the lid. Fix it to one long side with two or three hinges. Allow plenty of space for the lid to fold out of the way.

> ## USING ELECTRICAL APPLIANCES
>
> Make sure that the circuits in your house can handle the demands of all the appliances that you intend to use.
>
> ● **Power** Ensure that a hobby room has enough power points for all your appliances. Never try to run more than two items off one point.
> ● **Space** Check that there is plenty of space for air to circulate around the back of electrical machinery. This will prevent heat from building up to a dangerous level.
> ● **Flex** Tidy a flex by folding it into loops and slipping it into a cardboard tube.

ORGANIZING HOBBIES IN THE HOME

● **Tidying equipment** Keep small objects in sturdy plastic vegetable racks. If the racks are to hold items for several hobbies, label each section.

● **Ensuring safety** In areas used for tasks that create fumes and fire risks, make sure that there is good ventilation, and put up a "No Smoking" sign.

PLANNING CORRIDORS AND HALLWAYS

Areas between rooms can often be used for extra storage or living space, provided that you do not hinder access to rooms or create a fire risk by blocking doors. For example, you could adapt a corner of a wide hallway to form an office area, or fit shelving in a corridor.

FILLING EMPTY AREAS

● **Ensuring safety** Hallways, corridors, and stairs are all essential fire escape routes. Keep these areas clear of obstructions at all times.
● **Tidying coats** Position coat racks or hooks so that they do not obstruct a door. For small children, fit a second row of coat hooks below the first, at a height within easy reach.
● **Adding hanging space** Keep a collapsible dress rail in a spare room or wardrobe, and put it in a hallway to hold coats when you have a party.
● **Using temporary storage** Fit a shelf to hold items such as sports equipment, so that people can find the items easily when they need them.

USING STAIRWAYS

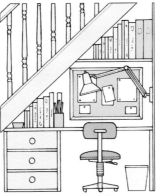

Creating a mini-office
Make an area for office work or homework by putting a desk in the space under a flight of stairs. Provide good lighting, preferably wall-mounted to save desk space, and a comfortable chair.

FILLING ODD CORNERS

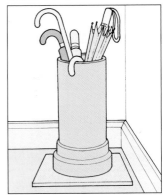

Holding umbrellas
Stand a length of earthenware pipe on a large ceramic tile, or in a shallow, waterproof container, to hold umbrellas and walking sticks. Put it in an inconspicuous place near the front door.

USING STORAGE SPACE

CUPBOARDS, SHELVES, AND OTHER STORAGE UNITS can be adapted to suit any home. Position them so that you make the fullest use of existing storage spaces, and fit extra units in otherwise unused parts of the home for long-term storage.

ORGANIZING CUPBOARDS

Take care of cupboards and their contents. Do not overload shelves or stand heavy items on top of cupboards. Group the contents so that they are easily accessible, and sort out cupboard space from time to time to clear away any rubbish that has accumulated.

CHOOSING CUPBOARDS

Cupboards can be purpose-built or they can be free-standing units. Each type has different advantages.

● **Built-in cupboards** Design these cupboards to fit a specific space. You can also adapt the interiors for items such as audio equipment.
● **Free-standing cupboards** It is quite easy to reposition these cupboards if changing the layout of a room, and you can take them with you when you move home.

CONSIDERING SCALE

● **Planning a small kitchen** To make the most of kitchen space, use wall cupboards in place of floor cupboards, since wall cupboards are less deep and take up less space. Check that items and appliances will fit on the narrow worktops and inside the cupboards.
● **Suiting your height** To check if a wall cupboard is positioned at the correct height for you, stand in front of it, and try to rest a hand flat on the upper shelf. If you cannot reach, lower the cupboard.

TIDYING INTERIORS

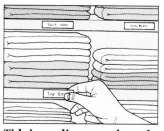

Tidying a linen cupboard
Sort linen into categories such as sheets and pillowcases. Label each shelf of a linen cupboard to show its contents. This will allow you to put the right type of linen in the right place every time.

POSITIONING CUPBOARDS IN A BEDROOM

This plan shows how to use space in a bedroom for different types of cupboard. Whichever room you are planning, use the following tips to make the most of cupboard space.

● **Ensuring free access** Leave sufficient space in front of cupboards so that you can open the doors fully.
● **Using awkward spaces** Place cupboards with sliding doors in areas without much clearance.
● **Filling recessed areas** Use a small cupboard in a recessed area such as a window bay.
● **Filling a fireplace** Stand a small, decorative cupboard in an old fireplace. Check that the chimney has been sealed. If not, brush out the fireplace regularly to remove soot deposits.

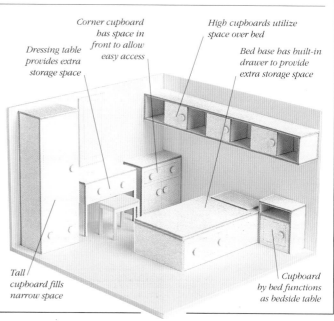

Corner cupboard has space in front to allow easy access

High cupboards utilize space over bed

Dressing table provides extra storage space

Bed base has built-in drawer to provide extra storage space

Tall cupboard fills narrow space

Cupboard by bed functions as bedside table

ORGANIZING WARDROBE SPACE

You can fit a great deal in a wardrobe if you make use of horizontal as well as vertical space. Before hanging or stacking items, group them by length or width, and separate those to be folded or kept in boxes. Put garments in the same place every time to keep the space tidy.

ARRANGING SPACE IN WARDROBES

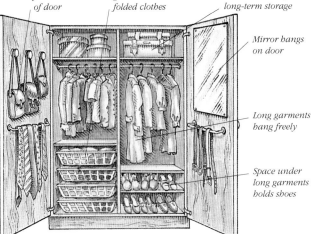

Accessories fit on inside of door

Wire trays under short garments contain folded clothes

Shelf above hanging rail holds items for long-term storage

Mirror hangs on door

Long garments hang freely

Space under long garments holds shoes

Arranging clothes and accessories

To keep your wardrobe neat, do not overload hanging rails or shelves. Leave enough room to remove and replace clothes and accessories easily. Make use of all the space, including the insides of doors. If you hang items on a door, do not overload it, since you could put stress on the hinges. Use doors to hang lightweight objects such as ties and costume jewellery, and use one hook for each item.

PROTECTING ITEMS

● **Covering delicate garments** Make or buy cotton covers to protect expensive clothes or fragile garments in a wardrobe. Alternatively, save the plastic bags from a dry cleaner, and use these to cover garments.

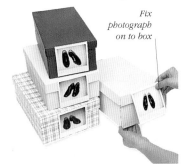

Fix photograph on to box

Storing shoes efficiently

Keep little-used shoes in boxes on a wardrobe floor or shelf. Take a photograph of each pair, and attach the picture to the relevant box so that you can find the shoes instantly.

SAVING SPACE

● **Compacting clothes** On wardrobe shelves, store non-creasing clothes such as thin sweaters by rolling them rather than folding them.

● **Utilizing doors** Fix a towel rail to the inside of a wardrobe door. Slip shower curtain hooks on to the rail, and hang belts and ties from them.

● **Fitting a mirror** In place of a free-standing mirror, fix a mirror to a wardrobe door. Choose a door with its back to the light, so that light falls on you and not on the mirror.

● **Using in a spare room** Fill a wardrobe in a spare room with seldom-worn clothes. Clear the wardrobe when it is needed for guests' use.

BRIGHT IDEA

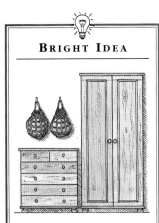

Sharing storage space
If children share a bedroom, assign each a colour. Paint units and hangers in these colours to show where each child's belongings are kept.

CREATING WARDROBES

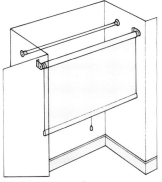

Making use of a recess

Fix a rail across a recess so that you can hang clothes there. Leave enough room between the rail and the back wall to fit hangers. If there is no space for doors, fit a roller blind to the front of the recess instead.

MAKING USE OF SHELVES

Shelves can both enhance the look of a room and provide storage space. They can be made from different materials for a variety of uses, such as wood for holding books and household equipment, and toughened glass for displaying ornaments, photographs, and small plants.

FILLING SHELVES

● **Filling shelves safely** Do not overload shelves, otherwise they may sag or break. If you plan to build shelves, add more supports than you think you will need. If adding objects to a shelf, make sure that the span is adequately supported to bear the extra load.

● **Organizing objects** Keep objects near where they are most likely to be used. Do not put frequently used items on shelves that are too high to reach comfortably.

● **Storing small objects** Create shelves within shelves to store small items. For example, put a spice rack at the back of a shelf, or use a wooden cutlery holder placed on its side.

● **Keeping shelves tidy** Label the fronts of shelves so that people can put objects back in the correct places after use.

USING OPEN SHELVES IN A LARGE ROOM

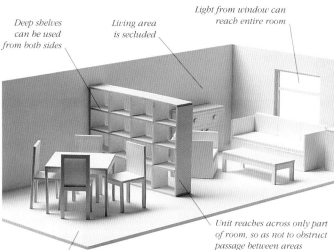

Deep shelves can be used from both sides

Living area is secluded

Light from window can reach entire room

Unit reaches across only part of room, so as not to obstruct passage between areas

Dining area is small and intimate

Dividing a large room
Use open shelves to divide a large room for different functions. For example, place open shelves between a living area and a dining area to form a practical screen. Make the shelves deep enough that both sides of the unit can be used for storage or displaying objects.

CREATING INSTANT SHELVES

You can construct simple shelves quickly and easily using only bricks and wooden boards, without the need for any special tools or equipment. It is best to choose attractive bricks that are in good condition, and sturdy wooden boards that are at least 15 mm (5/8 in) thick. Build one or two more shelves than you think you will need. As you work, make sure that each level is steady and properly supported.

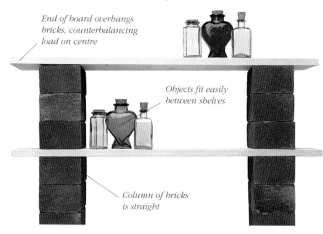

End of board overhangs bricks, counterbalancing load on centre

Objects fit easily between shelves

Column of bricks is straight

Making basic shelves
Arrange bricks in columns, each three or four bricks high, and lay a board across the bricks. Allow the ends of each shelf to overhang the bricks by a little way for stability. To add shelves, pile more bricks on top of the first shelf, following the original columns. When adding bricks, check that the height of each shelf will accommodate the objects that you intend to display.

MAKING USE OF DRAWERS

Drawers provide many different types of storage space, and can be large or small, deep or shallow, to suit particular items. It is possible to divide space inside drawers so that you can see the contents at a glance, and keep small items tidy and easily accessible.

PLANNING USE OF SPACE

● **Fitting drawers into spaces** When shopping for a set of drawers, take with you the dimensions of the space where you wish to stand it so that you can check that it will fit before buying.

● **Positioning a set of drawers** Allow enough room for an adult to kneel down in front of a set of drawers when a drawer is fully open.

● **Choosing units** If possible, select units with drawers of varying depths. Store items such as underwear in shallow drawers, and larger items such as sweaters in deep drawers.

● **Storing items flat** For large objects that must be kept flat, such as artwork or fabrics, use a plan chest, available from art shops. These chests have wide, shallow drawers designed to hold such items.

● **Using deep spaces** Consider fitting deep, sturdy drawers to store large objects such as board games or vinyl records.

KEEPING DRAWERS TIDY

Making drawer dividers
To organize items such as socks in a drawer, use a divider from a drinks box. Cut the divider to the size of the drawer, and push it in. Place small items in the spaces.

FILLING AND USING DRAWERS

Do not overfill a set of drawers. Every few months, clean out drawers to remove accumulated dust and rubbish. At the same time, examine each drawer for any signs of damage.

● **Filling drawer space** Leave at least 2.5 cm (1 in) between the top edge of a drawer and the top of the contents. This will keep the objects inside from spilling over and jamming the drawer.

● **Packing sharp objects** Wrap blades and sharp edges before storing items. Otherwise, bare metal points and blades could blunt each other, and could cut anyone using the drawer.

● **Limiting weight of contents** Never keep a very heavy object in a drawer. Even if the object fits in the space, its weight may put excessive strain on the bottom of the drawer.

● **Waxing runners** Rub a piece of soap, or the end of a wax candle, along drawer runners occasionally. This will enable the drawers to slide smoothly and keep them from sticking.

● **Making safety stops** If an old set of drawers has rails that separate the drawers, nail a line of corks into the underside of each rail. The corks will catch the back edge of each drawer so that it cannot be pulled out.

ORGANIZING CONTENTS

● **Labelling for clarity** Label the front of each drawer with details of what it contains. In the same way, label children's drawers with lists of the clothes that they each contain. Make separate labels for items such as socks, T-shirts, and sweaters.

● **Preserving clothes** Arrange clothes in drawers so that the most delicate items are at the top and the more durable garments are at the bottom. For example, store smart shirts on top of T-shirts. This will prevent the clothes from becoming overly creased.

● **Arranging implements** Lay long, thin objects such as ladles so that they all face the same way. This will keep them from becoming jumbled.

● **Keeping tiny objects** Put a miniature set of drawers on a shelf, desk, or table, to hold objects such as jewellery or sewing items that might get lost in a larger drawer.

CLEANING DRAWERS

● **Maintaining interiors** Line drawers with lining paper so that they will be quick and easy to keep clean. Replace the lining paper as soon as it becomes soiled.

● **Cleaning up spillages** To stop spillages in a drawer from congealing, wipe out instantly.

Place bottles behind elastic

Securing small bottles
Using drawing pins, fix a length of elastic to the left and right sides of a drawer. Tuck bottles inside the elastic. They will not fall over, and will be easy to remove.

MAKING USE OF OTHER SPACES

Many parts of your home have potential as storage space, in addition to purpose-built units and shelves. Consider using the spaces above doors and windows, the backs of doors, unused walls, and any nooks and crannies that could hold a small shelf or cupboard.

USING SMALL SPACES

● **Decorating windows**
Small, empty spaces can fulfil decorative as well as practical functions. For example, you could fit glass shelves across a window with no view. Display glass ornaments on them; the objects will catch the light coming through the window.

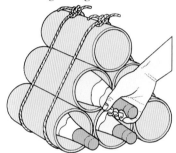

Improvising a wine rack
Make a wine rack from plastic drain pipe 12–15 cm (5–6 in) in diameter. Cut the piping into 30-cm (12-in) lengths. Glue these together in groups of six, and secure the groups with rope.

STORING UNDER BEDS

● **Creating storage units** Keep spare bedding, unused clothes, and children's toys in sturdy cardboard or plastic boxes. Before storing clothes and bedding, line the boxes with plain white paper. Tuck lavender sachets into fabrics to protect them from moths.

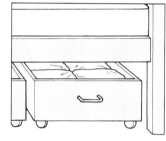

Making mobile boxes
Keep large, shallow boxes under high beds for extra storage. To make the boxes mobile, screw castors to the undersides at each corner. Fix a handle or loop of rope to the front of each box.

UTILIZING GAPS

● **Filling a niche** If there is a gap between kitchen units, slide a clothes rack into it to hold tea towels. Alternatively, if the space is high enough, use it to store brooms and mops or keep an ironing board.
● **Fitting shelves above doors** If there is a reasonable space between a ceiling and the top of a door, fit a narrow, well-supported shelf to hold ornaments or small objects.
● **Using empty wall spaces** Fit narrow shelves into the space between a door or window and a side wall. If a door opens out towards the wall, ensure that the shelves will not obstruct the door.
● **Using a child's room** Store rarely used items in high cupboards or on top shelves in a child's room. Ensure that the child cannot reach the area, so that he or she is not likely to pull items off and get hurt.

STORING ITEMS IN GARAGES AND SHEDS

Take care that you do not allow a garage or shed to become disorganized. It is only too easy to use the space as a dumping ground for objects instead of tidying them away immediately.

● **Arranging storage** Group items such as tools together so that you can find them easily.
● **Adding space** Fit second-hand kitchen cupboards to the walls. Fit locks to any cupboards used to store harmful substances.
● **Adding a work surface** Mount a fold-down table on one wall for repair work and other tasks.
● **Using electricity** If you plan to use the space as a workshop, install plenty of power points.

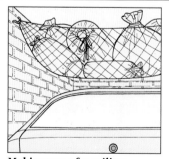

Making use of a ceiling
Hang a net across the ceiling of a garage to hold large, light items. If the garage door opens upwards, make sure that the net does not obstruct the mechanism. Do not overload the net, otherwise it may sag on to the roof of your car.

Hanging long tools on a wall
Cut a length of wood. Drill a line of holes along it, holding the drill at an angle, then fit dowelling pegs in the holes so that the pegs point upwards. Fix the wood to a wall. Hang tools on pegs with bristles or tines facing the wall.

STORING SPECIAL ITEMS

THINK CAREFULLY about how you organize space for bulky or valuable items. Keep large objects where they will not get in the way of daily life, unless they are in regular use. Put valuables well out of view of potential burglars.

ORGANIZING VIDEO TAPES AND MUSIC

Protect video tapes, cassettes, compact discs, and vinyl records from possible damage. Store them in a safe place near the equipment on which you play them, and keep the area tidy to prevent losses or damage. Set out collections logically, so that you can find items easily.

SORTING VIDEO TAPES
● **Labelling tapes** Label each tape with its contents and the date of recording.
● **Filing tapes** Set up a filing system, with categories such as "Films" and "Documentaries".
● **Dealing with old tapes** Review your video collection regularly, and wipe or discard tapes that you do not want.
● **Collecting clean tapes** Place labels on clean tapes so that they are ready to be written on directly after recording.

STORING COMPACT DISCS

Cut along lines with a fretsaw

Making a storage rack
Drill two lines of equally spaced holes down a length of plastic guttering. Fix the guttering to a stiff board. Mark lines to join pairs of holes, then cut to form slots.

PROTECTING ITEMS
● **Avoiding damage** Keep vinyl records and compact discs out of direct heat, which may warp them. Store tapes away from sources of magnetism such as the back of a television. Always put them back in their cases when not playing them.
● **Listing for insurance** Note the title of each item and whether it is a compact disc, cassette, vinyl record, or video tape. Update the list in case you need it for insurance purposes.

STORING BULKY OBJECTS

Positioning bulky items demands ingenuity and some lateral thinking. Work out which items must be accessible and which can be put away tidily in less reachable places. Be careful to position large or heavy objects safely so that you do not hurt yourself when moving them.

USING WALL SPACE

Stowing a bicycle
Hang a bicycle by its crossbar on a pair of brackets. Shape the tops of the brackets to make stoppers so that the bicycle does not slide off. Pad the brackets so that they do not scratch the bicycle.

KEEPING LEISURE ITEMS
● **Tidying sports equipment** Put durable items, such as footballs and hockey sticks, into a large, plastic laundry basket. Store the basket in a corner near an outside door.
● **Putting away sleeping bags** If sleeping bags do not have covers, roll them tightly, and tie them with fabric tape so that they occupy the minimum of space in a box or cupboard. Alternatively, use them with blankets as ordinary bedding.
● **Storing picnic items** Hang a coolbox out of the way on a strong hanging-plant bracket. Store plates, cutlery, and other picnic equipment inside it.

SAFEGUARD TIP

Securing a ladder
When you are not using a ladder, keep it out of the way by fixing it to a wall with securely fastened chains and padlocks. This will also stop burglars from taking it.

ORGANIZING PHOTOGRAPHS AND FILM

Photographs are precious mementoes. Store them in a cool, dry place to protect them from damage. Keep any that have particular value in a fireproof box or safe, or leave copies in the bank. Group photographs in boxes or albums to keep them tidy and accessible.

SORTING PHOTOGRAPHS

● **Labelling prints** If prints or packets do not already carry a date, write the month and year on the back of each print, along with the location.

Dividers are visible above prints

Arranging prints tidily
Store prints in shoe boxes instead of putting them in an album. To find photographs quickly, create a filing system using small cards as dividers. Label the cards to show the contents of each section.

KEEPING NEGATIVES

● **Avoiding marks** Handle negatives carefully, touching only the edges. Do not leave fingerprints on them, because this will result in poor reprints.

Filing negatives neatly
To store negatives flat, keep them in their plastic sleeves. Punch holes in the sleeves, taking care to avoid the negatives, and file in a ring binder. Label each sleeve to indicate the contents.

DEALING WITH FILM

● **Keeping undeveloped film** Heat damages film, so keep rolls in a refrigerator. Place them in a covered rack in the door, well away from food.
● **Storing exposed film** Put undeveloped rolls back in their original containers, and keep in a cool, dark place. Put negatives in the packet in which they were returned.
● **Developing film** Have film developed as soon as possible after using up a roll. If film is left for a long time, the images may deteriorate.
● **Taking films on holiday** In hot weather, wrap your camera and film in a plastic bag, and keep in a cool box to protect them from dust and heat.

STORING JEWELLERY

Keep valuable items of jewellery separate so that they do not scratch each other. Put these pieces and items of sentimental value in a safe at home, or in a safe-deposit box at a bank. Have jewellery valued for insurance, and tell the insurers if you sell or buy any pieces.

BRIGHT IDEA

Jewellery is laid flat

Disc is cut to fit can

Keeping jewellery safe
Open a food can at the base, empty it, and wash it. Fill it with jewellery wrapped in cotton wool, then plug the base with a disc of cork. Hide the can in a food cupboard.

KEEPING SMALL ITEMS

● **Tidying rings** Make a ring post for holding inexpensive rings. Cut a piece of dowelling 7.5 cm (3 in) long, and fix one end to a wood or cork base. Slip rings on to the post.
● **Grouping earrings** To store earrings for pierced ears, stick them into a pin cushion.
● **Hanging clip-on earrings** Fix a ribbon inside a drawer with drawing pins. Hang clip-on earrings on the ribbon.
● **Collecting items** Use a small tray or box to hold accessories that you wear every day. Make a habit of putting these accessories into the tray at night so that you will be sure to find them in the morning.

STORING NECKLACES

● **Arranging necklaces** Keep inexpensive necklaces in a long box or poster tube, or loop them on to a coat hanger, and hang them in a wardrobe.

Long necklace folded in half before hanging

Hanging up a necklace
Attach a cup hook to the inside of a wardrobe door. Store an inexpensive necklace or bracelet by hanging it on the cup hook.

ORGANIZING BOOKS AND PAPERS

The writer John Milton said "a good book is the precious lifeblood of a master spirit". Well-kept books give years of pleasure. Mark your place with a bookmark instead of folding the corners of pages. When you lend a book, note its title and the name of the borrower.

TRADITIONAL TIP

Preventing mildew

Sprinkle a little oil of cloves on wooden bookshelves to stop mildew from developing. Rub the oil into the shelves thoroughly so that it does not soak into the books.

PLANNING STORAGE

● **Setting up a system** Group your books into categories. For example, arrange them alphabetically by the authors' surnames, or by subject matter.
● **Allowing room** Leave at least 2.5 cm (1 in) between the tops of the books and the base of the shelf above so that you can remove books easily. Allow at least 2.5 cm (1 in) of shelf width for every book.
● **Arranging sheet music** Use a magazine rack to hold small quantities of sheet music. Sort large collections alphabetically, and allocate a shelf for them.

PRESERVING BOOKS

● **Minimizing humidity** Keep books in dry places. Combat humidity by putting a small moisture absorber near places that attract condensation, such as double-glazed windows.
● **Caring for covers** Protect paperbacks with plastic jacket covers. Wipe leather bindings occasionally with hide food.
● **Keeping down dirt** Remove books regularly, and dust them and the bookshelves.
● **Making dust shields** Tack 5-cm (2-in) wide leather strips to the fronts of shelves to keep dust off the books beneath.

STORING TOOLS

Garden and household tools are expensive, so look after them to prolong their useful lives. Keep implements with blades in a safe place, out of reach of children, and with the blades sheathed in thick cloth or bubble wrap. See page 27 for making a blade protector.

KEEPING IMPLEMENTS

● **Hanging tools** Protect tools from damage by hanging them up. Keep them on hooks or on a metal or wooden rack. If a tool has no hole by which to hang it, drill a hole in the handle, thread string through it, and tie to form a loop.
● **Storing small items** Use plastic storage boxes to keep garden items such as trowels, and household implements such as spanners and drill bits.
● **Maintaining implements** Clean all tools after you have used them. Wash soil-caked garden tools under an outside tap, then dry them carefully.
● **Storing for a season** At the end of the gardening season, clean all tools thoroughly. Oil metal parts to prevent rusting, and protect unpainted wood by rubbing it with linseed oil.

STORING LARGE ITEMS

● **Storing a wheelbarrow** Prop a barrow up against a wall. Put a brick in front of the wheel, and fix the handles to the wall with bungee cords.

Tidying a hose

Punch four holes in the base of an old enamel basin, and screw it on to a large softwood board. Screw the board to one wall of a garage or shed, then wrap the hose around the basin.

TIDYING A WORKSHOP

● **Utilizing work surfaces** Keep work surfaces clean and clear so that they are ready for use. Use shelves, or spaces under work surfaces, for storage.

Making a tool board

Wrap tools in clingfilm, and lay on a board. Fix nails where the tools are to hang. Spray the tools and board with paint, and leave to dry. Unwrap the tools, then hang them in the marked places.

SORTING OUT STORAGE

WHEN PLANNING STORAGE, first assess which items must be ready to hand and which are used only rarely. Lay out storage areas so that you can easily find everyday items, and utilize less accessible places for seldom-used objects.

ORGANIZING LONG-TERM STORAGE

For long-term storage, select areas out of the way of daily activities. Utilize all available spaces including rarely used containers such as luggage. For example, use suitcases for storing clothes; leave the clothes on a bed when you are away from home and using the suitcases.

PUTTING AWAY CLOTHES

Preserving delicate items
Fold white tissue paper carefully around delicate white clothes to protect the fabric from dirt, then wrap blue tissue paper over the white to block out light and keep the fabric from turning yellow.

PACKING OTHER ITEMS
● **Keeping blankets** Wrap woollen blankets in several sheets of newspaper. Seal the open edges of the paper with parcel tape. This will protect the blankets from moths.
● **Protecting hats** Store hats in hat boxes, which can be kept in any dry place.
● **Keeping leather bags** Clean the outsides and insides of leather bags. Fill with tissue paper so that they keep their shapes and do not crease. Put bags in a cardboard box, and store in a cool, dry place to protect the leather from mould.

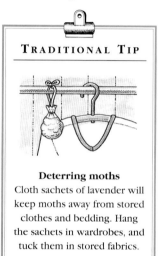

TRADITIONAL TIP

Deterring moths
Cloth sachets of lavender will keep moths away from stored clothes and bedding. Hang the sachets in wardrobes, and tuck them in stored fabrics.

STORING RARELY USED ITEMS

You can use secluded or even hard-to-reach places, such as a loft or a high shelf, for storing things that you seldom need. To remind yourself where you have put an item, note its location on a sheet of paper, and file the paper with your home maintenance log (see p. 45).

PACKING FRAGILE ITEMS

Dividers separate glasses

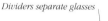

Wrapping glasses
Pad the insides of glasses with bubble wrap, then wrap the outsides in more bubble wrap. Store the glasses in a wooden wine box that contains dividers for holding bottles securely.

KEEPING DECORATIONS

Wire lies flat against card

Storing festive lights
Take a rectangular piece of stiff card, and cut a large notch in each of the short sides to form an "H" shape. Without twisting the lights, wind them carefully around the centre of the card.

STORING FOR A SEASON
● **Packing clothes** Designate an area for clothes that you do not need for part of each year. For example, one space could hold sweaters in summer and thin clothes in winter. Launder the clothes, and make any repairs, before packing them.
● **Keeping leisure equipment** Some items used for a limited season, such as skis and surf boards, are bulky. Hang them in a shed or little-used part of the house. If you do not often use such items,, consider hiring them rather than buying them.

STORING FREQUENTLY USED ITEMS

Ideally, store frequently used items as close as possible to the points where you use them. If they are needed in several different places, put them in portable containers, and carry them with you. Position the items in places that are easy to reach – preferably at about waist height.

KEEPING ESSENTIALS

The following is a list of items that you are likely to need every day. Keep them where you can find them instantly.

- Toiletries (see p. 80).
- Spectacles, if used.
- Medication, if needed.
- Outdoor wear.
- Clothes, shoes, and accessories for next day (see p. 79).
- Basic cooking equipment (see p. 48).
- Everyday foods.
- Cleaning fluids and cloths.
- Towels.
- Keys for house and car.
- Equipment and papers for work.
- Equipment and books that children need for school.
- Sports kit.
- Remote controls for audio equipment, television, and video cassette recorder.

PLANNING IN ADVANCE

- **Preparing for the next day** Every evening, make ready clothes, papers, and other objects that you will need for the next day. Put them in a place where you will see them easily the next morning.
- **Using lists** Each evening, make a list of objects that you need to find and errands for you to do the following day.
- **Checking personal items** Every time you use toiletries or cosmetics, ensure that they will be ready for use the next time. For example, renew used-up bars of soap, change blunt blades on razors, and sharpen blunt eye pencils.
- **Putting out breakfast items** Lay the breakfast table with crockery and cutlery the night before, and put out containers of non-perishable items such as cereals and preserves.

STORING CLEANING KIT

- **Setting out items** Decide which areas must be cleaned daily, such as the bathroom and the kitchen. Make up a cleaning kit to be kept in each of these areas.

Making a portable kit
Collect all the cleaning fluids, detergents, and cloths that you will need to clean a particular room. Keep these items together in a sturdy container that you can carry around while you work, such as a bottle carrier.

STORING HOUSEHOLD OBJECTS

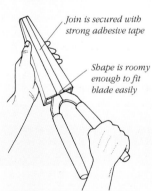

Join is secured with strong adhesive tape

Shape is roomy enough to fit blade easily

Making a blade protector
Trace the shape of a tool's blade on to card. Turn the tool over, and trace again. Cut out around both shapes, allowing enough room to form sides for the protector. Bend the card to fit the tool, then tape the join.

Keep fragile or dangerous items in places where people will not disturb them accidentally. Take care to put these objects out of reach of small children.

- **Protecting tools from damp** Keep tools in a cool, dry place. Never put them in a damp cellar or utility room, or in a small kitchen, because the humidity could cause them to rust.
- **Locking items away** Fit locks to medicine cabinets and cupboards storing cleaning products to stop children gaining access to them.
- **Positioning fragile objects** Keep breakable items out of reach of children. Make sure that these objects are not displayed where people are likely to brush against them or knock them over.

- **Protecting blades** Hang tools and kitchen implements with their blades pointing downwards so that people will not injure themselves on the sharp edges.
- **Shielding points** Push corks on to the points of sharp items such as knives and skewers. This will stop the points from becoming blunt or injuring people.
- **Storing metal objects** Wrap sharp objects in cloth, or keep them on a magnetic rack. Do not store them in a drawer, because they will become blunt through contact with other items.
- **Housing cleaning equipment** If you have small children, store cleaning fluids in high cupboards that the children cannot reach. Use floor-level cupboards for buckets, bowls, and cloths.

Setting Up Routines

QUICK REFERENCE

Cleaning the Home, p. 29

Organizing Laundry, p. 35

Planning for
Decorating, p. 37

Maintaining the
Home, p. 43

Ensuring Security
and Safety, p. 46

*B*Y SETTING UP SYSTEMS *for completing basic
household tasks, you can greatly simplify
domestic life and make your home a neat
and pleasant place. You will then have plenty
of time left for both work and leisure. Plan
each stage of major tasks such as decorating,
and set aside blocks of time each week for
routine tidying and cleaning. Encourage
everyone in your household to participate
so that your home is kept running smoothly.*

LAUNDRY AND CLEANING EQUIPMENT

Buy the best equipment that
you can afford, and look after it
well. Cheap items are not usually
as effective as good-quality ones
and may not last long, so buying
them can be a false economy.

● **Buying cleaning items** To save
money, buy cleaning products
that can do more than one task,
such as washing-up liquid which
you can use to clean worktops.
This will save you from having
to keep items that you use
infrequently for one job.
● **Protecting health** Make sure
that anything used to clean
cutlery or crockery is non-toxic.
● **Preserving hands** Wear
household gloves whenever
you carry out any wet or dirty
tasks. Use disposable gloves
for very messy jobs such as
polishing metal objects.

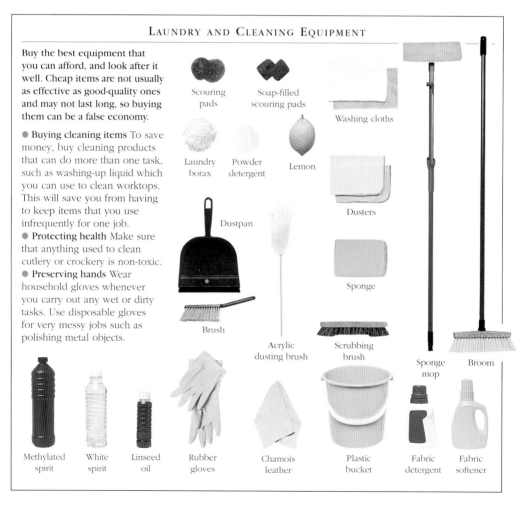

Scouring
pads

Soap-filled
scouring pads

Washing cloths

Laundry
borax

Powder
detergent

Lemon

Dusters

Dustpan

Sponge

Brush

Acrylic
dusting brush

Scrubbing
brush

Sponge
mop

Broom

Methylated
spirit

White
spirit

Linseed
oil

Rubber
gloves

Chamois
leather

Plastic
bucket

Fabric
detergent

Fabric
softener

CLEANING THE HOME

Try to dust and clean regularly, even if you do only a few rooms each week. By carrying out small amounts of cleaning at frequent intervals, you will be able to keep your home looking tidy with a minimum of effort.

WORKING EFFICIENTLY

Divide housework into manageable groups of tasks, and choose the time of day when you will have most energy to do them. Try not to spend too much time on any one task. Find the most comfortable way to work so that you make the best use of your physical energy.

ORGANIZING EQUIPMENT
● **Keeping items accessible**
Situate cleaning equipment as near as possible to the places in which it will be used, and store related items – such as dusters and polish – together.
● **Sorting by function** To limit the spread of bacteria, keep equipment for floors and toilets separate from other cleaning items. Never use these items for cleaning other areas.
● **Cleaning equipment** After use, take a few minutes to wash brushes and brooms, rinse buckets and bowls, and wipe spilt liquid off bottles.

CLEANING WITHOUT STRAIN

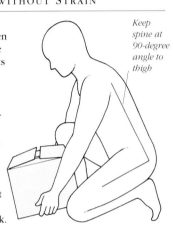

You will work most efficiently by conserving your energy. When cleaning, take up a comfortable position, and take frequent rests to prevent fatigue. To move an object, come close to it so that you exert your full strength without straining your muscles.

Keep spine at 90-degree angle to thigh

Lifting an object
Kneel with one foot flat on the ground for balance. As you lift, keep your spine straight and at a 90-degree angle to the leg on which you are kneeling, so that you take the weight with your legs and do not strain your back.

SETTING UP A DAILY CLEANING ROUTINE

You will need to do certain tasks every day. If you are out all day and do not wish to tackle them when you return, set your alarm clock earlier than usual and do them before you go. If you are at your best later in the day, set aside a convenient time in the evening.

CLEANING EVERY DAY

Quick cleaning tasks such as the ones listed below can be done in small groups at the beginning or end of a day.

● **Kitchen** Wash up after every meal. Tidy and wipe all the work surfaces.
● **Bathroom** Clean toilets. Wash down bath or shower areas after every use.
● **Beds** Fold back bedding to let perspiration escape.
● **Airing** Open windows to air heavily used rooms.
● **Pets** Clean food dishes.

MAINTAINING HYGIENE
● **Disinfecting a toilet** Clean inside the bowl to kill bacteria. Apply toilet cleaner under the rim, leave it for a few hours, then flush to rinse the bowl.
● **Cleaning worktops** Wipe surfaces with a product that will kill bacteria. Never allow pets to walk on worktops where food is prepared.
● **Wiping a waste bin** Wipe the lid of a kitchen waste bin every day. Even if it is not obviously dirty, it may have collected bacteria through contact with waste items.

TIDYING UP

Collecting clutter
Fold up the bottom of an apron. Sew the sides together, and stitch two equidistant lines down the front, making three pockets. Drop small items into them as you tidy up, and sort the items later.

PERFORMING WEEKLY TASKS

The main general task to be performed weekly is cleaning surfaces. Dust any non-washable surfaces, and vacuum or wash all floors at least once a week. You could either tackle a different room each day, or go through the whole house once a week. Tidy any area that needs it, as well.

CLEANING TOOLS

Push teeth of comb into bases of bristles

Removing fluff

Use the wide-toothed end of an old comb to clean fluff from a vacuum cleaner attachment or the bristles of a brush or broom. After removing debris, wash the comb and bristles with soap, and leave them to dry thoroughly.

TIDYING BEDROOMS

● **Making beds** Change bedding weekly, and allow mattresses and pillows to air.
● **Fitting a clean duvet cover** First remove the dirty duvet cover. Turn the fresh one inside out, reach into it, and grasp the two corners furthest from the opening. Fit these corners on to two corners of the duvet, then shake the cover down over the duvet.
● **Cleaning toys** To clean plastic or wooden toys, wash them in a mild disinfectant solution, then leave to dry.
● **Dusting** Remove dust from bedside lamps, mirrors, and pictures once a week.

TIME-SAVING TIP

Making a brush carrier
Cutting at an angle, slice the base off a large plastic bottle. Cut slits on the long side, and thread the bottle on to a belt. Use the bottle as a holster to hold brushes while you work.

PERFORMING MONTHLY TASKS

Make a note of monthly jobs in your diary, together with the time likely to be needed to complete them. Schedule the tasks for different weeks in the month, and carry out one or two at a time. In this way you can tackle everything without facing a mountain of work all at once.

CLEANING VALUABLES

● **Washing glassware** Rinse valuable glass items thoroughly, and dry them with care. To remove stains, soak the items in a weak solution of bleach.
● **Polishing metal** Use a long-lasting polish where possible. If the objects are not on show or in regular use, store them in tarnish-proof bags, or wrap them in acid-free tissue paper.
● **Cleaning fragile items** Wash small, breakable ornaments in a solution of soap flakes or washing-up liquid. Wash them one at a time so that they do not chip or scratch each other.
● **Dusting delicate china** Wear clean cotton gloves, and run your fingers gently over delicate china. Use a small paint brush to dust crevices.

CARING FOR MATTRESSES

● **Turning over** Turn over a mattress as often as the maker recommends. Flip it over, then swivel it so that the head rests where the foot used to be.

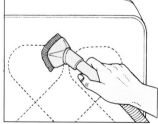

Cleaning a mattress
Use a soft brush on low suction to clean a sprung mattress, and use a crevice tool on foam. As well as removing dust, this will get rid of dust mite droppings, which aggravate asthma.

CLEANING FITTINGS

● **Wiping switches and sockets** Turn off the electricity. Moisten a cloth with methylated spirit, and wipe the socket or switch. Do not get liquid into sockets.

Hold bulb firmly

Dusting a light bulb
Switch off the light, and remove the bulb when it has cooled. Wipe with cotton wool or a damp cloth moistened with methylated spirit. Allow the bulb to dry before fixing it in position.

PERFORMING OCCASIONAL TASKS

Tasks that are done only occasionally, such as washing carpets or cleaning paintwork, can be time-consuming. Allow enough time for you to finish them within a day. These tasks tend to be physically tiring, so do not attempt to do more than one of them in a single day.

CLEANING LIGHTING

Plastic sheet is tied to light

Spray close to fitting to dislodge dirt

Washing a chandelier
Tie a plastic bag over each cooled bulb and fitting. Put newspaper underneath and a plastic sheet around the chandelier. Dust with an acrylic brush. Apply cleaning solution with a plant sprayer.

TASKS TO BE DONE OCCASIONALLY

Schedule a set time for each task. When you have finished, note in your diary the next date for the task to be done.

● **Washing windows** Clean the insides of windows two or three times a year, when they start to look grimy. (The outsides will need to be cleaned more often.) Do not clean windows on a hot day, because they will dry too quickly and look streaky.
● **Cleaning paintwork** Wash paintwork whenever it appears grubby. Once it is clean, use spare paint (see p. 42) to touch up scuffed or damaged areas.

● **Cleaning loose covers** Check the labels on loose furnishing covers, or ask the manufacturer whether the fabric can be washed. Never assume that a cover can be washed simply because it can be taken off.
● **Shampooing carpets** When cleaning a carpet, leave strips so that you can still walk across part of the carpet. If you do not need to use the room, clean the whole carpet, working towards the exit door, and leave to dry.
● **Protecting wet carpets** Put aluminium foil under furniture legs, so that the legs do not become damp and leave marks.

ORGANIZING A FULL CLEAN

This type of cleaning is done once or twice a year. It is often called "spring cleaning", but you can do it whenever you have a spare day or weekend. It is best to clean rooms one by one. To keep up your enthusiasm, vary the tasks, and take a break every few hours.

LISTING TASKS

Include the following tasks in your work. Note them in a log (see p. 34) for convenience.

● **Curtains and blinds** Take down, and clean. Before replacing them, wipe curtain tracks and window areas.
● **Surfaces** Shampoo carpets. Clean walls and dust ceilings.
● **Cupboards** Empty out and clean interiors. Dispose of stale food and old clothes.
● **Shelves** Clear surfaces. Dust shelves and contents.
● **Hangings** Take down, and clean. Dust walls behind.
● **Furniture** Polish wood and steel. Wipe plastic surfaces.
● **Doors** Clean. Oil fixings.
● **Laundry** Wash and air items to be stored for a season.

CLEANING SURFACES
● **Repairing damage** Treat any stains before cleaning. Touch up chipped enamel, damaged plastic, or discoloured wood once the surface is clean.

Blend liquids in bowl before bottling

Making wood cleaner
Mix 15 ml (1 tbsp) turpentine and 15 ml (1 tbsp) linseed oil with 1 litre (1¾ pints) warm water. Pour into a screw-top bottle, and shake. Apply on a soft cloth, then rub off. Leave to dry, then polish.

BRIGHT IDEA

Timing yourself
Make a list of tasks, and note an estimated time for each job. Before you begin a task, set a timer for the end of the scheduled period. Make a note of the actual time taken. Keep the finished list for reference when you have your next major clean.

CARRYING OUT A QUICK CLEAN

You may not always have time to clean the house thoroughly. For day-to-day tidiness, confine your efforts to bedrooms, kitchen, and main living areas. If you are expecting visitors, clean only the places that they are likely to see, and keep the doors of other rooms firmly shut.

DOING ESSENTIAL JOBS

● **Cleaning bathrooms** Keep toilets and basins squeaky clean however busy you are.
● **Cleaning floors** Sweep or vacuum the most heavily used areas of the home, or those that are noticeably dirty.
● **Tidying up** Ask the family to help remove clutter. Even small children can empty waste bins, throw out dead flowers, and wash up petfood bowls.
● **Dusting quickly** Dust and wipe obviously dirty areas. If you are short of time, dust only places in direct sunlight.

TASKS FOR A QUICK CLEAN

The following tasks take very little time but will make a room appear clean and pleasant.

● **Clearing up** Put clutter into a large box. Hide the box, and sort out the contents later.
● **Dusting** Remove obvious dust from polished surfaces or areas such as television screens.
● **Removing rubbish** Throw out dead flowers and cigarette ends.
● **Neatening furniture** Plump cushions on chairs and sofas. Remove human or pet hairs.

● **Cleaning bathrooms** Tidy bathrooms, especially if guests are likely to use them. Clean toilets, and put out fresh towels.
● **Tidying bedrooms** If people are coming to stay, ensure that beds are made up and surfaces are dusted. Clean the most visible spots such as bedside tables and dressing tables.
● **Clearing a kitchen** Tidy food and equipment into cupboards. For speed, put items in the nearest free spaces. Remember to sort them out later.

WASHING UP

This is a job that you cannot escape. Do not let washing up collect over the course of several meals. This is unhygienic, and the task will then take hours. However, you do not have to wash up straight after eating. Soak very dirty items, to make the dirt soft and easy to remove.

WASHING UP EFFICIENTLY

By washing up in this order, you will make the best use of water and will not have to waste time changing it.

1 Fill very dirty items with water, and leave to one side. Soak cutlery in a jug of warm water. Rinse glasses in cold water, then wash in a plastic bowl of hot water.

2 Soak greasy crockery in detergent solution. Meanwhile, wash cutlery, cleaning items individually.

3 Wash crockery. Remove egg, starch-based foods, and milk with cool water (not hot, which will set the dirt).

4 Scrub pans and very dirty items in the water used for soaking, then wash them in a bowl of fresh, hot water.

WASHING UP BY HAND
● **Protecting hands** Wear rubber gloves, but first check the water temperature without them. If you have long nails, shield them by fixing small pieces of sticking plaster inside the finger ends of the gloves.
● **Caring for glasses** Slip glasses sideways into hot water to reduce the chance of cracking. Dry glassware, and put it away before you wash any other items, especially if you have only a small draining area.
● **Rinsing glasses** Add a little vinegar to the rinse water to produce a sparkling finish.

MAKING USE OF A DISHWASHER
● **Conserving water** Do not run a dishwasher until it is full. If this involves leaving items for more than one day, run a rinse cycle over what is already in the machine.

CLEANING GLASSES

Drying without smears
Once you have rinsed each glass, fill it up with hot water. Stand it on the draining board while you rinse and fill the next. Tip out the water just before you dry each glass with a clean, dry tea towel.

● **Saving energy** If items are not too dirty, use the machine on a low temperature setting.
● **Deodorizing inside** To clear odours, run the machine when empty using a special cleaner.

ORGANIZING HELP

If you live in a large home or lead a very busy life, you may need help with cleaning and maintaining your home. Write out a list of tasks that need to be done every day. If you require particular jobs to be done in a certain way, include this information on the list.

INVOLVING CHILDREN

Hanging out washing
Fix another washing line below the main one, at a height that children can reach. Let children hang up underwear and some of their own clothes.

USING OUTSIDE HELP

● **Contacting agencies** If you need help on a regular basis, consider hiring someone from an agency. These workers are checked, insured, and usually bring their own equipment.
● **Finding casual help** You could contact local teenagers and unemployed people for help. Brief them thoroughly.
● **Consulting friends** If you know someone who employs a cleaner, ask if they would recommend that person.

BRIEFING A CLEANER

Take up references before you hire anyone. Draw up a brief including the following points. Give a copy to the cleaner.

● **Tasks** Write a list of tasks for the cleaner to do.
● **Pay** Agree the rate of pay and hours to be worked.
● **Security** If you give the cleaner a key or a security code, note this in the brief.
● **Insurance** Provide details of your insurance cover.

CREATING A FAMILY ROSTER

There is no reason why all family members, other than babies and toddlers, should not lend a hand with the household chores. Make a roster of daily tasks and weekly jobs, and agree them with your family. Put the roster in a prominent place, such as on a kitchen wall.

ALLOCATING TASKS

● **Occupying young children** Four- to eight-year-olds can easily tidy their own rooms, make their beds, empty small waste bins around the house, and deposit their dirty clothes in the laundry basket.
● **Organizing older children** Eight- to twelve-year-olds can lay the table, wash up, put things away, and dust.
● **Enlisting teenagers' help** Teenagers should be able to tackle most household chores. They may be stronger than their parents, so could be useful for moving furniture and rolling up carpets.
● **Fitting jobs to people** Allow for each person's abilities and limitations. For example, do not ask young children to carry out demanding tasks.
● **Planning free time** Schedule free evenings for children with lots of homework or exams. Allow yourself free time, too.

SAMPLE FAMILY ROSTER				
DAY	ADULT 1	ADULT 2	CHILD 1	CHILD 2
Monday	Wash up after meals	Free day	Free day	Lay table for meals
Tuesday	Lay table for meals	Collect waste for recycling	Wash up after meals	Free day
Wednesday	Free day	Lay table for meals	Free day	Wash up after meals
Thursday	Carry out weekly shopping	Wash up after meals	Help with weekly shopping	Lay table for meals
Friday	Lay table for meals	Empty waste bins	Wash up after meals	Free day
Saturday	Wash up after meals	Change towels and bedding	Hang out washing	Lay table for meals
Sunday	Empty kitchen bin	Free day	Lay table for meals	Wash up after meals

Making a Cleaning Log

Create a log to help you to plan a full clean (see p. 31). Divide the log into sections for each area or type of object to be cleaned. List the tasks and the equipment to have ready for each task, and specify time limits. The chart below indicates how to organize tasks in a log.

Gathering Information

- **Using a log** Carry your cleaning log on a clipboard. Tick each task as you finish it.
- **Making extra notes** Fix a sheet of paper behind the log, and use it for recording any problems or shortcuts.
- **Storing records for appliances** Keep instruction manuals and servicing records for appliances with your cleaning log.
- **Planning ahead** Note the date of the next cleaning session in a diary or on a wall planner.

Organizing Logs

Keeping templates
Draw templates for cleaning logs in advance so that they are ready for use. Keep the templates in a ring binder until you need them.

Filling in Information

List all cleaning items used for each task

Listing equipment
Gather cleaning items so that you can see at a glance what you will need. Fill in the log to show the items needed for each task.

Tasks to Include in a Cleaning Log

Items	Tasks	Equipment Required	Time Needed
Ceilings and walls	**Dusting** Dust crevices.	Duster, broom.	10 minutes.
	Washing paintwork Wash grubby areas of paintwork.	Bucket of hot water, cleaning fluid, sponge.	30 minutes.
Windows	**Frames** Dust and wipe clean.	Duster, damp cloth.	5 minutes.
	Glass Wash insides and outsides of panes.	Chamois cloth, bucket of warm water, cleaning fluid.	15 minutes.
Fixtures	**Plug sockets** Clean surfaces.	Cloth, methylated spirit.	1 minute.
	Sinks Clean plugholes.	Toothbrush, cleaning fluid.	2 minutes.
Objects	**Picture frames** Clean glass.	Duster, soft cloth, vinegar.	5 minutes.
	Bookshelves Empty and dust.	Duster, cloth, oil of cloves.	30 minutes.
Bedding	**Foam pillows** Hand-wash.	Wash liquid, rubber gloves.	10 minutes.
	Beds Clean mattresses.	Vacuum cleaner, crevice tool.	10 minutes.
Appliances	**Toaster** Clean out crumbs.	Newspaper to catch crumbs.	5 minutes.
	Kettle Removing scale.	Scale remover or lemon juice.	10 minutes.
Floors and carpets	**Hard floors** Clean corners.	Cleaning fluid, toothbrush.	10 minutes.
	Carpets Clean and deodorize.	Bicarbonate of soda.	40 minutes.

ORGANIZING LAUNDRY

WORK OUT A LAUNDRY ROUTINE THAT SUITS YOUR LIFESTYLE. For example, a family of four may need several machine loads and one hand wash every week. Allow time for extra tasks such as dry cleaning and simple repairs.

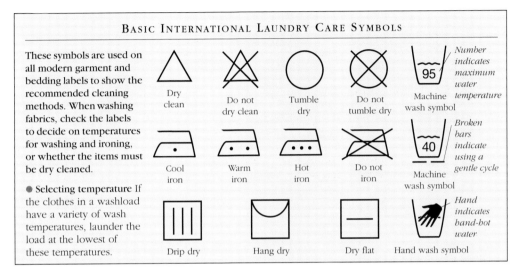

BASIC INTERNATIONAL LAUNDRY CARE SYMBOLS

These symbols are used on all modern garment and bedding labels to show the recommended cleaning methods. When washing fabrics, check the labels to decide on temperatures for washing and ironing, or whether the items must be dry cleaned.

- **Selecting temperature** If the clothes in a washload have a variety of wash temperatures, launder the load at the lowest of these temperatures.

Dry clean

Do not dry clean

Tumble dry

Do not tumble dry

Machine wash symbol — Number indicates maximum water temperature

Cool iron

Warm iron

Hot iron

Do not iron

Machine wash symbol — Broken bars indicate using a gentle cycle

Drip dry

Hang dry

Dry flat

Hand wash symbol — Hand indicates hand-hot water

SORTING OUT A WASHLOAD

Before laundering, group fabrics into whites, bright colours, and dark colours. Check pockets for tissues, which disintegrate and cover fabrics in fluff, or coins, which may damage the washing machine. Fasten zips so that they do not become snagged inside the machine.

TREATING STAINS
- **Cleaning a shirt collar** Rub a little liquid detergent into a dirty shirt collar to dissolve marks before washing.

Soak fabrics in a clean plastic bucket

Soaking delicate fabrics
Mix 30 ml (2 tbsp) cream of tartar with 4.5 litres (1 gallon) hot water, then leave to cool. Soak delicate items in it for a few hours before washing to remove stains.

GROUPING ITEMS
- **Washing nylon tights** Put nylon tights in a pillowcase so that they do not become tangled in the wash.

Fold socks around ring

Keeping socks together
Wrap each pair of socks securely around a shower curtain ring. Make sure that the sock feet are left free so that water can get to them during the wash cycle.

WASHING EFFECTIVELY
- **Saving energy** Wash at the lowest recommended temperature to save energy. Wash white cotton at the full temperature occasionally to maintain the brightness.
- **Loading a machine** For economy, fill a machine to the maximum permitted weight or set it to a half-load capacity.
- **Washing heavy items** Do not put objects such as duvets in a domestic washing machine in case they damage the drum.
- **Hand-washing** Squeeze items gently, then rinse until clear water runs from them.
- **Softening fabrics** Add 30 ml (2 tbsp) of white vinegar to a washload before rinsing, as an inexpensive fabric softener.

DRYING CLOTHES AND OTHER FABRICS

Make sure that you dry clothes as much as necessary for the next stage of care. Items to be ironed should be slightly damp. Fabrics that should not be ironed can be dried fully. Both ironed and fully dried items, particularly bedding, should be aired thoroughly before use.

REMOVING WATER

Using a rolling pin
To squeeze excess water from a garment, put the item between two towels, and run a rolling pin firmly over it. The towels can be dried and reused for bathing.

DRYING NATURALLY

Fitting an indoor line
Fix a line over the bath so that you can dry clothes indoors. Fit a type that can be retracted when not in use, or a double line to support heavy garments.

TUMBLE DRYING

● **Loading a dryer** Do not overload a dryer, otherwise the contents will not have enough room to move around. Fill it half full at any one time.
● **Removing lint** Always clear lint from the filter of a dryer before putting in a fresh load. If the filter is clogged, the dryer will work inefficiently, wasting energy and money.
● **Avoiding damage to wool** Do not tumble dry woollen garments. The heat in the dryer may cause the fibres to shrink. In addition, woollen garments may shed fluff in the dryer.

FOLDING AND IRONING FABRICS

Before ironing, check that the ironing board is set at a comfortable height. Iron garments systematically, starting with any awkward parts such as collars and sleeves, and finishing with large areas. Keep the plate of the iron clean so that it will not mark or stick to any fabric.

SAVING ENERGY
● **Caring for non-iron clothes** Many items, especially those that have been tumble-dried, can be left to air without ironing, then folded. Mixed-fibre shirts do not need ironing if hung immediately on plastic or wire hangers. Do not use wood, because this can stain.
● **Pulling out creases** When hanging clothes and bedding on a line, take time to pull the items into shape and remove creases. Once they are dry, they may not need ironing.
● **Putting clothes in order** Group clothes according to the ironing temperatures that they need; check the labels to be sure. To make the best use of an iron's heat, start work on clothes that require the coolest setting, and work up to the hottest temperature.

MAKING SURE YOU ACHIEVE THE BEST RESULTS
● **Working systematically** Iron shirts and dresses in the following order: collar, yoke, cuffs, fronts, back. For each of these sections, iron on the wrong side of the fabric.

Keeping garments damp
To ensure that silk clothes stay damp enough for ironing, roll several garments together. Put the roll of fabric on a waterproof surface. Do not leave it on top of another fabric or on wood, which could stain the clothes.

● **Avoiding creases** Collars and gathers can be difficult to iron without adding wrinkles. For a collar, work from the points to the centre. For a gather, iron inwards towards a seam.

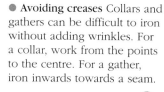

Cleaning a steam iron
Remove scale from a steam iron by using a mixture of equal parts of white vinegar and boiled water. Pour the mixture into the tank, and let the iron steam until dry. Rinse with water, shaking it through the steam holes.

PLANNING FOR DECORATING

I F YOU HAVE A HECTIC LIFESTYLE, you might consider employing a professional decorator. On the other hand, you may find it rewarding to do your own decorating. Start with a small area, and practise before trying special effects.

DECORATING EQUIPMENT

The implements shown here are used for preparing and decorating surfaces. Buy good-quality tools, because they will work effectively and last for a long time. To maximize the working lives of your tools, clean and dry them as soon as you have finished work.

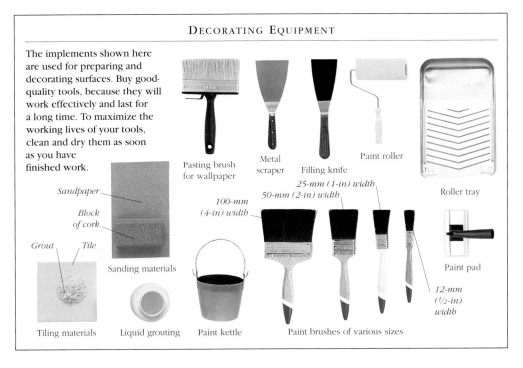

Pasting brush for wallpaper

Metal scraper

Filling knife

Paint roller

Sandpaper

Block of cork

Grout   Tile

Sanding materials

Tiling materials

Liquid grouting

Paint kettle

100-mm (4-in) width

50-mm (2-in) width

25-mm (1-in) width

Roller tray

Paint pad

12-mm (½-in) width

Paint brushes of various sizes

PLANNING A NEW LOOK

Take time for planning before you opt for a new décor. It is usually best to decorate your home in a style appropriate to that of the building. Other considerations include the sizes of the rooms, the amount of light available, and the intended functions of the spaces.

CHOOSING MATERIALS

● **Looking at samples** Gather samples of paint, paper, and fabrics. Leave them in the area to be decorated so that you can judge how they will look (see p. 38). Some shops make a small charge for providing samples, but usually refund this when you place an order.
● **Using existing furniture** A complete new look will be expensive, even if you do it yourself, so plan new schemes around items of furniture and pictures that you already own.

COVERING SURFACES

● **Protecting furniture** If pieces of furniture are to stay in a room during decoration, place them in the centre of the room. Cover with dust sheets.
● **Covering a floor** Spread a thick layer of old newspaper on the floor. Avoid using plastic sheeting, because this can be slippery when it is wet.
● **Covering light fittings** Put plastic bags over any light fittings that you will not use while you are working. Tape the bags to the fittings.

THINGS TO REMEMBER

Before you start to decorate, ensure that all the necessary preparation has been done.

● **Time** Allow enough time for all the tasks to be done, so that you do not rush the work or leave it unfinished.
● **Clothes** Use safety goggles when working above the level of your head.
● **Safety** To guard against ill effects from chemicals, cover your skin, and keep windows open to let fumes disperse.

MAKING A DECORATING LOG

Plan a decorating scheme in detail before you begin the work. Collect samples of materials to form a decorating log, so that you can see at a glance if the materials complement each other. Leave the log in the area to be decorated to check if your plan will suit the room at all times.

COLLECTING MATERIALS

● **Storing samples** Use a box to hold bulky samples, such as hard flooring and carpet, that will not fit in your log. A box file is ideal for this purpose.

● **Choosing new items** If you are buying new objects from a catalogue, cut out the pictures. Add these images to the log.

● **Recording room contents** Photograph the furniture, fittings, and objects that you already have in a room, and put the pictures in the log.

PUTTING TOGETHER A DECORATING LOG

Use pinking shears to cut neat edges

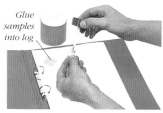

Glue samples into log

1 Cut small squares from your chosen papers and fabrics. Use pinking shears to cut any material that is likely to fray. Dab squares of paint or other liquids on to card, and cut out.

2 Stick the samples to sheets of paper, and store in a ring binder. Group samples of materials to be used together, such as paint and decorative paper for a wall with a dado.

INFORMATION TO INCLUDE IN A DECORATING LOG		
MATERIAL	**FACTS TO RECORD FOR EACH MATERIAL**	
Fabric	● **Design** Record the name, colour, reference number, fabric type, and make of each fabric design. ● **Maintenance information** Put the care label into the log.	● **Colour** If fabric has a colour record along the selvedge (fabric border), cut it off. Take it with you when buying other materials so that you can match the fabric.
Paint	● **Reference** Record the colour, batch number, type, and make. ● **Volume** Note the amount needed per square metre/yard, number of coats, and area to be covered.	● **Undercoat** Include the make, number, and drying time. ● **Cleaning information** List the specific materials needed to clean the different sorts of paint used.
Wallpaper	● **Reference** Record the colour, name, batch number, and make. ● **Measurements** Write down the dimensions of an average roll and the area to be covered.	● **Pattern** Note the length of the pattern drop in metres/yards. Keep a length of the wallpaper. ● **Lining paper** Note the batch number, make, type, and thickness.
Wood treatment	● **Reference** Note the colour and number, batch number, and make. ● **Volume** Note the amount needed per square metre/yard, number of coats, and area to be covered.	● **Time** Write down the drying time of the treatment per coat. ● **Maintenance information** Note renewal times for treatment, and if the surface should be sanded first.
Carpet	● **Reference** Write down the colour, batch number, and make. ● **Measurements** Record the length and width of the rolls, and the total floor area to be covered.	● **Maintenance information** Place the care label in the log. ● **Additional items** Note the type of underlay. Specify the items used to secure the carpet to the floor.

ESTIMATING QUANTITIES

The area that can be covered by a material is usually specified on the package. Measure the total area to be covered. Divide this total by the area covered by one can of paint, roll of paper, or flooring for the amount of material needed. Buy a little more than you require.

CALCULATING AMOUNTS OF MATERIALS

WALLPAPER	LIQUID COVERINGS	TILES AND FLOORING
● **Working out roll area** Most wallpapers are 10 m (33 ft) long and 52 cm (20½ in) wide, and are available ready-trimmed. For untrimmed paper, allow for the area to be trimmed when calculating how much you need. ● **Calculating surface area** Measure the height of a wall from the base to the ceiling or cornice, and measure the width. Multiply the two totals together. ● **Calculating amount** Divide roll length by wall height to find the number of "drops" per roll. Allow enough paper to match patterns, and 5 cm (2 in) extra at the ends of each drop.	● **Assessing surface area** Measure the length and width of each surface to be covered, and multiply the two figures to give the surface area. Add all the area figures to find the total area. ● **Working out volume** The manufacturer's instructions will indicate the area covered by a can of paint or other covering. Divide the total surface area by the figure for one can to work out how many cans you need. ● **Allowing for extras** If you plan to paint a light colour over a very dark colour, allow for more coats than usual to produce the desired shade.	● **Finding number of tiles** Sizes of tile vary. Work out the total area to be covered, and divide this figure by the area per tile to find the number of tiles needed. ● **Planning tile layout** Draw a sketch to show the number of tiles to use and how they will fit together. This will allow you to see if you need to trim any tiles. ● **Measuring an irregular area** If the area to be covered is an irregular shape, draw a plan of it, and divide this into square or rectangular blocks. Calculate the areas of these smaller blocks, then add the figures together to give the total surface area.

PREPARING FOR WALLPAPERING

Surfaces to be papered should be smooth and clean, with holes and cracks filled in. Do not skimp on preparation, since uneven surfaces can cause bumps and bubbles that can be difficult to remove, and the wallpaper may not match exactly at the edges as a result.

STRIPPING OLD PAPER

Soaking with a spray
To soak a small area of wallpaper, use a house-plant spray. You will then be able to strip the wallpaper quickly with a scraper. For large areas, use a garden spray, which holds more water.

PREPARING SURFACES

● **Clearing large areas** If you need to clear large areas of paper, hire a steam stripper.
● **Checking plaster** When you have completely stripped the surface, look at the condition of the plaster. If it is poor, you may need to replaster the area. Plaster takes a long time to dry, so allow for delays.
● **Filling small holes** Using a metal scraper, enlarge holes to take filler. Remove debris with a wire brush. Push the filler in, and level it off with a knife. Sand smooth when dry.
● **Repairing large holes** Pack large holes in plaster with damp newspaper, add filler on top, and sand when dry.

REMOVING FITTINGS

Marking holes for fittings
Remove fittings, nails, or screws from a wall. Hang the wallpaper. While it is damp, push matches through it into the holes left by the items. You can then see where to replace the fittings.

PREPARING FOR PAINTING

Paint shows more flaws on wall surfaces than wallpaper, so surfaces must be clean and smooth before painting. If a surface has been painted before, simply wash it with sugar soap solution after filling any cracks. If it has been papered, remove wallpaper and adhesive.

AVOIDING SPLASHES

● **Covering your hair** Shield your hair from paint splashes with a disposable shower cap.
● **Caring for skin** Keep white spirit or turpentine handy for removing paint from skin.

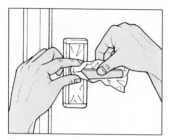

Covering a door handle
Before painting a door, cover the handle and plate with aluminium foil or cling film. Secure the edges of the covering with masking tape. Remove as soon as the door is dry so that adhesive from the tape does not leave marks.

TRADITIONAL TIP

Keeping paint off glass
Before painting a window frame, dampen a bar of soap, and smear it thickly across all the glass. The soap will prevent paint splashes from sticking to the glass, allowing you to remove them easily.

PROTECTING SURFACES

● **Anticipating splashes** Before you start painting, assemble equipment for removing accidental splashes. Whenever possible, clean up any paint while it is still fresh. Remove water-based paint by sponging with cold water. Scrape off oil-based paint with a spoon, then dab the stain with white spirit.
● **Shielding a floor** Use small sheets of cardboard to protect the edges of a floor surface where it meets the walls. As you work, rest the edge of a sheet against the wall, at right angles to the base. You can then paint down to the floor without marking it.
● **Lining containers** Before filling roller trays and paint kettles, line them with plastic bags so that you can remove the paint easily after work.

STARTING WORK

● **Removing old decoration** Strip off any existing surfaces, such as wallpaper, unless you wish to paint over them. Sand and wash the stripped area.

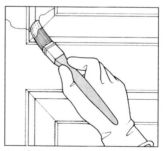

Applying paint stripper
Use an old paint brush or cloth to apply paint stripper to awkward areas, such as the edges of door panels. Wear thick rubber gloves to protect your hands. Take care not to inhale the fumes.

PREPARING TO PAINT

Cover any surface that you do not intend to paint, including already-decorated areas.

● **Hangings** Take down and remove from the room. At the same time, remove or cover fixtures for the hangings.
● **Furniture** Remove as much as possible from the room.
● **Fittings** Cover sockets and switches with cling film. Secure around the edges with masking tape.
● **Lights** Remove shades. Mask light bases that join a wall or ceiling to be painted.
● **Walls** Mask any small areas that are not to be painted.
● **Floor** Fix a covering over areas that you will not paint.
● **Doors and windows** Seal edges with masking tape to keep out dust as you work.

TREATING SURFACES

● **Clearing flaky paint** Scrape large areas carefully with a chisel. Remove dust and small flakes with a vacuum cleaner. Sandpaper each area, then wash and leave it to dry.
● **Filling holes** Brush away debris. Dampen the holes, and pack them with filler. Leave to dry, then sand smooth.
● **Removing grease** Paint will not hold on greasy wallpaper. To remove grease, rest brown paper on the area, and run a warm iron over the paper.
● **Preparing a painted surface** First ensure that the surface is clean. Apply sugar soap with a large sponge to give a suitable surface for the new paint. Alternatively, use a solution of household detergent. Wipe the area dry with a lint-free cloth.

PREPARING TO LAY FLOORING

For flooring to lie properly, the sub-surface must be smooth and level. Sand wooden boards, and punch down protruding nail heads. Concrete floors are usually level, but you can smooth any unevenness by laying a thin layer of screed or covering with sheets of hardboard.

CONSIDERING FLOORING BASICS

● **Fitting carpet tiles** Avoid laying carpets in kitchens and bathrooms. If necessary, use washable carpet tiles that can be easily lifted and washed.
● **Fixing gripper strip** Before laying gripper strip for a carpet, find any central heating pipes under a floor. Put the heating on full, and walk across the floor in bare feet. If you feel heat where a strip will go, glue the strip rather than nail it.
● **Positioning tiles** Lay a wooden batten against a row of correctly spaced tiles. Mark the tile widths on the wood. Use to mark the positions of rows and columns on an area.

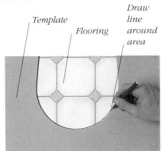

Template   Flooring   Draw line around area

Making a template
To fit sheet flooring in an awkward area, such as around the foot of a basin, draw the shape of the area on paper, and cut this out to make a template. Trace around the template on to sheet flooring, and cut out.

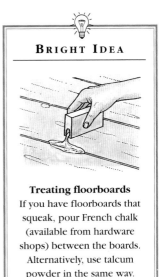

BRIGHT IDEA

Treating floorboards
If you have floorboards that squeak, pour French chalk (available from hardware shops) between the boards. Alternatively, use talcum powder in the same way.

PLANNING A SEQUENCE OF TASKS

Take time to schedule your decorating tasks before starting work, especially if you have several jobs to do in one area. Allow plenty of time for each, so that you do not need to leave work unfinished. Include blocks of time during which wet surfaces can be left to dry.

WORKING IN ORDER

Work from top to bottom in each room. Follow the relevant stages below to paint or wallpaper a room.

● **Papering ceiling** Apply lining paper to the ceiling. Leave to dry before painting.
● **Painting** Prepare and paint ceiling and walls.
● **Decorating woodwork** Apply paint, stain, or varnish.
● **Papering walls** Hang lining. Allow to dry completely before adding wallpaper.
● **Tiling** Mark area with tile layout. Fix tiles in place.
● **Cleaning** Wash tools while decorated areas are drying.
● **Carpeting** Lay new carpet.
● **Putting up fittings** Add or replace fittings.

PAINTING IN STAGES

● **Starting work** Paint from the ceiling down, so that new paint is not splashed. Work away from the source of light.
● **Applying primer** Use primer on any surface that has not been painted before.
● **Using undercoat** Apply as many coats as necessary to cover an old surface colour.
● **Adding topcoats** Allow enough time to paint a whole area at once, so that you do not leave unsightly tidemarks when you finish work.
● **Coating wood** Seal knots with knotting before applying coats of paint or varnish.
● **Removing masking tape** Take off tape before the paint is totally dry, so that the tape does not pull off new paint.

PAPERING IN ORDER

● **Planning work** Start work at a focal point or light source. End in an inconspicuous area because you are likely to need to cut the paper to fit.
● **Hanging lining paper** Apply lining paper horizontally to walls so that the seams do not match those of the top paper. Allow 12 hours to dry.

TILING IN SEQUENCE

● **Marking surface** When marking the guidelines for placing the tiles, allow space around obstructions to fit cut tiles of equal size.
● **Using adhesive** Score ridges in tile adhesive to create suction to hold the tiles fast.
● **Spacing tiles** Cut matches in half to use as tile spacers.

CARING FOR MATERIALS

You may not need decorating equipment for a long time once you have used it, so clean it well and store it safely. Properly maintained tools will last for years. Keep leftover materials such as tiles, rolls of paper, and small amounts of paint. Store these away from light and heat.

DEALING WITH PAINT

● **Washing out emulsion paint** To clean a brush, scrape off as much paint as you can with a flat-bladed knife, then rinse the brush well in warm water.

● **Removing oil-based paint** Squeeze the brush between sheets of newspaper. Put a little solvent in a plastic bag, and seal loosely around the handle. Rub the bag against the brush to work the solvent into the bristles. Wash with detergent and warm water.

● **Using solvents** Before you remove oil-based paint, look at the can to see if any special solvent is recommended.

● **Keeping spare paint** Pour a little paint into a clean, glass screw-top jar. Label with the colour, reference number, and manufacturer's name, and note where the paint was used.

SAFEGUARD TIP

Disposing of glaze
Glaze is highly flammable; rags soaked in glaze may catch fire without warning. Wear rubber gloves when handling them. Seal the rags in an old can before throwing them away.

MAINTAINING BRUSHES

● **Drying off brushes** Shake brushes vigorously to get rid of excess water, then dry with a clean, lint-free cloth. Take care not to harm the bristles.

Wrap card around bristles

Storing a paintbrush
Wash and dry a paintbrush, then straighten the bristles. Cut a rectangle of card from an old cereal packet. Wrap this around the bristles to cover them, and secure with an elastic band.

CLEANING TOOLS

● **Wiping wallpaper tools** To remove wallpaper paste from a paper-hanging brush, seam-roller, or pair of scissors, wipe with a damp, clean cloth. Put the tools away in a dry place.

Washing tiling tools
Rinse tiling tools in warm water immediately after use. To avoid clogging drains, wash tools in a bucket, and let the residue settle. Pour the water away, then tip the residue into a can for disposal.

CARING FOR ROLLERS

● **Removing excess paint** Run the roller firmly across layers of newspaper, discarding each layer as it becomes dirty. Clean paint pads in the same way.

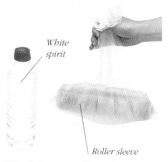

White spirit

Roller sleeve

Washing a roller sleeve
To remove oil-based paint from a roller sleeve, put the sleeve in a plastic bag, and soak it in white spirit. Wash the sleeve with detergent and warm water to remove the white spirit.

STORING MATERIALS

● **Storing paint pads** Once you have cleaned a paint pad, put it in a plastic bag to stop dust from settling on the mohair. Seal the bag around the pad's handle with an elastic band.

Hook

Tube is hung from hole in flap

Insulating tape

Hanging up a tube
To hang up a tube, such as a tube of grout, fold a 15-cm (6-in) length of insulation tape over the end, leaving a flap. Pierce a hole in the flap so that you can hang the tube from a hook or nail.

MAINTAINING THE HOME

YOUR HOME WILL FUNCTION AT ITS BEST if you keep the structure in good repair and ensure that systems such as fuel and water operate efficiently. As well as being pleasant to live in, a well-kept home will maintain its financial value.

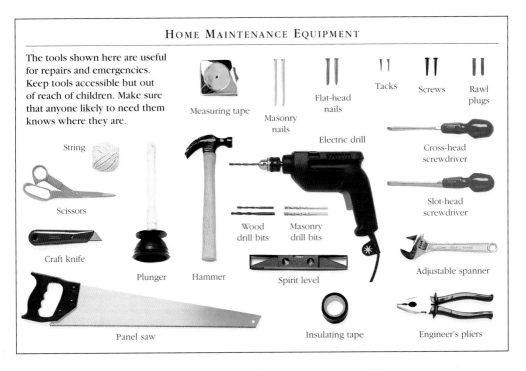

HOME MAINTENANCE EQUIPMENT

The tools shown here are useful for repairs and emergencies. Keep tools accessible but out of reach of children. Make sure that anyone likely to need them knows where they are.

Measuring tape

Masonry nails

Flat-head nails

Tacks

Screws

Rawl plugs

Electric drill

Cross-head screwdriver

Slot-head screwdriver

String

Scissors

Craft knife

Wood drill bits

Masonry drill bits

Plunger

Hammer

Spirit level

Adjustable spanner

Panel saw

Insulating tape

Engineer's pliers

MAKING REGULAR CHECKS AND REPAIRS

Look over your home regularly so that you know what the systems and structure are like when they work normally. You will then be able to spot any problems as they occur. Make repairs as soon as you can; even minor problems may become serious if left untreated.

CARRYING OUT REPAIRS

● **Fixing wallpaper** If using spare wallpaper for repairs, hang it in the appropriate room until it fades to the same shade as the paper on the wall.
● **Checking window areas** See that blinds and curtains work easily. Spray sticking curtain tracks with furniture polish.
● **Oiling metal parts** Oil door and window hinges often, and catches occasionally. Lubricate cylinder locks with graphite powder instead of oil, since oil traps dirt in the mechanism.

FREEING A DOOR

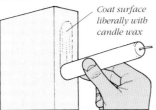

Coat surface liberally with candle wax

Coating surface with wax
If a wooden door sticks in its frame, warm the end of a wax candle. Rub the warm end along the parts of the door and frame that stick to make these parts slide easily against each other.

MAINTAINING OBJECTS

● **Inspecting equipment** Make sure that repair equipment, such as long ladders and step-ladders, is safe. Look out for loose joints or worn treads.
● **Examining furniture** Check that drawers and cupboard doors open easily. Repair any sticking runners or loose hinges as soon as possible.
● **Listing first-aid kit** Attach a list of the contents to the lid of your first-aid box. Mark on the list when an item has been used, and be sure to replace it.

MAKING MAINTENANCE CHECKS

The best way to keep track of household maintenance is to make regular inspections of your home and note what needs to be done. By making regular checks you are unlikely to run into major difficulties. However, if problems do arise, there are many clever solutions.

USING A WATER SYSTEM

● **Checking a water tank** Inspect the water tank once a year. Look out for brown or white areas, which signal corrosion and must be treated.
● **Monitoring water flow** Test seldom-used basins, bidets, or toilets to check that the water flows freely. Let taps run for a few minutes, and flush toilets.
● **Keeping drains clear** To stop drains in baths and basins from becoming blocked, pull hairs out of plugholes.
● **Inspecting drainage** Check gutters for cracks, and remove debris. Examine down pipes to make sure that they are firmly fixed to the wall.
● **Locating stopcocks** Make sure that everyone knows where the stopcocks are, and how to turn them off.

SAFEGUARD TIP

Insulating a pipe
In almost any climate, the temperature at night may fall low enough to freeze water in unprotected pipes. To prevent this from occurring, use insulation material to cover water pipes in unheated areas of a home.

MAINTAINING PLUMBING

● **Testing radiators** With the heating on, feel each radiator. If the top is cooler than the base, air is present. Remove air by using a radiator key.
● **Stopping drips** Store spare washers. If a tap starts to drip, replace the washer instantly.

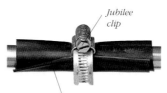

Jubilee clip

Bicycle inner tube

Fixing a pipe quickly
If a metal pipe leaks, cover the leak until it can be repaired. Cut a length of bicycle inner tube. Slit it lengthways, and wrap it over the leak. Pull the tube tight, and fasten with a jubilee clip.

CHECKING ELECTRICS

● **Inspecting connections** Make sure that there are no cracks in plugs, sockets, or electrical flexes. Pull flexes gently where they meet plugs to check that wiring is not loose.
● **Identifying problems** A warm plug or flex is a sign of faulty wiring. Switch off the appliance. Use it again only after the wiring is repaired.
● **Maintaining safety** Do not attempt to repair electrical wiring on an appliance. Call a qualified repair person to deal with the problem.

MAKING STRUCTURAL CHECKS FOR DAMP

● **Inspecting walls** Look at the surfaces of inside and outside walls for damp patches.
● **Preventing damp** Clear away any leaves or debris heaped against outside walls.

PREVENTING PROBLEMS

To stop a simple problem from becoming an emergency, take preventative action.

● **Saving water** Before draining the water supply, collect cold water in large containers so that you can wash, cook, and use the toilet while the water supply is turned off.
● **Unblocking drains** Take immediate action if you notice that water drains sluggishly. If a drain is totally blocked, use a plunger before trying liquid drain cleaner.
● **Removing grease** Never use liquid cleaner to clear sink blockages containing fat. For grease-blocked pipes, pour in a handful of washing soda, followed by 1 litre (1¾ pints) of boiling water.

CHECKING SAFETY ITEMS

Testing a smoke detector
To ensure that a smoke detector registers smoke, move a lit candle gently under it. If it fails to work, remove dust from the detector with a vacuum cleaner, and replace the batteries.

● **Looking at roofs** Examine flat roofs and the ceilings beneath them. Check for damp patches, which may be caused by condensation or leaks and will need to be treated.

MAKING A HOME MAINTENANCE LOG

Having made an initial inspection of your home, compile a log of areas that need to be examined regularly. Leave space to tick and date each check, and add any comments. Use a new log for each inspection. The log will also be handy for briefing professional repair people.

USING A LOG

● **Making initial checks** Make a log as soon as you move into a new home so that you can repair problems straight away.

● **Compiling information** File the completed logs in a ring binder, with the most recent at the top. Keep the file in the same place as your other household documents.

● **Monitoring changes** When compiling a new log, examine previous logs to identify any potential problems. Note these trouble spots on the new log and check them first.

KEEPING RECORDS

● **Storing instruction manuals** When you buy a new electrical appliance, the manufacturers should supply an instruction manual and a guarantee. File these in a safe place with the log so that you can find them if an appliance becomes faulty.

● **Servicing items** Arrange to have features such as a central heating system or a burglar alarm serviced about once a year by professionals. Keep a servicing record for each item with the log so that you are aware of potential problems.

DOING OTHER TASKS

● **Recording damage** If an object is too badly damaged for you to repair, write down exactly what is wrong with it and anything that you do to fix it temporarily. Discuss these notes with a professional when you arrange for the object to be repaired.

● **Replacing materials** Make a note of any spare parts that are worth buying and storing for future use. For example, it is worth keeping extra washers for taps and one or two spare flexes for electrical appliances.

CHECKS TO INCLUDE IN A HOME MAINTENANCE LOG			
ITEM	NATURE OF CHECK	ITEM	NATURE OF CHECK
Roof: outside	● **Roofing** Material is intact. ● **Gutter** Guttering and pipes are intact, rust-free, and clear. ● **Structure** All parts are sound.	Loft	● **Insulation** Material is packed securely, with no gaps. ● **Floor** There is not any excessive stress from objects stored in attic.
Walls: outside	● **Surfaces** Walls have no cracks, damp patches, or broken pieces. ● **Drains** Pipes and drain covers beside walls are free of debris.	Walls: inside	● **Surfaces** Paint and other surfacings are in good order. ● **Condition** Damp, mould, and pests are not present.
Floors	● **Surfaces** Flooring is intact. ● **Condition** Damp is not present. ● **Water exclusion** Outside-door seals are watertight.	Doors and windows	● **Seals** Devices are watertight. ● **Catches and locks** Parts work freely, and are not stiff or loose. ● **Frames** Surfaces are sound.
Pipes and stopcocks	● **Materials** Pipes are intact, rust-free, and do not leak water. ● **Stopcocks** Taps turn easily.	Central heating	● **Heating system** Boiler is working efficiently. ● **Radiators** Pipes are free of air.
Water fittings	● **Drains** Sinks and baths drain freely. Toilets are not blocked. ● **Shower** Head is not clogged. ● **Taps** Taps turn and do not leak.	Electrical fittings	● **Lights** All bulbs and switches are working correctly. ● **Wiring** Exposed wires are intact and secure.
Safety and security equipment	● **Burglar alarm** This works correctly. ● **Fire equipment** Extinguishers and blankets are in good order.	Electrical appliances	● **Functions** Items work correctly. ● **Wiring** Flexes, plugs, and sockets are in good order.

ENSURING SECURITY AND SAFETY

IT IS WISE TO MAKE YOUR HOME SAFE, both to protect your possessions and to ensure peace of mind. By purchasing or making security equipment and planning ahead, you will be able to prevent many problems before they occur.

HOME SECURITY EQUIPMENT

A home security system need not be elaborate, but it must be effective. Fit locks to windows and outside doors, especially in areas that are not often used. If you have an alarm system, ensure that everyone in the household is able to use it. Keep the instructions in a safe place.

● **Fitting locks** Before you fit a lock, check that the door or window and its frame are sound. If not, the lock may not deter burglars.

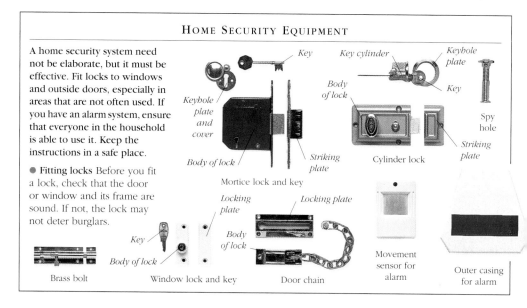

Key · Key cylinder · Keyhole plate · Key
Body of lock · Spy hole
Keyhole plate and cover · Body of lock · Striking plate · Cylinder lock · Striking plate
Mortice lock and key
Locking plate · Locking plate · Body of lock
Key · Body of lock
Brass bolt · Window lock and key · Door chain · Movement sensor for alarm · Outer casing for alarm

MAKING YOUR HOME SECURE

Examine your home for weak spots such as rarely used doors and basement or ground-floor windows. Fit locks to these points, and check regularly to ensure that the locks work properly. Establish a sensible security routine, such as locking doors every time you go out.

DEALING WITH CALLERS
● **Checking identification** Cut the logos from letters sent by suppliers such as an electricity company. Fix them to a sheet of paper, and label them. Use the paper to check identity cards when officials call.
● **Accompanying strangers** Stay with strangers while they are in your home. Keep them in one room if possible, and close the doors to all other rooms. Never leave a handbag or wallet in a room with a stranger.
● **Giving information** When recording a message on an answerphone, make sure that you do not indicate whether or not you are at home.

PREVENTING BURGLARY
● **Using a door chain** Put the chain on the door whenever a stranger calls. However, do not keep the chain on all the time, since it may stop people from escaping in an emergency. Instead, keep the door locked.
● **Blocking a sliding door** Put a broom handle in the track of a sliding door to stop burglars from opening the door even if they have broken the lock.
● **Using plants** Grow bushy, prickly plants outside ground-floor windows to deter burglars from reaching the windows.
● **Securing windows** Fit locks to any upper-storey windows situated near a flat roof.

KEEPING KEYS SAFE

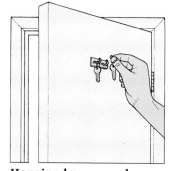

Hanging keys on a door
To keep window and door keys safe, fix a hook to the back of the relevant room door, and hang the keys from it. Ensure that they will not be visible to people looking through the windows.

PROTECTING ITEMS WITHIN ROOMS

To protect valuables from theft, keep them in an undetectable place or in a container such as a strong box. Compile security records, including pictures of the objects and notes of security marks. Use these to help you or the police to identify objects if they are ever stolen.

MAKING A MINI-SAFE FROM A BOOK

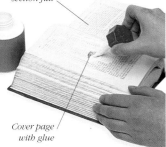

Keep glued section flat

Cover page with glue

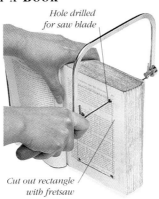

Hole drilled for saw blade

Cut out rectangle with fretsaw

1 Find an unwanted hardback book. Separate a thick section of pages in the centre. Glue together all of the pages in the sections at the beginning and end. Leave to dry, then glue together all of the pages in the central section.

2 When the central section is dry, mark a rectangle in the middle of it, leaving a border of about 4 cm (1½ in). Cut out the rectangle with a fretsaw. Glue the border to the end section. Put valuables in the safe, and keep on a shelf.

RECORDING SECURITY MARKS

Keep identification notes for the following objects. If they have reference numbers, write these down. If not, use an ultraviolet pen to mark your postcode or house number in an inconspicuous place.

- Television.
- Video cassette recorder.
- Audio equipment.
- Personal stereo.
- Computer: hard drive, monitor, keyboard, and accessories.
- Bicycle.
- Sports equipment.
- Kitchen appliances.
- Valuable furniture.
- Antique objects.
- Valuable clothes.

MAKING YOUR HOME SAFE

More accidents happen in the home than in any other place. However, it takes only a little forethought to prevent many crises. Look around your home to identify the possible hazards, and make sure that you have enough equipment to deal with dangers such as fire.

AVOIDING FIRE HAZARDS

● **Showing fire escapes** Draw plans for each floor, and mark which doors or windows to use as fire exits. Display the plans in a prominent place.

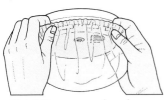

Shielding a smoke alarm
Place a smoke detector in any room with potential fire hazards, such as a kitchen. Put a shower cap over it while you are cooking to prevent a false alarm. Remove the cap immediately afterwards.

PREVENTING ACCIDENTS

● **Disposing of sharp items** Wrap pieces of glass or metal in several layers of newspaper before throwing them away.
● **Preventing scalds** Before pouring hot water into a sink, partially fill the sink with cold water. This will prevent steam from rising and scalding you.
● **Making glass doors safe** Stick adhesive shapes on to glass doors. This will make the glass obvious so that children and animals do not run into it.
● **Avoiding electrical fires** Do not hide an electric flex under a carpet or a loose rug. If you cover a flex in this way, it may overheat and catch fire.

SECURING RUGS

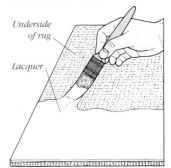

Underside of rug

Lacquer

Making a rug stay in place
If a rug is not valuable, paint the underside with lacquer. Leave to dry, then wipe over with laundry starch, and let this dry. Fix a strip of rubber to each edge to enable the rug to grip the floor securely.

PREPARING FOOD

QUICK REFERENCE

Maintaining a
Kitchen, p. 50

Buying Food and Other
Goods, p. 52

Organizing Food
Stores, p. 54

Preserving Food, p. 56

Cooking, p. 60

Entertaining Guests, p. 62

FOOD PREPARATION WILL BE EASIEST and most enjoyable if your kitchen is clean, well organized, and well stocked. Keep as much equipment as you need for the amount of cooking that you do, and take good care of it so that it will work properly and last for a long time. To avoid running out of food, make sure that you always have enough of essential supplies, and set aside blocks of time to prepare meals in advance. Plan carefully for special occasions such as dinner parties.

BASIC EQUIPMENT FOR FOOD PREPARATION

The equipment shown here should be sufficient for all your everyday cooking requirements. Buy the best that you can afford, and ensure that the items are easy to handle. Do not buy items that are too heavy to carry.

● **Choosing vessels** Buy pots, pans, and bowls in two or three sizes so that you can prepare different volumes of food.
● **Selecting colanders** Choose a metal colander rather than a plastic one. Plastic may melt if you pour hot water on it.
● **Buying chopping boards** Plastic is easier to clean than wood, and can be washed in a dishwasher. If you buy wooden chopping boards, choose thick ones, which should not warp after washing.

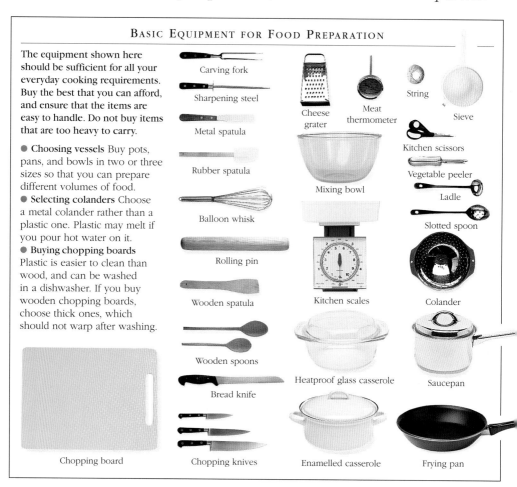

Carving fork

Sharpening steel

Metal spatula

Rubber spatula

Balloon whisk

Rolling pin

Wooden spatula

Wooden spoons

Bread knife

Chopping knives

Chopping board

Cheese grater

Meat thermometer

Mixing bowl

Kitchen scales

Heatproof glass casserole

Enamelled casserole

String

Sieve

Kitchen scissors

Vegetable peeler

Ladle

Slotted spoon

Colander

Saucepan

Frying pan

FOOD-STORAGE CONTAINERS

Keep a range of containers for preserving fresh foods and storing long-life goods. To obtain the best use from food containers, follow these practical guidelines.

● **Storing dried foods** To maximize the lifespan of dried foods, take them out of the packets in which they were bought, and transfer them into airtight containers. Label the containers clearly.

● **Fitting corks into bottles** To fit a swollen cork into a bottle or jar, soak the cork in boiling water for a few minutes. It will then be soft enough to be squeezed into place.

● **Checking seals** Regularly inspect corks in bottles and rubber seals on preserving jars to ensure that they have not perished or changed shape.

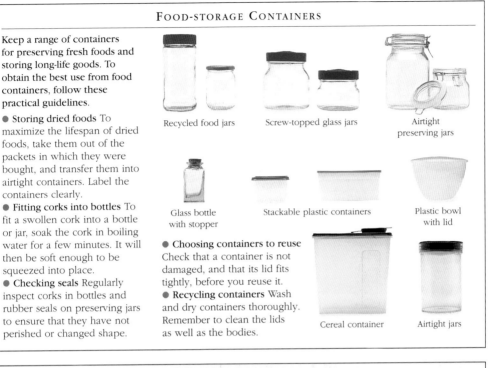

Recycled food jars   Screw-topped glass jars   Airtight preserving jars

Glass bottle with stopper   Stackable plastic containers   Plastic bowl with lid

Cereal container   Airtight jars

● **Choosing containers to reuse** Check that a container is not damaged, and that its lid fits tightly, before you reuse it.

● **Recycling containers** Wash and dry containers thoroughly. Remember to clean the lids as well as the bodies.

UTILIZING ELECTRICAL KITCHEN APPLIANCES

FOOD PROCESSOR

● **Preparing cheese for pasta** Chop cubes of hard cheese until they resemble crumbs.

● **Removing odours** Chop pieces of bread to clean the interior.

TOASTER

● **Defrosting bread** Thaw single slices of bread by heating them in a toaster on a low setting.

● **Cleaning** To dislodge crumbs, blow through a drinking straw.

BLENDER

● **Making breadcrumbs** Chop stale bread in a blender to make fresh breadcrumbs.

● **Cleaning interior** To remove soft food from the blades, put warm water in the blender, and run it for a few seconds.

ELECTRIC CAN OPENER

● **Opening pet food cans** Use a separate can opener for pet food cans to avoid contaminating other foods.

● **Cleaning cutting wheel** Remove dried food with an old toothbrush.

HAND WHISK

● **Improving sauces** Whisk sauces while they are still in the pan to remove any lumps from the liquid.

● **Whisking hot drinks** Whisk hot milk or cocoa to make extra froth.

COFFEE PERCOLATOR

● **Improvising filter paper** If you run out of filter papers, use a sheet of strong kitchen paper.

● **Cleaning** Add 10 ml (2 tsp) baking soda to water, and brew.

FOOD MIXER

● **Making muesli** Use a cake mixer tool to mix dry muesli.

● **Drying blades** After washing, dry blades in a warm oven to avoid cutting your fingers.

ELECTRIC CARVING KNIFE

● **Straightening a blade** Press a bent blade between a heavy object and a flat surface.

● **Slicing gateaux** Use an electric knife to slice a gateau while it is frozen.

Maintaining a Kitchen

By keeping kitchen equipment clean and in good repair, you can ensure that it works properly and lasts as long as possible. Keep blades sharp and surfaces clean. Store pots and pans so that the insides are protected from dirt.

Keeping Work Surfaces Clean

To maintain hygiene, keep all work surfaces clean. Wipe the surfaces with a product containing a bactericide, especially if food has fallen on to them. Avoid resting hot containers on work surfaces, since scorched areas can harbour germs and are difficult to clean.

Using Work Surfaces
- **Preparing food** Do not prepare food directly on a work surface; this is unhygienic and could damage the surface. Use a chopping board instead.
- **Resting hot pans** To avoid scorching work surfaces with hot pans, keep a heatproof pan rest, thick wooden board, or large earthenware tile by the hob. Use a perforated trivet if you need food to cool.
- **Cleaning awkward areas** Dip a toothbrush in diluted bleach to scrub inaccessible surfaces such as the grout between tiles.

Using a Sink Area
- **Avoiding stains** Keep steel pan scourers in a container when wet so that they do not leave rust stains on a draining board.
- **Draining cutlery** Stand cutlery in a plastic holder with a perforated base to drain. Clean the holder regularly to stop dirt from collecting in it.
- **Peeling vegetables** After washing, lay vegetables on a drainage rack to drain. Peel washed vegetables over a drainage rack to stop peels from clogging the plughole.

Providing Drainage

Sink — *Tray with holes*

Improvising a drainer
Find an inexpensive plastic tray that fits over your sink. Drill holes in the base at 5-cm (2-in) intervals. Use the tray as an extra surface for draining wet items.

Storing Equipment

Organize pots and pans, and their lids, so that they are accessible and take up the minimum of space. Store them in cupboards to keep them clean. If you store them on open shelves, wash them regularly. Always protect the interiors of non-stick pans from scratches.

Stacking Saucepans

Stand pan on centre of trivet

Using a trivet
A lid can be damaged when two pans are stacked on each other. To avoid this, invert the lid of one pan. Lay a trivet on it, and place another pan on top. The trivet will take the weight of this pan.

Protecting Surfaces

Keeping a wok clean
Never clean a seasoned wok with washing-up liquid, since this will strip the seasoning from the inside. Wipe the wok clean with paper towels, then wrap in aluminium foil before storing.

Storing Other Items
- **Tidying lids** Fix a narrow, plastic-covered rack to the door of a cupboard to hold lids for pans and casseroles.
- **Organizing equipment** Store mixing bowls and measuring jugs near work surfaces. Keep two or three of each so that you do not need to interrupt food preparation to wash up.
- **Keeping specialized items** Do not keep a specialized utensil, such as a pasta-cutting machine, unless you are sure that you will use it often. It will only take up space that could house necessary items.

KEEPING UTENSILS

Keep items such as knives and ladles safely so that they will not be damaged and will not cause injuries. Hang up long, thin items, or those with holes in their handles, to keep them out of the way of work surfaces. Clean utensils regularly so that they are always ready for use.

TIDYING METAL ITEMS

● **Keeping knives** Use a knife block. Do not put knives in a drawer – they will rub against other items and become blunt.

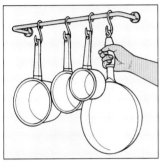

Hanging objects on a rail
Fix a towel rail high on a wall, and attach butcher's hooks to it. Use the rail to hang lightweight pots and pans, or utensils such as ladles, sieves, and slotted spoons.

MAINTAINING WOOD

● **Cleaning utensils** Wash wooden spoons and spatulas regularly, even if you have not used them. If you stand them in a container by your cooker, clean the container as well to remove dust and grease.
● **Combating dryness** If any wooden utensils appear dried out, coat them lightly in oil. Wipe off excess oil with paper towels. Oil feeds wood and restores its appearance.
● **Cleaning chopping boards** Scrub wooden boards with a wire wool pad after use to remove all traces of food. If possible, keep separate boards for raw meat, poultry, and fish, since these foods may contain bacteria that could be transferred to other foods.

BRIGHT IDEA

Using a toothbrush
Keep an old toothbrush for cleaning items such as cheese graters and garlic crushers. To remove odours from the items, dip the toothbrush bristles in bicarbonate of soda before use.

MAKING A CANVAS ROLL FOR KITCHEN KNIVES

If you do not have a magnetic knife rack or a knife block, make a knife roll from canvas. Allow 7.5 cm (3 in) of width for each knife. The roll can be made to hold knives of various sizes, with pockets shaped so that you can remove knives easily. Wash the roll regularly so that dirt is not transferred to the knives.

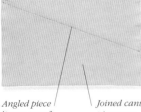

Angled piece lies on top of straight piece

Joined canvas pieces are turned right side out

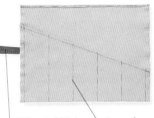

Ribbon is folded double and sewn at centre

Seams form pockets for knives

End of handle is exposed

Roll up tightly so that cloth holds knives securely

1 Cut two pieces of canvas 2.5 cm (1 in) longer than your longest knife. Trim the top of one piece at an angle. Hem the top edges. Align the pieces, wrong sides facing, and join at the bottom edges.

2 Sew the sides together. Mark lines down the angled piece at 7.5-cm (3-in) intervals, and sew through both pieces along these lines. Cut 50 cm (20 in) of strong ribbon for a tie, and sew it behind the longest pocket.

3 Slide knives into the pockets, in order of size. Roll up the canvas, starting from the end containing the shortest knife. To secure the roll, wrap the two halves of ribbon around it, and tie with a double bow.

BUYING FOOD AND OTHER GOODS

PLAN EVERY SHOPPING TRIP so that you can make the most economical use of your money, time, and energy. This is particularly important if you will be accompanied by young children, or if you are working to a tight budget.

PREPARING TO GO SHOPPING

Work out the practical details, such as how much you will spend and when to travel, in advance. Allow sufficient time for your trip, including a little extra time in case of delays. Try not to go shopping when the roads will be busy or the shops will be crowded.

CHECKING SUPPLIES

When writing a shopping list, check your home for supplies of the following items.

● **Food and drink** Plan meals, and check long-term supplies in your cupboards, freezer, and drinks stores.
● **Household goods** Check cleaning supplies for kitchen and bathroom, and items such as light bulbs and batteries.
● **Toiletries** Check with all members of the household to see which toiletries need to be replenished for them.

COMPILING A SHOPPING LIST

Wire hooks hold roll of paper

Touch-and-close tape on pencil

Touch-and-close tape fixes pencil to wood when pencil is not in use

Wire holds paper taut on wood

Making a shopping-list holder

Drill two holes towards each end of a piece of wood. Thread wire around the back of the wood and through one pair of holes. Bend each end to form a hook. Fix a roll of paper between the hooks. Thread wire through the other holes to secure the loose end of the paper.

PLANNING TO SHOP

● **Making a list** Arrange entries in groups, such as canned foods or dairy products. If you know the layout of a shop, list items in the order in which you will find them. By sorting out your list in this way, you can limit your time in a shop and avoid forgetting anything.
● **Leaving children** Try not to take small children on major shopping trips, which are unpleasant for most children. Arrange to leave them with a friend for whom you can return the favour in the future.
● **Organizing your route** If you have many different items to buy, leave food shopping and heavy or bulky items until last. This will reduce the risks to perishable foods and limit the carrying of heavy bags.

VISITING SHOPS

● **Eating beforehand** Always eat something before you go shopping. If you are hungry you will not shop efficiently, and may be tempted by items that you do not really need.
● **Dressing comfortably** Wear flat shoes so that you can move fast. Put on a sweater or jacket that you can remove easily if you get hot.
● **Using a shopping list** Take a pen or pencil with you so that you can tick off items on your shopping list as you buy them. If you do not have a pen or pencil, make dents in the list with a fingernail.
● **Protecting frozen foods** If you have a cool bag or freezer blocks, take these with you to keep frozen or perishable goods cool on the way home.

MONEY-SAVING TIP

Keeping foods cool
If you do not have a cool bag or freezer blocks, take some old newspapers with you when you go shopping. Wrap frozen foods in several sheets of newspaper before packing them. The wrapping will help to keep the foods cool during the journey home.

SHOPPING EFFICIENTLY

To make the best use of your money, keep track of your spending while you are in a shop. Plan a route around a shop so that you can move quickly with no distractions. As you gather and pack goods, arrange them so that they will not be damaged during transport.

USING MONEY WISELY

● **Keeping track of costs** Take a pocket calculator with you, and add up prices as you collect goods so that you will be able to see immediately if you go over your budget.

● **Buying fruits and vegetables** Buy loose items, which will be cheaper than those that are already packaged.

TAKING CONTAINERS

● **Carrying easily** If you are going by car, take boxes with you. Load your shopping into them so that it does not roll around in the boot. If you are walking or travelling on public transport, take a holdall or rucksack so that you can carry the shopping comfortably.

MANAGING SHOPPING TRIPS WITH CHILDREN

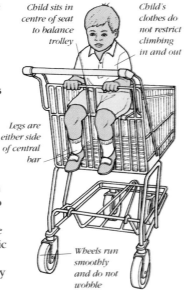

Child sits in centre of seat to balance trolley

Child's clothes do not restrict climbing in and out

Legs are either side of central bar

Wheels run smoothly and do not wobble

● **Keeping children occupied** If you have to take a small child shopping, let the child take a toy that is easy to carry. If the child sits in a shopping trolley, tie the toy to the trolley handle with string to prevent the child from dropping it.

● **Finding suitable shops** Call the head offices of shops to find out whether they have any local outlets with supervised children's play areas.

Checking a trolley
When selecting a trolley in a shop, check that the trolley runs smoothly and that the child seat or baby seat is safe. If the trolley is fitted with a safety belt, make sure that it is working properly.

PACKING YOUR PURCHASES

As you place items into a supermarket basket or trolley, arrange them so that they are not crushed. Pack them similarly in your shopping bag.

● **Collecting goods** Load trolleys and baskets so that fragile items rest on top of heavy ones. At the checkout, unpack the heaviest goods first so that you can fill bags and boxes in the same way.

● **Letting children help** Ask older children to arrange goods in a trolley and unload them at the checkout. This will free you to choose and pay for the goods.

Organizing items in a bag
When loading a shopping bag, start with heavy or hard objects. Include toiletries and cleaning fluids so that these will not leak over food. Put more fragile items above, packing them securely so that they will not fall out.

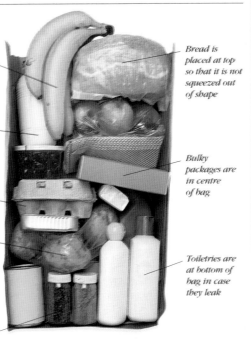

Fruits and vegetables are packed at top so that they are not squashed

Soft bottles and cartons are near top so that they are not crushed

Egg-box is secured in middle

Heavy potatoes are near bottom of bag

Metal and glass containers are in bottom of bag so that they do not squash fragile objects

Bread is placed at top so that it is not squeezed out of shape

Bulky packages are in centre of bag

Toiletries are at bottom of bag in case they leak

ORGANIZING FOOD STORES

KEEP YOUR FOOD STORES TIDY so that you will always know what is in stock and where to find items. Group foods of the same type together, and write the use-by dates on food packets if they are difficult to see at a glance.

KEEPING DIFFERENT FOODS

Put strong-smelling foods such as garlic in plastic containers or cardboard packets so that their odours are not transferred to other foods. Whenever you transfer food from one container to another, make sure that the new container is clean and dry before doing so.

STORING ESSENTIALS

Maintain a stock of these foods so that you always have the basis for a quick meal.

- Cereals.
- Coffee and tea.
- Dressings and sauces.
- Dried herbs and spices.
- Flour.
- Lemon juice.
- Meat and vegetable extracts.
- Cooking oil.
- Pasta.
- Pulses.
- Rice.
- Salt and pepper.
- Canned food.
- Stock cubes.
- Sugar.
- Long-life drinks.

PRESERVING QUALITY

● **Using a rack** Keep long-life fresh foods, such as citrus fruits and onions, on a plastic or wire vegetable rack. Ensure that air can circulate around the foods, since this will inhibit the growth of mould.
● **Preserving potatoes** Store potatoes in a cool, dark place. This will keep them fresh, and slow the development of sprouts or green patches.
● **Avoiding contamination** Do not store damaged vegetables or fruits with unblemished foods, since the damaged items may contaminate any neighbouring ones. Keep the imperfect items separate, and use them up quickly.

STORING FRESH FOODS

● **Preserving perishables** Store perishable vegetables and fruits such as cucumbers and melons in the salad drawer of a refrigerator (see p. 57).

Preparing spring onions
Wash fresh spring onions, then cut off the leaves down to the bulbs. Put the bulbs into sealed plastic bags to stop the odour from escaping, and keep them in a refrigerator until needed.

STORING CAKES

Put sugar by cut part of cake

Reducing humidity
Store cake in an airtight container, and place one or two sugar lumps in the container with the cake. The sugar will absorb moisture from the air, and this will keep the cake fresh.

TIDYING CANS

Organizing pet food
Cut a slot, slightly larger than a pet food can, in one end of a wide plastic pipe. Stand the pipe with the slot at the base. Drop cans into the top. Take cans from the slot to use the oldest first.

KEEPING DRIED FOODS

● **Storing dried herbs** Buy dried herbs in small amounts. Light makes them taste musty, so keep them in the dark.
● **Checking for pests** Inspect dried foods regularly. Discard any with pests or droppings.

SAFETY

Be careful never to buy or use canned foods that show any of the following signs.

● **Punctures** These allow air to contaminate the food.
● **Domed ends** The food is rotting and generating gas.
● **Foul smell** The food is bad.

MANAGING A STORECUPBOARD

When you put away food that you have just bought, push it to the back of the cupboard, and move other items forwards so that you use these up first. Check use-by dates and the condition of fresh foods regularly, and throw out food that is past its best.

STORING BASIC SUPPLIES
● **Keeping extras** Choose an area of your storecupboard for keeping back-up supplies of food. Keep these supplies away from frequently used shelves and their contents.
● **Storing drinks** Always keep some long-life milk and fruit juice among the supplies.
● **Monitoring supplies** Check the store area regularly, to see that supplies have not run out.
● **Keeping olive oil** If you buy olive oil in a plastic bottle, decant it into a glass bottle after opening to ensure that it keeps well. An empty wine bottle is an ideal container. Store in a cool, dark cupboard or in the refrigerator.

USING DOOR SPACE

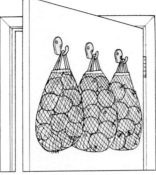

Hanging items in bags
Fix cup-hooks to the back of a kitchen door to hold string bags of fruits and vegetables. Ensure that the weight of the bags and their contents does not put too much stress on the door and its hinges.

ADAPTING SHELVES
● **Saving space** Stand small jars and bottles on a spice rack against a wall so that they take up a minimum of space.

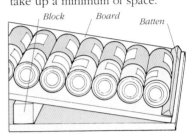

Block   Board   Batten

Keeping cans in order
Make a sloping shelf for food cans by resting one end of a thick board on a block of wood. Fix a batten to the front to stop cans from rolling off. Lay cans on the shelf with the newest at the back.

SUGGESTED MAXIMUM STORAGE TIMES FOR NON-PERISHABLE FOODS

FOOD TYPE	STORAGE TIME	FOOD TYPE	STORAGE TIME
Canned foods	2–5 years In a hot climate, use the foods before the eat-by date. Humidity may rust cans and so spoil food.	Grains and pulses	1 year Refined grains and dried pulses last for up to 1 year. Wash grains and pulses before cooking them.
Flours	3–6 months Refined white flour lasts the longest. Whole-grain flour should be used within 3 months.	Dried herbs	6 months Whole leaves retain more flavour than chopped herbs. Use before the aroma starts to fade.
Cereals	6 months Keep in an airtight container, since humidity can cause cereals to become soft and stale.	Spices	6–12 months Keep small amounts, and use before the aroma fades. Whole spices last for up to 1 year.
Pastas	1 year Use dried pasta without egg, such as spaghetti, within 1 year. Keep egg pasta for as little time as possible.	Condiments	1 year This applies to items made with vinegar, such as tartare sauce, tomato relish, or prepared mustard.

PRESERVING AND CHILLING FOOD

THERE ARE MANY WAYS to extend the lifespan of food. Traditional methods of preserving foods can improve their flavour as well as prolonging their lives, while chilling by refrigeration or freezing can maintain their freshness.

PREPARING FOOD FOR PRESERVING

Techniques such as pickling and jam making can enable you to store large quantities of inexpensive fruits and vegetables, and to make the most of home-grown produce. Whichever method you use, ensure that the food is clean and that containers are sterilized and airtight.

PRESERVING FRUITS
● **Straining fruits for jelly** Tie a muslin cloth or bag to the legs of an upside-down stool to hold it steady. Pour the fruits through the muslin into a bowl.
● **Bottling fruits** When pouring syrup over fruits to be bottled, add the syrup in stages to stop air bubbles from forming.
● **Handling jam jars** Once you have filled jars with hot jam, put them on a wooden board or folded towel. Do not stand them on a cold work surface, since the glass may crack.
● **Labelling jam jars** Wait until the glass is cold before you label a jar. Adhesives will not hold on warm or hot glass.

STERILIZING GLASS JARS

Using a microwave
Wash empty glass jars, rinse them well, then remove the rubber seals and place them where they will stay clean. Put the clean jars into a microwave oven, and run it on High for two minutes.

TRADITIONAL TIP

Drying celery
To preserve celery, first cut it into 2-cm (¾-in) pieces. Dry the pieces on a tray in a warm, open oven. Cover with parchment, and store in a jar. To use, boil until tender.

USING FRESH HERBS

To make the most of herbs, buy them fresh rather than ready-dried, or grow your own. Store them by freezing (see p. 58), drying, or preserving in oil.

CHOOSING HERBS
● **Buying herbs to store** Shake fresh herbs before you buy them. If the herbs are in good condition, their leaves will stay attached to the stalks.
● **Gathering sprigs** Pick home-grown herbs just before they flower so that they will keep their flavour when stored. Gather them early in the morning, before the sun has started to dry the plants.

DRYING AND STORING
● **Hanging bunches** Hang herbs upside-down to dry in a warm, dry place. Prick air-holes in a brown paper bag, and put this over the herbs to keep out light and dust, and to trap leaves that fall off.
● **Labelling bunches of herbs** Fix an adhesive label to one stalk of a bunch of herbs. Write on it the name of the herb and the date when it was bought or picked. Use the herbs within one year.
● **Packing dried herbs** Once herbs are dry, strip the leaves from the stalks, grind them if desired, and store them in airtight containers. Keep in a cool, dark place to preserve the flavours of the herbs.

Close top so that bottle is airtight

Making flavoured oils
Drop sprigs of fresh or dried herbs, such as tarragon, basil, or rosemary, into fresh bottles of olive oil. Leave the bottles in a cool place for one or two weeks. The flavoured oils can then be used for dressings.

USING A REFRIGERATOR

Keep refrigerator shelves tidy so that you make the best use of the available space. Arrange foods by type so that you can find items easily. Every week, look through the contents of the refrigerator, and throw away any foods that have passed their use-by dates.

CHILLING FOOD SAFELY

● **Storing cooked foods** Cool hot foods before placing them in a refrigerator. If you put hot foods in a refrigerator, they will transfer heat to nearby items, encouraging the growth of bacteria in those items.

● **Keeping raw foods** Wrap raw meat and fish, and put them on the lowest shelf. Never let these foods touch or drip on to other items, since the juices may transfer bacteria.

● **Allowing air movement** Arrange foods so that there is a little space between items. This will allow cool air to circulate and keep all the foods at an even temperature.

PREVENTING PROBLEMS

● **Maintaining temperature** Shut the door as soon as you have used a refrigerator. If you leave the door open for even a few minutes, the air inside will warm up, and it will take some time to return to the correct temperature.

● **Storing odorous foods** Seal strong-smelling foods, such as spring onions or mature cheeses, in sealed containers or plastic bags. This will stop odours from tainting other items such as milk or chicken.

● **Banishing smells** Put charcoal in a saucer at the back of each shelf to dispel odours. Change the charcoal every few months.

WRAPPING FOOD

Wrap each banana in foil

Preserving ripe bananas
Cover ripe bananas individually in aluminium foil, and store them in the salad drawer of a refrigerator. The foil will halt the ripening process, keeping the bananas from turning brown.

GROUPING FOOD IN A REFRIGERATOR

FOODS FOR UPPER SHELVES

Keep frequently used foods on the topmost shelves of a refrigerator so that they are easily accessible and you can see immediately if supplies are low.

● Condiments.
● Butter.
● Margarine.
● Eggs.
● Cheese.
● Cooked items other than meat.
● Convenience foods.

FOODS FOR LOWER SHELVES

Put the following foods on the bottom shelves so that their aromas or juices will not taint other items. Cover raw meat, poultry, and fish loosely with clingfilm so that air can circulate around them.

● Raw meat.
● Cooked meat.
● Raw poultry.
● Fish.
● Shellfish.
● Yoghurt.
● Cream.

FOODS FOR SALAD DRAWERS

Put each type of food in a separate polythene bag so that it will not flavour any others. Store root vegetables in brown paper bags to keep out light.

● Broccoli.
● Cauliflower.
● Root vegetables.
● Salad leaves.
● Fresh herbs.
● Soft vegetables.
● Soft fruits.

FOODS FOR DOOR COMPARTMENTS

Keep bottles and cartons in a refrigerator door. However, if items such as milk turn sour when stored there, try to fit them on an interior shelf.

● Mineral water.
● Fruit juices.
● Milk.
● Bottled drinks.
● Cream in an aerosol can.

PREPARING FOOD FOR FREEZING

You can put most fresh foods straight into a freezer, but many will retain their flavours and textures longest if prepared beforehand. Seal foods tightly in strong packages. Label the packages clearly, because some foods can be unrecognizable once they are frozen.

CLEANING & COOKING

● **Preparing fresh meats** Clean meat and fish thoroughly before freezing them. Prepare them so that they are ready to cook when defrosted. For example, skin chicken pieces.
● **Treating fruits and vegetables** Clean fresh items (except soft fruits) thoroughly in cool, running water. Make sure that the fruits and vegetables are totally dry before freezing, otherwise any water on them will turn to ice and damage the texture of the foods.
● **Freezing cooked foods** Cool cooked items completely before freezing. To cool foods quickly and safely, place them in a bowl surrounded by cold water or ice cubes.
● **Packing herbs** Tie fresh herbs in bunches, then pack loosely in plastic bags. If you wish to flake the leaves, crumble the frozen herbs while they are inside the bag.

PREPARING FRUITS & VEGETABLES FOR FREEZING

FOODS TO PUT IN SYRUP	FOODS TO BLANCH
Mix together 450 g (1 lb) sugar, 1 litre (1¾ pints) of water, and juice of 1 lemon to make a basic cold syrup. ● Pineapple. ● Citrus fruits. ● Mangoes. ● Apricots. ● Peaches. ● Papaya.	Plunge the foods into boiling water for the times given below, then drop into iced water. ● Corn on the cob: 2–4 mins. ● Peppers: 1 min. ● Onions: 1 min. ● Peas: 1 min. ● Leeks: 30 secs. ● Spinach: 10 secs.

FOODS TO PURÉE	FOODS TO OPEN FREEZE
Pulp the foods in a liquidizer, or mash through a sieve. ● Strawberries. ● Tomatoes. ● Peaches.	Freeze flat on a tray, then pack into a container. ● Gooseberries. ● Redcurrants. ● Raspberries.

WRAPPING POULTRY

● **Using fresh wrapping** Rinse raw poultry in cold water, then wrap in clean aluminium foil.

Wrap foil tightly around poultry

Packing in portions
Buy poultry for freezing in bulk, and divide it into batches for single portions or meals. Wrap individual pieces in aluminium foil or clingfilm before freezing so that they will defrost quickly.

PACKING FOODS

● **Fitting foods together** Put a plastic bag into a container. Pour food into the bag, and freeze. Take the bag out of the container, and place it directly in the freezer. Use the same container again to produce shapes that stack together.
● **Filling containers** Solids and liquids expand when they freeze, so never fill containers to the top, otherwise the food will push off the lid of the container or even crack it.
● **Keeping air out** Because air can spoil frozen foods, arrange loose items so that the spaces between them are small. When freezing food in a bag, first squeeze the air out of the bag.

PREPARING SWEET FOODS

● **Sealing ice-cream cartons** To stop ice-cream from picking up smells from other foods in the freezer, seal the carton in a plastic bag. Label the bag.
● **Keeping chocolate** Store bars of chocolate in the freezer to keep them firm. Remove them half an hour before eating.
● **Making sorbets** Add two teaspoons of gelatine to each 500 ml (1 pint) of mixture before freezing. This will keep the sorbet icy when served.
● **Freezing biscuit mixture** Roll biscuit mixture to form a 5-cm (2-in) diameter log. Wrap the log in greaseproof paper, and freeze. Slice the log to make biscuits when required.

STOCKING A FREEZER

Freeze only foods that you know you will eat. Bargains in shops may seem tempting, but the food could be wasted if nobody likes it. Keep the freezer tidy. Label packages, place food types in groups, and discard anything that has been there for more than six months.

STORING FOODS

The information given here is a rough guide to storage times. Always check freezing instructions on packets.

- **Poultry** Chicken and turkey keep for about nine months. Lean birds can be frozen for longer than fatty ones.
- **Fish** Most types of fish keep for up to three months, but the taste of some may deteriorate before then.
- **Spiced foods** Keep for up to three months. After this time spices may lose flavour.
- **Ice-cream** Use within two months. After this time, the structure of the ice-cream may start to break down.

PLANNING AHEAD

- **Saving wine** Pour leftover wine into ice cube trays, and freeze. Add the frozen cubes to dishes such as casseroles.

Freezing a casserole
Before freezing a casserole, put a clean, empty plastic cup upright in the centre of the container. This will serve to reduce the thawing time of the casserole.

MONEY-SAVING TIP

Filling unused space
Freezers run most efficiently when full. Fill empty spaces with crumpled newspaper. Put the paper in plastic bags before leaving it in for a long time, since otherwise it may become damp.

MAINTAINING A FREEZER

NATURE OF TASK	METHOD	TIMING
Using up food	● **Labelling** Name and date packs before freezing. Use different colours to show each type of food. ● **Listing** State contents, when bought, use-by date, and amount.	● **Sorting out foods** Check the foods in a freezer every 3 or 4 months. Use foods in order of date of purchase. ● **Disposing of foods** Throw out foods that are old or past their use-by dates.
Defrosting	● **Thawing** Put old towels in the base of a freezer, and stand bowls of hot water on each shelf. ● **Dislodging ice** Use a spatula to prevent damage to the walls.	● **Choosing time** Defrost a freezer whenever the ice on the inside is more than 1 cm (⅜ in) thick. Keep the contents cool by storing them in a cool box, or working on a cool day.
Cleaning	● **Wiping interior** Wipe any thawed water from the interior of a freezer before starting to clean it. ● **Washing** Use a bicarbonate of soda solution, and leave to dry.	● **Combining tasks** Wash out the interior of a freezer whenever you defrost it. Sort out which foods to save and which to throw away, if you have not done this recently.
Checking regularly	● **Testing seals** Shut the door or lid on a piece of paper. If you can pull out the paper when the freezer is shut, the seal may be faulty and could have to be replaced.	● **Carrying out checks** Test the seal every 3 or 4 months. To monitor temperature, keep a thermometer in a freezer. Check it every few days to see that the temperature is constant.

COOKING ECONOMICALLY

PLAN COOKING SESSIONS IN ADVANCE to save fuel and time. Use forward planning to eliminate the need for expensive ready meals. Make sure that you always stock sufficient fresh, canned, or dried foods to make a quick meal easily.

PLANNING MENUS IN ADVANCE

It is a good idea to work out every week's meals in advance. This will allow you to plan your shopping list in detail. Make sure that you include a number of foods that can be reused as ingredients for different meals, so that you will be able to save money on shopping bills.

SAVING TIME

Slide pancake on to greaseproof paper

Preparing pancakes
Cool pancakes on a plate, then put them in a container between circles of greaseproof paper. Refrigerate for up to three days. To use, reheat in a warm oven.

FEEDING VEGETARIANS
● **Planning a balanced diet**
When choosing foods for vegetarian meals, ensure that they contain enough vitamins and minerals. Consult a diet book, or ask for dietary information from your doctor.
● **Adapting meat dishes** If only one member of a household is a vegetarian, plan menus so that there is always an interesting vegetarian option. Make dishes such as spaghetti or risotto. Divide the pasta or rice in two, and serve one portion with a meat sauce and the other with vegetables.

MAKING ECONOMIES

The following tips show how to use leftovers in new dishes. For safety, reuse only foods in good condition, and never reheat meat more than once.

● **Potatoes** Reheat baked skins and serve with dips.
● **Pasta and rice** Use boiled rice or pasta to make a salad.
● **Vegetables** Purée cooked vegetables to make soup, or cook slowly to make stock.
● **Fish** Flake cooked fish, and use in fish pies or fish cakes.
● **Meat** Dice meat or poultry, and make stew or curry.

COOKING IN BULK

You can save time and money by buying large quantities of fresh foods and making several dishes at once. Freeze dishes as soon as they have cooled after cooking. Label the containers, listing any ingredients to be added when the food is defrosted, prior to reheating.

PRE-COOKING FOODS

Set aside a morning or afternoon for cooking a range of dishes. If you regularly eat one type of meat or vegetable, always keep ingredients for several different flavourings ready for use.

● **Buying fruits and vegetables**
When you go shopping, look for fruits and vegetables that are blemished or about to pass their sell-by date. These foods may be less expensive than fresh ones. Cook them in dishes such as stews, in which their appearance will not matter.

Preparing mince
Divide a large amount of cooked mince into batches, and freeze. Reheat the mince with herbs, vegetables, and sauces to make different meals such as chilli con carne or spaghetti bolognese.

PREPARING INGREDIENTS
● **Using up tomatoes** Skin tomatoes in bulk, remove the seeds, and purée. Freeze in ice cube trays, then add the cubes to soups or pasta.
● **Cooking stock** Simmer scraps of meat, fish, or vegetables slowly to make enough stock to last for several weeks. Check the stock regularly to make sure that the pan does not boil dry and burn.
● **Freezing pastry** Make up a large amount of pastry, and freeze it in batches ready for you to use at a later date.

Using a Cooker Efficiently

A cooker uses a lot of expensive energy, so make the most of this power by filling the oven when using it. It may be most economical to use a microwave for small quantities of food, or to avoid making dishes that require a lengthy cooking time, such as casseroles or roasts.

Arranging Food Inside an Oven

Roast potatoes are in hottest zone

Chicken is placed above pudding, so pudding is not affected by aroma

Filling an oven
Cook foods with similar cooking times together. If there are areas of different temperature in the oven, use the hottest area for foods that must be cooked at a high temperature or cooked until crisp. Put strong-smelling foods above other dishes to avoid transferring aromas.

SAFEGUARD TIP

Cooking in aluminium foil
When wrapping aluminium foil over a roasting dish, make sure that the foil fits closely so that it will not touch the sides of the oven - the hot surfaces could set the foil alight.

PART-COOKING FOOD
● **Parboiling potatoes** Before roasting potatoes, boil them for half the usual time. Drain and dry them, then roast. The potatoes will take less time to roast than raw ones, and the insides will be soft and fluffy.
● **Baking food lightly** Foods such as pies and quiches can be stored when they are only partly cooked. You can then reheat them later at a fairly high temperature, and they will not overcook or burn.
● **Making bread** Bake bread rolls until they have just begun to turn brown, then remove them from the oven, and freeze. You can then take out as many as you need for each meal. Always save a few rolls from the freshly baked batch to eat straight from the oven.
● **Preventing food poisoning** Do not part-cook any dishes that contain chicken or pork. Never eat part-cooked meat if you are pregnant. It could be contaminated with listeria, which can cause miscarriage.

SAVING ENERGY
● **Cooking vegetables** To cook two types of vegetable at once, boil one vegetable and steam another over the same pan. If you do not have a steamer, use a metal colander or sieve, and cover with a saucepan lid.

COOKING ECONOMICALLY
● **Adapting methods** Try not to use two energy-intensive cooking methods at once. For example, do not cook a dish in an oven while frying potato chips on a hob. Instead, cook the chips in the oven as well.

MAKING USE OF A MICROWAVE

Microwaves are invaluable for rapid cooking, defrosting, and reheating. To ensure that a microwave heats food evenly, rearrange food half-way through cooking. If food varies in thickness, place the thinnest parts in the centre of the oven.

● **Reducing baking time** Wash and dry baking potatoes, and pierce the skins. Put them along the edges of a microwave turntable, and cook on High for 5 minutes. To crisp the skins, use a browning facility, or transfer to a conventional oven.
● **Cooking a fish fillet** Put a fish fillet on a plate, and cover with clingfilm. Pierce the film. Cook on High for 4–6 minutes.

Add small sprigs of thyme

Making a deodorizer
Put some sprigs of thyme and slices of lemon into a heatproof glass measuring jug with 250 ml (9 fl oz) water. Heat the mixture until it boils. The aroma will deodorize the microwave.

ENTERTAINING GUESTS

INVITING GUESTS TO YOUR HOME is a pleasant way to socialize, and can be cheaper and more relaxing than going to a restaurant. Plan the menu in advance, and do as much as possible before guests arrive so that you can enjoy yourself.

ORGANIZING A SPECIAL MEAL

Do not be overly ambitious when working out a menu. Even a formal dinner party should not be a stressful occasion. It is more sensible to keep to familiar recipes, and to prepare the food and setting well, than to try out dishes that you have never cooked before.

PLANNING IN ADVANCE

Before a special meal, make a list of preparations. The chart below indicates numbers of days before a meal, and tasks to do on those days.

21
- Select date and time of meal.
- Decide on guests and invite them.
- Choose menu.
- Do shopping list.

10
- Buy drinks.
- Buy packaged foods such as peanuts.
- Buy napkins and similar items.

5
- Gather cutlery, crockery, glasses, and cooking equipment.
- Buy any non-perishable foods.

2
- Buy fresh foods such as vegetables.
- Plan cooking schedule.
- Prepare items that will not spoil.

1
- Cook dishes that can be prepared in advance. (Cook others on the day.)
- Wash crockery, cutlery, and glasses.
- Make dessert.
- Tidy up kitchen, living room, and dining area.

LOOKING AFTER GUESTS

- **Checking diet** When inviting guests for the first time, ask whether they have any special dietary requirements or if there are particular foods that they do not eat.
- **Organizing seating** If you are inviting more than four guests, prepare a seating plan.
- **Helping guests mingle** Before a meal, try to make sure that guests talk to people who will not be sitting near them at the table. Later, you may like to move some guests to different seats before dessert so that they can talk to other people.
- **Keeping records** Write up a dinner party log with the date of each meal, the guest list, and the menu. In this way you can avoid serving the same meal twice to the same guests.

SAVING TIME

Egg-cup   *Coffee cup*

Cereal bowl   *Plate*

Laying a table in advance
Set out cutlery and crockery in advance so that you will not have to supply items during a meal. For a special breakfast, put a cereal bowl on a plate, and add an egg-cup and a coffee cup.

PREPARING A FLORAL DISPLAY

Bag allows space around flowers

Flowers are already arranged

Bag is tied securely around vase

Arranging in advance
Put flowers in a vase the day before you need them. Fill the vase with water. Mist the flowers and foliage with water, then cover with a plastic bag. The bag will trap moisture, and keep the flowers fresh. Remove it one hour before the guests arrive.

ORGANIZING A CHILDREN'S PARTY

Plan all the activities for a children's party in advance. Organize help for the day of the party. You will need another adult for taking small children to the toilet, preparing games and food, and mopping up tears. Another parent, or a friendly teenager, may be happy to assist.

SCHEDULING EVENTS

● **Planning meal time** Have a meal half-way through a party. Schedule boisterous games for before the meal so that the children work up an appetite.
● **Preparing games** Decide on games well in advance, and assemble props in a box or basket. Games do not always last as long as you expect, so plan several spare activities. Be prepared to play popular games more than once.
● **Alternating activities** Balance noisy games with pastimes such as listening to stories. This will keep children from becoming tired and upset.

PREPARING FOODS

● **Minimizing mess** Make bite-sized party foods that will not be messy. Put a plastic sheet underneath the eating area to catch crumbs and spills.

Making mini-pizzas

Cover dough bases or halved bagels with tomato paste and cheese. Cook in advance, then freeze. Reheat the pizzas on the day that you need them, and let them cool down before serving.

PREPARING DRINKS

Decorating glasses

Cut stars and crescent moons out of coloured card. Glue matching pairs together around each straw, and attach more shapes to the glasses. Keep some spare shapes in case any are damaged.

ORGANIZING A PARTY FOR TEENAGERS

● **Selecting foods** Select items that will not drip or be spilt.
● **Preparing foods** Let the host prepare simple foods such as French bread with cheeses.

● **Protecting surfaces** Cover tables with cling film, then lay cloths on top. This will protect the surfaces from spills, and the cloths will look attractive.

PLANNING SECURITY

● **Looking after guests** For a teenage party, ask a young adult you trust to keep order, watch over the guests, and act as a bouncer if necessary.

ORGANIZING ENTERTAINMENT FOR CHILDREN

If you are planning to provide entertainment for children, leave a clear space for it. Lay cushions, sleeping bags, and mattresses on the floor to make seats. Make sure that everyone who needs to go to the toilet does so before the show starts.

● **Setting time** Schedule the entertainment for the end of the party. The children will look forward to it, and sitting down for a while will calm them so that they are not over-excited when they go home.
● **Keeping children happy** When you book entertainment such as a magician's show, check that it will be suitable for the age of the children, so that they will not be bored or worried by it.

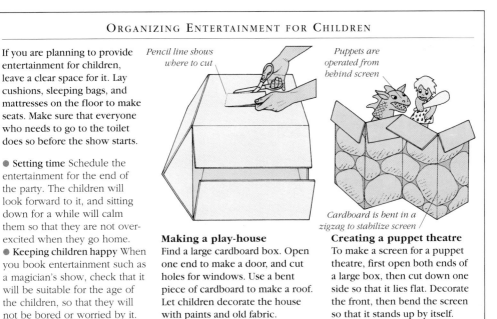

Pencil line shows where to cut

Puppets are operated from behind screen

Cardboard is bent in a zigzag to stabilize screen

Making a play-house

Find a large cardboard box. Open one end to make a door, and cut holes for windows. Use a bent piece of cardboard to make a roof. Let children decorate the house with paints and old fabric.

Creating a puppet theatre

To make a screen for a puppet theatre, first open both ends of a large box, then cut down one side so that it lies flat. Decorate the front, then bend the screen so that it stands up by itself.

PLANNING A THEMED PARTY

This is one activity in which planning and organization can be especially fun. Devising a theme for a party can be as enjoyable as hosting the event itself. Remember to inform all your guests of the theme, either on the invitation or individually over the telephone.

CHOOSING A THEME

To increase the impact of a theme, apply your idea to several aspects of the party.

● **Mediterranean** Use bright red-checked gingham for tablecloths. Alternatively, choose "Italian culture", with music from Italian operas and guests in full evening dress, or "Renaissance", with people dressed as figures from history or works of art.
● **Under the sea** Fit blue lightbulbs, make decorations from aluminium foil, and drape netting over the walls. Serve sea food on shells.

IMPLEMENTING A THEME

● **Reducing outlay** Choose a theme that will allow guests to be creative with their own clothes, or to use inexpensive items such as paper masks.
● **Choosing a host's costume** If you are the host, make sure that your costume will not hamper you during the party.
● **Selecting foods** You can serve conventional party foods if you give each dish a name that suits the theme of the party. For example, if the theme is "horror", name sausages "victims' fingers", and at a French party, name a fruit punch "Moulin Rouge".

CREATING ATMOSPHERE

Cut shape in skin so that light will shine through

Making a fruit lantern
Hollow out a hard-skinned fruit, such as a watermelon, and save the pulp for eating. Slice off the end to form a base. Cut shapes in the fruit, then put a night-light candle inside. Stand it on a plate.

PLANNING A PICNIC

To guarantee an enjoyable time on a picnic, it is best to plan the event in advance. For example, have a picnic in a place that you already know well, or go to look at a new spot before the picnic. Keep some items of basic picnic equipment in your car at all times.

BASIC PICNIC EQUIPMENT

Take plastic utensils, which are lightweight and hard-wearing. Pack paper napkins and a damp cloth for wiping hands. Use cool boxes and packs to preserve food on the journey. Take insect repellent to prevent stings.

● **Sitting comfortably** Take plastic sheeting to keep rugs and cushions dry, and a folding table and chairs for those wishing to use them.

Damp cloth in plastic bag

Cool packs

Bowl   Plastic cups

Insect repellent

Paper napkin

Plastic cutlery

Plastic plate

Eating equipment

Cool box

PREPARING DRINKS

Fill beaker two-thirds full to allow liquid to expand when freezing

Transporting fruit drinks
Dilute fruit cordial to the desired strength, pour it into plastic beakers with lids, then freeze. Pack the frozen drinks around picnic foods to keep them cool on a journey. When you arrive, thaw the drinks in a warm place.

PLANNING AN OUTDOOR PARTY

A n outdoor party can be fun as long as the weather is dry. Make an emergency plan in case of bad weather. For example, put aside a tarpaulin as a roof for an enclosed area. Do not invite more people than you can fit in your home if you have to hold the party indoors.

COOKING FOOD ON A BARBECUE

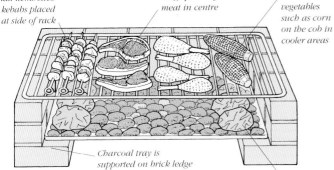

Small items such as kebabs placed at side of rack

Large pieces of meat in centre

Whole vegetables such as corn on the cob in cooler areas

Charcoal tray is supported on brick ledge

Foil-wrapped potatoes on embers

Building a simple barbecue
Build a long brick wall with short walls at right angles to either end. Build a brick ledge in the wall using a single line of bricks set sideways, then add another two courses in the normal way. Use a heatproof surface, such as a metal sheet, to hold the charcoal, and place this on the ledge. Lay an old oven shelf on the top of the barbecue.

LIGHTING AND TENDING A BARBECUE
● **Heating charcoal** Start a barbecue at least half an hour before the party begins. Wait until the charcoal is white hot before starting to cook.

● **Protecting yourself** Grilled foods tend to spit, particularly if marinated. Wear oven gloves and a long apron, especially if you are dressed in thin clothes.

BRIGHT IDEA

Storing drinks
For a party, clean out a wheelbarrow thoroughly, fill it with ice, and keep cans and bottles cool in it. To use the ice cubes in drinks, spray them with soda water so that they will not stick together.

PROTECTING FOOD
● **Preserving freshness** Cover all dishes with clingfilm until you cook or serve them.
● **Keeping foods cool** Keep perishable items chilled in a refrigerator until you take them outside. Foods such as mayonnaise deteriorate if left in direct sunlight, so place them in bowls filled with ice.
● **Protecting food in the open** Cover food in the open air with cloths or nets to keep insects and birds at bay.

SAFETY

Remove all obstacles from the garden before the guests arrive.

● **Tools** Place all garden tools in a locked shed or garage.
● **Garden chemicals** Do not apply chemicals to plants on the party day, so that guests are unaffected by the residue.

PREPARING FOR AN OUTDOOR PARTY

A party can be a good excuse for tidying a garden. Mow grass, tidy flower beds, and move obstacles such as plant pots.

● **Buying beakers** Buy plastic or acrylic beakers instead of glasses. Unlike glasses, the beakers should not break if dropped on the ground.
● **Deterring insects** Have cans of insect repellent spray handy for guests to use. Protect the cans from direct sunlight and hot spots such as a barbecue.
● **Fencing off plants** Put up a temporary fence around any valuable or poisonous plants that you cannot move.

Improvising lights
Cut strips of coloured paper to wrap around small glass jars, and cut decorative shapes in the strips. Tape the strips around the jars. Put night-light candles inside, and light them. Use to decorate garden tables.

Structuring Work

QUICK REFERENCE

Setting Up a Home
Office, p. 67

Managing Work
Time, p. 71

Communicating
Effectively, p. 74

Keeping
Records, p. 76

W*HETHER YOU WORK in an office or in your home, make sure that you function as efficiently as possible. Assess all aspects of your work, from the environment to the tasks that you do, to determine whether they suit you and meet the demands of the job. Take time to plan schedules for your work, and organize your office so that equipment and information are instantly accessible.*

PLANNING A HOME OFFICE

If possible, set up a home office in a room that is away from the main living areas. Otherwise, use a quiet part of a living room or dining area, or adapt an empty space such as the area underneath a staircase (see p. 17). If you plan to work in an area that is also used by others in the household, set aside a place to store office items once you have finished work. Make sure that you have ample lighting for your needs, and fit extra plug sockets if necessary. Make a floor plan to decide where to position furniture. Allow at least 1-metre (39-in) clearance around each large item. Organize your desk area, shelving, and cabinets so that you do not have to move far in order to find information.

● **Arranging an office** Position equipment so that vital items, such as a telephone, are within easy reach. At the same time, make sure that there is enough space on the desktop for work.

● **Siting power points** Ask an electrician to fit power points near all electrical items so that you will not have to trail flexes across a floor.

● **Securing flexes** If you have to lay flexes across a floor, secure them to the floor with insulating tape so that people will not trip over them.

● **Using daylight bulbs** Make sure that the work area is lit properly. If possible, fit lighting with daylight bulbs, which will minimize strain on your eyes.

● **Minimizing clutter** Keep the floor area and desktop free of clutter. If your work area is tidy you will be able to find items easily and will always have clear space for your work.

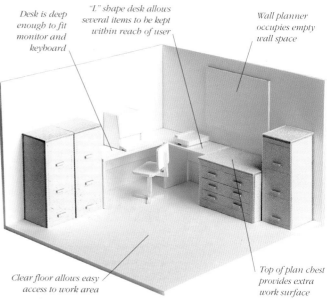

Desk is deep enough to fit monitor and keyboard

"L" shape desk allows several items to be kept within reach of user

Wall planner occupies empty wall space

Clear floor allows easy access to work area

Top of plan chest provides extra work surface

Deciding on an office layout
When you lay out an office, consider how often you will need each piece of equipment. Keep essential objects within reach of your desk, and use areas away from your desk to store items that you seldom need.

SETTING UP A HOME OFFICE

LIST THE TASKS THAT YOU WILL BE DOING in your home office, and the equipment that you will need to do them. Determine the amount of space that you will need for your office, and work out a budget to spend on equipping it.

ORGANIZING AN OFFICE LAYOUT

Plan a layout so that the items you use most often are within easy reach of your desk. Store seldom-used objects out of the way on high shelves, or in another room. As well as planning space for equipment and files, allow room for you to lay out papers while you work.

USING SPACE CLEVERLY

● **Utilizing corners** If you have a small work area, fit a triangular desk in a corner.
● **Mounting items on walls** If you have limited space for work surfaces, mount items such as a telephone and a desk lamp on a wall.
● **Using a trolley** Keep a trolley to hold items that you use every day. Push the trolley under your desk when you have finished work.
● **Laying out stationery** Keep out only as much stationery as you will need for a few days. Store the rest out of the way.

UTILIZING SHELF SPACE

● **Fitting shelves** When you fit shelves, allow more shelf space than you immediately need so that you have room to store extra items in the future.
● **Using furniture** Use the tops of cupboards and cabinets as shelving for lightweight objects. Make sure that you do not overload these surfaces.
● **Storing books** Put reference books on a shelf by your desk so that you can reach them without leaving your chair.
● **Storing files** Put filing trays on deep shelves to keep your work surface clear.

CREATING STORAGE

Improvising filing trays
Clean a set of unused, stackable vegetable racks, and use them instead of a filing tray to hold papers. Stand the racks on an accessible work surface or shelf.

DISPLAYING DATA

● **Using wall space** Display visual information such as planners and notices on a wall in front of your desk, where you can see the information without turning around.
● **Making pinboards** To make an inexpensive pinboard, collect several dozen corks, cut them in half lengthways, and glue the pieces together on a wooden board.
● **Using spaces under shelves** If you have shelves just above your desk, fit a panel of cork or pinboard between the lowest shelf and the top of your desk so that you can make use of the wall space.

MAKING AN OFFICE MEMO BOARD

1 Pad a piece of chipboard with a sheet of foam. Cut a piece of scrap fabric to cover the board, leaving a 5-cm (2-in) border of fabric all around the edge. Lay the foam-covered board on top of the material, and nail the excess material to the back.

2 Lay thin ribbons on top of the fabric in a criss-cross pattern. Fasten the crossing points to the board with drawing pins, and pin the ends of ribbon to the back of the board. Mount the memo board on a wall, and tuck cards and notes under the ribbons.

EQUIPPING AN OFFICE

You do not always need to buy new office equipment. Second-hand objects are often much cheaper than new ones, and may be hardly worn. Consider improvising some items, particularly for storage and filing, in order to save money when fitting out a work area.

CHOOSING EQUIPMENT

Select the following items to equip your work area. These items should enable you to carry out all usual office tasks.

- Desk.
- Comfortable chair(s).
- Computer or typewriter.
- Telephone.
- Answering machine.
- Fax machine.
- Calculator.
- Files.
- Address book.
- Diary.
- Notice board.
- Clock.
- Paper and envelopes.
- Pens and pencils.
- Postage stamps.
- Paper clips and adhesives.

STORING SUPPLIES

- Collecting mail items Keep a supply of stamps, new or recycled envelopes, air mail labels, and forms for couriers.

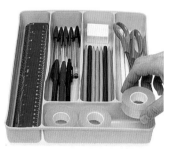

Keeping small items tidy
Put a cutlery divider in a drawer, and keep small items such as pens, rulers, and adhesive tape in it. Every couple of months, remove the divider, and dust it.

MONEY-SAVING TIP

Making a desk tidy
Cut the neck off a plastic bottle. Fix the base to a board, together with a can and an aerosol can lid. Decorate the desk tidy with paint, then keep small items in it.

MAINTAINING SUPPLIES OF OFFICE STATIONERY

- Buying in bulk To save money, buy stationery in bulk. Form a group with other people working from home so that you can place joint orders.

- Checking stock Make a list of stationery items. Before you have used up supplies of an item, cross it off the list. Replenish the stock regularly.

RECYCLING PAPER

- Minimizing waste Take waste paper to a recycling centre, or give it to a firm that recycles their paper. Keep old envelopes in a box for reuse.

CLEANING AND MAINTAINING EQUIPMENT

Every few weeks, set aside time for cleaning office equipment. Done correctly, this regular cleaning will prolong the lifespan of the equipment. Check to see if any item is faulty, and arrange for problems to be repaired.

- Keeping a computer dust-free Wipe the screen every day with an anti-static cloth. Cover the keyboard and screen when you have finished using a computer. Buy a plastic cover, or make your own from lint-free cloth.
- Cleaning a telephone Wipe the mouth and earpiece with disinfectant. Use a soft brush to dust the key pad or dial.

- Cleaning a keyboard Always switch off a computer completely before cleaning a keyboard. Rub the characters on the keyboard gently, using a toothbrush and methylated spirit.
- Using chemicals safely Before you start to use chemicals such as cleaning fluid on a computer, always open a window so that you will not suffer any ill effects from any fumes that are given off.
- Dusting a mouse mat Keep your mouse mat clean so that the mouse can move over it easily. To lift dirt off a fabric-covered mat, wrap adhesive tape around your fingers, sticky side outwards, and rub it lightly over the mat.

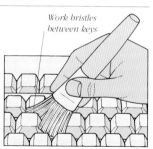

Work bristles between keys

Dusting a keyboard
Use a large, soft brush, such as a blusher brush, to remove dust from the crevices in a keyboard. Check that the brush is clean, then rub the bristles on your hand to create static electricity, which will attract the dust.

KEEPING VALUABLE ITEMS SAFE

Take care of valuable office equipment and confidential data to protect them from loss or damage. Take precautions such as turning off electrical items and locking the office when you finish work. Protect sensitive information so that it cannot be misused by anyone else.

MAKING SAFEGUARDS IN AN OFFICE	
OBJECT	METHODS OF KEEPING ITEMS SECURE
Computer	● **Maintaining flexes and plugs** Check plugs, connectors, and flexes regularly to ensure that they are not loose or damaged. When using the computer, do not rest your chair leg on a flex. ● **Tidying wires** To keep trailing wires out of the way, anchor them to a wall, or thread them all through a length of plastic drainpipe laid next to a wall. ● **Hiding a lap-top computer** Store a portable computer in a lockable drawer until you need to use it. Keep the power cable and any accessories in the drawer with the computer. ● **Recording identification** Make a note of the model names and identification numbers for each part of your computer, including accessories such as speakers.
Filing cabinet	● **Maintaining a cabinet** Check rarely used drawers in a filing cabinet to ensure that they open and shut smoothly. If you have to tug at the drawers, you may pull the cabinet over. ● **Preventing accidents** Never overload drawers or stand heavy items on top of a filing cabinet. Shut drawers as soon as you have finished with them. ● **Making a cabinet secure** Lock a filing cabinet whenever you are out of the office. Store the keys in a safe place, such as a lockable box. Keep spare keys in another place. Keep a note of the storage places. ● **Protecting files** If you have confidential papers, devise code names for the files so that other people cannot easily find them.
Telephone and fax	● **Installing a line for business** If possible, have a dedicated line for work. Fit a lock on the work telephone so that nobody can use it when you are not there. ● **Encoding contact names** If you enter often-used numbers into a telephone, write each contact's initials, rather than their name, on the handset. This will ensure that they cannot be identified by anyone using your telephone. ● **Sending a fax** When sending a fax with private information, such as bank account details, remove the document from the machine immediately, and file it in a safe place to ensure that it is not read by someone else. ● **Using a mobile telephone** Put a mobile telephone away in the same place each time you have finished using it so that you will be unlikely to mislay it.
Documents and money	● **Keeping certificates safe** Deposit certificates and other important documents in the strong room of a bank. If you wish to keep these documents in your home, store them in a wall or floor safe. ● **Handling cash** If you need to give money to strangers, have it ready before they arrive. Do not let callers see where you keep your cash supply. ● **Storing petty cash** Put money in a lockable box. Hide the cash box, or screw it to the floor or the inside of a drawer. Keep a record of petty cash used, for tax purposes and for your reference. ● **Identifying credit cards** Make a photocopy of each card, and file the copies in a safe place. You can then quote the numbers to the bank or credit card company if the cards are stolen.

WORKING IN COMFORT

You will work most efficiently when you are comfortable. Plan your work area to suit your physical needs. Take regular breaks to exercise your muscles and relax the eyes. Remember to rest your mind as well, perhaps by taking a stroll or chatting to a friend.

AVOIDING REPETITIVE STRAIN INJURY

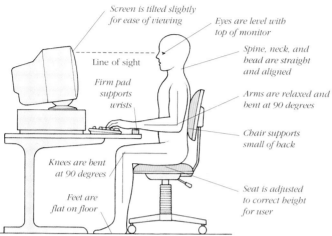

Screen is tilted slightly for ease of viewing

Eyes are level with top of monitor

Line of sight

Spine, neck, and head are straight and aligned

Firm pad supports wrists

Arms are relaxed and bent at 90 degrees

Chair supports small of back

Knees are bent at 90 degrees

Feet are flat on floor

Seat is adjusted to correct height for user

Positioning yourself to use a computer

Repetitive strain injury (RSI) is pain or muscle damage that occurs when you repeatedly over-use your shoulders, arms, or hands. If you use a computer regularly, adjust your computer, desk, and chair so that you can work comfortably. Make sure that your back, feet, and wrists are well-supported. When you use the keyboard, regularly flex and relax your hands so that they do not become stiff and painful.

IMPROVING CONDITIONS

● **Lighting work areas** Prevent headaches and eyestrain by fitting overhead lighting that is bright and does not flicker.

● **Using a desk lamp** Angle a desk lamp so that it lights your work without dazzling you. If you use a lamp near a computer screen, make sure that the light does not reflect off the screen into your eyes.

● **Regulating temperature** Use equipment such as a portable heater or an electric fan to maintain the air around you at a comfortable temperature.

● **Adding plants** Plants release oxygen, which improves air quality. They also emit water vapour, which restores the moisture to dry air. If you wish to upgrade the air in which you work, position a few pot plants around your work area.

REDUCING WORK-RELATED STRESS

Excessive stress can reduce your efficiency and make you ill. Take action as soon as you start to feel over-tired or unhappy. Do not allow stress to persist for a long time.

● **Relaxing eyes** From time to time, look up from your work and focus your eyes on objects at different distances.

● **Relieving face muscles** Frowning can create mental as well as physical tension, so try the following exercise to relieve this stress. Tense all of your face muscles, hold for a moment, and then relax the muscles. Repeat several times.

● **Staying active** To keep your energy levels high, do some form of exercise at least two or three times a week.

● **Having lunch** Make time to eat lunch in a relaxed manner. This will stop your blood sugar level from dropping and prevent indigestion.

● **Playing music** If you are not doing written work, relax by listening to music while you work. The music can block out background noise as well as give you pleasure.

● **Scheduling leisure time** Try not to let work extend beyond office hours. Keep in regular contact with your family and friends, so that you do not become lonely.

● **Boosting morale** Write a list of all your achievements, including minor ones. Refer to the list whenever you feel depressed or uncertain to boost your confidence.

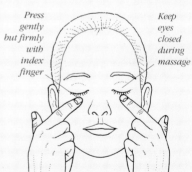

Press gently but firmly with index finger

Keep eyes closed during massage

Relaxing tired eyes

Using your index fingers, rub small circles just above the centres of your eyebrows, changing direction every 10 circles. Pinch the bridge of your nose several times, then rub small circles on the centres of your cheekbones. Finish by stroking large circles around your eye sockets, working outwards from the bridge of your nose.

MANAGING WORK TIME

PLAN ALL OF YOUR WORK IN ADVANCE, allowing sufficient time to complete each task on schedule. If you make a habit of dealing with work punctually, you will minimize stress and give others confidence in your reliability.

WORKING EFFECTIVELY

Assign each task a level of importance or urgency, and schedule a specific duration. Be realistic about how much you can achieve, allowing more time than you think you will need. Discipline yourself to do difficult jobs at the scheduled time instead of putting them off.

SCHEDULING TASKS

● **Making a task list** At the end of each day, list tasks to do the next day, with the most important at the top. Cross off each task as you finish it. Put any unfinished tasks at the top of a list for the following day.
● **Planning ahead** When you write a task list, check your diary entries for the next few days to ensure that you include tasks recorded there.
● **Breaking down tasks** If a project is lengthy or complex, divide it into small tasks, each with its own deadline.

MAKING USE OF TIME

● **Filling spare minutes** Make a list of small jobs such as filing, making telephone calls, or tidying your desk. If you have a little free time, carry out two or three of these tasks.
● **Working during travel** If you have to travel a long way to attend a meeting, take some work to do on the journey. When travelling by train or aeroplane, you could catch up on reading or make notes. If you travel by car, take a pocket dictaphone and record plans or answer letters.

CLASSIFYING JOBS

Drawing a chart
Divide a page into quarters. Title the columns "Urgent" and "Routine", and the rows, "Simple" and "Complex". Note tasks in the relevant areas to help you to plan a schedule.

ORGANIZING YOURSELF AND OTHERS

To keep to your work schedule, try to make it easy to accomplish tasks. Arrange the work to suit you so that you will maintain your motivation. If you work with other people, make appointments in good time, and brief others carefully before delegating jobs to them.

THINGS TO REMEMBER

Note down any arrangements that you make with other people, or any discussions that you have. Keep these notes for future reference.

● **Appointments** As soon as you make an appointment with someone, write it in your diary. Confirm the time and place the day before.
● **Discussions** If you discuss an important or contentious subject face to face or on the telephone, write a letter to the other person to confirm what was said.

MAKING WORK EASY

● **Selecting times** Do your most demanding work when you are most alert. For example, if you are at your peak in the morning, schedule demanding jobs for that time, and use the afternoon for routine tasks.
● **Setting financial goals** If you are concerned about money, set financial targets that will be easy to achieve, rather than overstretching yourself.
● **Planning rewards** Schedule rewards for completing tasks on time. For example, have a mid-morning coffee break, or a swim at the end of a day.

LIAISING WITH OTHERS

● **Briefing someone else** When you ask someone to perform a task, give them a date or time by which you want the work.
● **Scheduling a meeting** Give others a choice of times for a meeting so that they can opt for the most convenient time.
● **Preparing an agenda** List the subjects for discussion in a meeting, and set a specific time for each. Send the agenda to everyone who is to attend.
● **Saving time** Meetings are not always necessary. If you simply need to pass on information, send a letter or a fax instead.

ALLOCATING WORK TIME

To calculate the best use of your time, first define how you already spend your working hours. Make a pie chart of your working week so that you can see which activities take up the most time. You can then decide whether or not to alter the way in which you divide your time.

MAKING A PIE CHART OF YOUR WORKING WEEK

ACTIVITY	NUMBER OF HOURS SPENT															HOURS SPENT	FRACTION OF TIME	DEGREES ON CHART
	1	2	3	4	5	6	7	8	9	10	11	12	13	14	15			
Meetings	✓	✓	✓	✓	✓	✓	✓	✓	✓	✓	✓	✓	✓	✓	✓	15	$\frac{1}{4}$	90
Travel	✓	✓	✓	✓	✓	✓	✓	✓	✓	✓	✓	✓	✓	✓	✓	15	$\frac{1}{4}$	90
Administration	✓	✓	✓	✓	✓	✓	✓	✓	✓	✓						10	$\frac{1}{6}$	60
Practical tasks	✓	✓	✓	✓	✓	✓	✓	✓	✓	✓						10	$\frac{1}{6}$	60
Correspondence	✓	✓	✓	✓	✓											5	$\frac{1}{12}$	30
Lunch breaks	✓	✓	✓	✓	✓											5	$\frac{1}{12}$	30

1 Make a chart to collect data for a pie chart. Draw rows to represent activities. Label the rows and use different colours to show the activities. Draw columns to show the hours spent on each activity. Over the course of a week, add a tick to the appropriate row for each hour taken up by an activity. Include the time taken for commuting and other work-related travel, and for breaks.

2 Divide the total work time by the hours for each activity. Write the answers as fractions of the total time. To calculate the proportions for each activity on a pie chart, multiply 360 (the number of degrees in a circle) by each fraction.

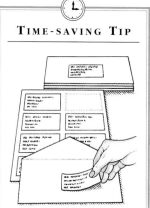

TIME-SAVING TIP

Pre-printing labels
Have batches of labels pre-printed so that you do not have to spend time writing or typing them individually. Set up templates on a computer for labels and forms, or type out master forms that you can photocopy as needed.

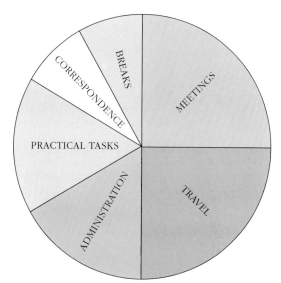

3 On a fresh sheet of paper, draw a large circle for the pie chart. Using a protractor, divide the circle into sectors of the correct size for each activity. Colour in the sectors, using the same colours as on the original chart, and label them. You will then be able to see at a glance each activity as a proportion of your total work time.

MAKING A WORK LOG

At the end of each day, make a list of things to do the next day. Write down what each task involves, and by when the task must be finished. Organize the information into a chart to make a work log. The chart below gives examples of information to include in a log.

USING LOGS
● **Reusing work logs** Make a template for a work log, and mount it on a sheet of card. Cover with clear adhesive film. Fill in the log with water-based ink, and reuse it each day.

PRIORITIZING TASKS
● **Highlighting tasks** Mark the most important tasks for each day with a large asterisk, or mark them in highlighter pen. You can then prioritize your work easily during the day.

COMPARING GOALS
● **Grouping information** If you keep a year planner on your wall, display your work log beside it so that you can regularly compare your long-term and short-term goals.

INFORMATION TO INCLUDE IN A WORK LOG			
ACTIVITY	TIME AND PLACE	PEOPLE TO INVOLVE	ACTION TO TAKE
Meetings	● **Time** Note the day, time, and duration. ● **Location** Include the address and contact numbers if necessary. ● **Travel** Note the time needed (if applicable).	● **Attending** Name the people who are to attend the meeting. ● **Briefing** List people to have agendas or briefing. Note any people to be informed of the outcome.	● **Agenda** List all the subjects on the agenda. ● **Reference** Note any extra information to be circulated. ● **Aim** Write down the goal of the meeting.
Practical tasks	● **Time** Record the day, time, and expected duration for each task. ● **Travel** Note the time needed (if applicable). ● **Deadline** Give the date for completion.	● **Recipient** Name the person who is to receive the finished work. ● **Assistants** Give the names of any assistants. ● **Suppliers** List suppliers of objects or information.	● **Outline** Write down each part of the task. ● **Equipment** List the tools, materials, and information needed. ● **Priority** Note the importance of the task.
Correspondence	● **Duration** Note the time to allow for correspondence. ● **Deadline** Write down the latest time by which to contact each correspondent.	● **Recipient** Note the name, address, e-mail address, and contact numbers of the recipient. ● **Copies** List any people to receive copies of the correspondence.	● **Contents** List the main points of each subject to be discussed in correspondence. ● **Information** Note any extra information to give a correspondent.
Tasks to be delegated	● **Briefing** Note when to brief a person on a task. ● **Duration** Record the time allowed for a task. ● **Deadline** Give the date for completion.	● **Name** Write down who is to carry out the task. ● **Number** Record the location and contact numbers of the person carrying out the task.	● **Instructions** List the tasks to be done. ● **Information** Give the names of sources that can be used to provide extra information.
Engagements outside work	● **Time** Note the day, time, and duration. ● **Location** Record the location of the activity. ● **Travel** Note the time needed (if applicable).	● **Companions** List the names and numbers of anyone else involved. ● **Other contacts** Note whom to tell in case of delay or cancellation.	● **Nature** Write down a brief description of the engagement. ● **Equipment** List extra items needed, such as sports equipment.

73

COMMUNICATING EFFECTIVELY

P UT POINTS ACROSS in simple, direct statements to enable others to understand your ideas. Before communicating with anyone, decide exactly what you wish to express. After an important discussion, confirm the details in writing.

PLANNING TELEPHONE USE

T o make the best use of a telephone, plan calls in advance. Allow time each day for telephoning, and let regular callers know when you will be available to talk with them. Take notes while you are talking. Keep records of important telephone calls related to your work.

TAKING MESSAGES

When taking a message for someone else, record all of the following information.

● **Name** Note the full name, in case the recipient of the message knows other people with the same first name.
● **Telephone number** Take the number, even if the recipient of the message knows it.
● **Time** Record the date and time of the call.
● **Message** Write down the content of a message after you have noted the relevant names and numbers.

MAKING CALLS

● **Planning a call** Write out points to discuss before you call someone. Keep the notes in front of you for reference while you are talking.
● **Staying on hold** If you are put on hold when you call someone, wait for only one minute. If the other person has not answered by then, leave a message or try later.
● **Speaking pleasantly** Try to sound pleasant without being false. Imagine that the person is in front of you and smiling at you. Smile back, and your voice will reflect your mood.

FOLLOWING UP

● **Recording details** As soon as you have finished an important call, note the date and time of the call, and summarize the points that were discussed.
● **Confirming information** After discussing an important matter with someone, write a letter to that person to confirm any decisions that you made.
● **Leaving a message** If you have to leave a message for someone, specify a time by which that person should respond. Note this time in your diary, and call again if the person has still not answered.

ORGANIZING CORRESPONDENCE

D eal with business correspondence regularly so that it does not pile up. Allow adequate time in your schedule, and make sure that you are not disturbed during that time. File letters and faxes, together with photocopies of your replies, as soon as you have dealt with them.

PLANNING STRUCTURE

● **Making a draft** On a sheet of scrap paper, note the points to be covered in a letter. With each main point, note any related minor points. Write a rough draft of the letter, and make any last changes on this before writing the final version.
● **Arranging information** Set out the main points of a letter or fax in brief paragraphs so that the recipient can read the information quickly. Allow one paragraph for each major point, and one sentence for each idea within a paragraph.

LAYING OUT TEXT

● **Giving a heading** Begin a fax or letter by giving a heading to the text. Write the heading in bold type or capital letters, or underline it. This will enable a reader to see at a glance what the document will be about.
● **Highlighting facts** Give each paragraph a number or a heading. Place this above the paragraph, and underline it or print it in bold type.
● **Listing points** When writing a list of items in the text of a letter, mark each one with a bullet (●) to give it emphasis.

WRITING LETTERS OF COMPLAINT

Be direct and accurate. Say only what is necessary, and try not to become emotional.

● **Defining a goal** First, decide what you wish to achieve by writing, such as receiving compensation or a refund.
● **Keeping it simple** Keep to the point. Support your message with facts, not with vague or emotive language.
● **Including evidence** Always send photocopies rather than original documents.

SETTING OUT INFORMATION IN DOCUMENTS

DOCUMENT	CONVEYING ESSENTIAL INFORMATION
Curriculum vitae	

Curriculum vitae

Keep your curriculum vitae (CV) brief. If possible, fit it on to one side of a page of letter paper. Put your name and address clearly at the top. Use one paragraph for each stage of your career.

● **Arranging facts** Mention the most important parts of your work history first. If you are in work, start with your current job, and work backwards. If you have just left school or college, list your examination passes first, starting with the most recent.

● **Highlighting skills** Mention any practical skills that may be useful for a job, such as the ability to drive or to speak a foreign language fluently.

● **Listing leisure interests** Describe leisure activities so that they appear relevant to the job. For example, if you belong to a sports team, you could emphasize teamworking skills.

● **Checking for errors** Because you are aiming to make a good impression on a stranger, it is vital that your CV is error-free. Check what you have written carefully, and use a dictionary to check the spellings and meanings of words.

● **Adding a covering letter** Enclose a short covering letter with a CV. State the job for which you are applying, and how you heard about it. Explain briefly why you are interested in the job, and why you may be suited to it.

Letter

Make your points briefly, because the recipient of the letter may have only a few minutes to look at it. Give your address, contact numbers, and e-mail address so that people can contact you. Put the recipient's address in a prominent place on the page.

● **Saving time** Write a letter only if you are sure that this is necessary. For a brief message, consider sending a fax or making a telephone call.

● **Defining structure** Give each letter a beginning, middle, and end. Begin by saying why you are writing. Give the main points in the body of the letter. Finish by summing up your message or inviting the other person to reply.

● **Quoting a reference number** If you are replying to a letter, quote the date and reference number of that letter in your first paragraph.

● **Adding enclosures** If you have enclosed extra information, mention each enclosure in the paragraph for the relevant point so that the reader can refer to it instantly.

● **Giving your title** If you prefer to be addressed by a particular title, such as Ms or Dr, include this when you give your name at the end of a letter.

● **Reading aloud** Read a letter aloud once you have finished writing it. If the text sounds good, and you can read it smoothly, it should be easy for the other person to follow.

Invoice

Include your name and address, and that of the recipient. Give the date and any reference number for the work. Briefly describe the work, and note the amount to be paid. Sign the invoice.

● **Planning format** Set up a master form on a computer, or type it. Keep some pre-printed forms ready for use.

● **Defining costs** If an invoice is for several pieces of work, give the cost for each item, and write the total amount beneath these figures.

● **Listing extra costs** When including costs such as tax or postage, give both the price of the work and the total figure including these extra costs.

● **Using reference numbers** Devise a system for numbering your invoices so that you can identify them easily for personal reference or tax purposes.

● **Giving a reply date** Write on your invoice the date by which you will expect payment (usually 30 days). Even if this has no legal force, it will be useful for future reference.

● **Sending an invoice** Mail or fax an invoice as soon as you have finished the work, or include it with the last instalment of the work.

● **Noting dates of payments** Keep photocopies of all the invoices that you send out, and write on each of them the date when you are paid.

KEEPING RECORDS

T AKE CARE TO KEEP RECORDS for both business purposes and personal reference. Whether you store records on paper or by electronic means, organize the information clearly and neatly, and in such a way that you can easily refer to it.

SETTING UP A FILING SYSTEM

A rrange information into general categories. If necessary, subdivide the information in each category. For example, subdivide a banking file by each account that you have. Enter all information in chronological order, with the most recent items at the front of a file.

LABELLING & GROUPING

● **Identifying contents** Label files clearly with a general subject and the different categories within the subject.
● **Colour-coding files** Use a different-coloured file for each subject, so that you can identify files at a glance.
● **Labelling shelves** If you keep magazines or pamphlets that do not show their titles on their spines, group the items by title, and label the shelves underneath each title.

MONEY-SAVING TIP

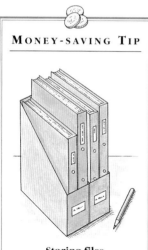

Storing files
Clean out a couple of large detergent boxes. Cut off the tops, and slice a diagonal piece from the upper corners of each. Cover each box with adhesive plastic, and label to indicate the contents.

MAKING A CONTAINER FOR HANGING FILES

Dowelling is slightly longer than box

Slot is 2.5 cm (1 in) deep

1 Find a wooden box that will hold hanging files. Mark the width of a file on the front and back of the box, near the top edges. Drill holes at the marks, and cut these into slots. Fit lengths of dowelling into them.

2 Place the files in the box so that they hang from the dowelling. Leave the box open for easy access, or add a cover to protect the files. Label the front of the box clearly to indicate the contents.

ORGANIZING DATA

● **Grouping data for vehicles** Keep a file for each vehicle. At the front, insert a sheet of paper giving the make, age, registration number, and date of purchase. Include all tax and insurance documents, and receipts for repairs.
● **Keeping data for pets** Keep a photograph of each pet, and record its breed, identification marks, and distinctive physical features. Include insurance documents, veterinary data, and any breed certificates.
● **Labelling floppy disks** Attach an adhesive label to each disk. Note the general category of information on the disk and, if there is room, the name of each file or folder.

FILING ON A COMPUTER

● **Cleaning a hard drive** Check your hard drive regularly, and remove any files and software programs that you do not use. This will free up memory for recent or important data.
● **Tidying folders** Delete all unnecessary documents. If you wish to keep copies, print them out and file them with the rest of your papers.
● **Recording file names** If you use coded names for files, keep a list of the codes and real names in a safe place.
● **Storing letters** Do not keep copies of letters on your hard disk. For maximum space on the computer, photocopy the printed letter once you have signed it, and file the copy.

KEEPING IMPORTANT DATA

Protect information such as financial records, legal documents, and confidential business data. Organize files and information carefully so that you have easy access to all of the material. Keep the most sensitive information in a secure place such as a coded file, a safe, or a bank.

STORING ON PAPER

● **Storing receipts** Keep files to hold receipts for valuable items. Set up one file for office equipment, and make another for household objects. You can then refer to the receipts if you need to value an object or prove your ownership. File any guarantees together with the relevant receipts.

● **Keeping hard copies** File a hard copy of every important document on your computer, in case the machine breaks down or is stolen and you cannot retrieve the documents.

● **Using an address book** List people in an address book or card index using only their initials and surnames. This will protect people's privacy if the information is lost or stolen.

USING FLOPPY DISKS

● **Keeping copies of files** Store copies of essential files on floppy disks. Put the disks in a lockable box. Keep the box in a secure place, away from heat and magnetic sources that could damage the disks.

Keeping business cards
Collect business cards in a small photograph album for quick and easy reference. Either file them alphabetically by surname or company name, or categorize them by profession.

ORGANIZING FINANCE

● **Monitoring your budget** Keep up-to-date files of your recent spending, and allocate space for planning ahead.

● **Keeping receipts** Save receipts for credit cards and counterfoils for paying-in slips so that you can check them against bank statements.

● **Studying statements** As soon as a bank statement arrives, check each entry against your credit card receipts, cheque book, and counterfoils for paying-in slips. Notify the bank instantly if you find any errors.

● **Saving money** Open separate savings accounts for different purposes. For example, have one for emergencies and one for treats such as holidays.

● **Managing financial matters** Take a bookkeeping course to learn how to organize your accounts and deal with taxes.

KEEPING DATA SECURE

● **Storing vital facts** Make a list of data such as the numbers and expiry dates of your credit cards and the numbers of your bank accounts and insurance policies. File the list in a secure place.

● **Encoding data** To keep information safe from other people, encode it in a way that you will easily understand.

● **Storing copies** Keep two copies of essential documents in separate safe places. This way, you will always have a back-up if the original, or one of the copies, is lost.

● **Depositing with a lawyer** Leave important information, such as the location of your will and the combination of a safe, with your lawyer.

ENSURING MAXIMUM SECURITY

Keep valuable business and legal documents in a highly secure place such as a safe in your home or in a bank. Keep a list of any items that you store in such places.

● **Choosing a personal safe** If you wish to have easy access to documents or objects, install a safe in your home or office. Fix the safe securely into a wall or floor in an inconspicuous position.

● **Storing in a bank** Use a safety deposit box in a bank if you need documents or objects to be well guarded. Your access to them will be limited to the bank's working hours, so check these in advance. Take identification, such as a passport, with you when you wish to view the items or to remove them.

SAFEGUARD TIP

Destroying a credit card
On receipt of a replacement credit card, cut the old one into small pieces immediately. Throw the pieces into different waste bins to make sure that the card cannot be reconstructed. Always sign a new credit card as soon as you receive it.

RUNNING A HOUSEHOLD

QUICK REFERENCE

Personal Care, p. 79

Childcare, p. 82

Special Needs, p. 87

Medical Care, p. 89

Planning Petcare, p. 92

Maintaining Family Transport, p. 94

Planning Special Events, p. 96

Dealing with Crises, p. 98

*O*RGANIZING YOUR HOME LIFE *can be a complex operation, whether you have children to care for, hold down a demanding career, or have special physical needs. If you set up systems that run smoothly, you should find yourself with some free time to enjoy. Break down complex tasks into a number of simple jobs so that you can handle them easily, or delegate them to other members of your household. Plan carefully for major family events, and find out how to prepare yourself for any possible crises that may arise.*

MAKING AND USING A HOUSEHOLD ORGANIZER

Make and display an organizer like the one below so that everyone in your household knows what they and the rest of the household will be doing each day. Use it not only for logging activities, but also for listing any equipment needed for them, such as swimming gear or library books.

● **Using an organizer** Plan each week's activities in advance, and refer to the organizer so that you do not forget any details. Make a habit of updating the organizer every evening.

Spread glue on underside of picture

1 Take a photograph of each member of your household. On each photograph, draw a square around the person's face, and – following the lines – cut out the face. Make sure that the trimmed photographs are all the same size.

2 On a piece of card, draw a column at the left, then a column for each photograph. Draw a row for each activity. Leave the first column empty, and glue the photographs at the tops of the other columns.

Symbols indicate regular activities

Members of household

Wipe chart clean with soft cloth every day

3 In the first column, draw a symbol to represent each activity. Once you have finished the chart, cover it with clear adhesive plastic, and display it in a prominent place, such as on a kitchen wall. To fill in the organizer, use a pen with ink that can be wiped off. Tick the activities that each person is to do on a particular day, and add any other useful details.

ORGANIZING PERSONAL CARE

Good grooming is an important element of personal organization. If you take the time to arrange your wardrobe so that it is easy to present yourself tidily, you will feel confident and will make a good impression on other people.

PUTTING TOGETHER A WARDROBE

Group clothes so that you can find them easily. Keep frequently worn garments in accessible places. Do not hang clothes that need to be cleaned or mended. Instead, put them in a prominent place, and make time to deal with them as soon as possible.

GROUPING BELONGINGS

● **Grouping by use** Put casual clothes, smart clothes, sports kit, and formal wear in groups.

● **Matching accessories** Hang accessories such as scarves on the same hangers as outfits. Group shoes, bags, belts, and gloves so that you can quickly match them to outfits.

● **Matching cosmetics** If you like to wear certain cosmetics with particular outfits, make labels listing these items, and attach the labels to the hangers holding the relevant clothes.

● **Keeping outdoor wear** Hang coats next to an outside door so that they will be easily accessible without taking up space in a wardrobe.

GROUPING BY COLOUR

Coordinating clothes
Arrange clothes of each type (such as daywear or sportswear) into similar or complementary colours, so that you can select coordinated outfits quickly and easily from your wardrobe.

KEEPING ESSENTIALS

Check that your wardrobe contains a selection of basic garments that you can mix and match to form outfits. Include the following items.

● Underwear for at least 2 weeks.
● 6 sets of nightwear.
● 3 smart skirts and/or pairs of trousers.
● 5 smart shirts or blouses.
● 5 casual shirts.
● 2 jackets.
● 2 jumpers.
● 3 pairs of smart shoes.
● 2 pairs of casual shoes.
● 1 smart overcoat.
● 1 casual overcoat.
● Accessories.

TIME-SAVING TIP

Assembling an outfit
The evening before an important occasion, assemble a complete outfit, including accessories, on a hanger. Hang it in a prominent place, and put the shoes underneath.

CHOOSING CLOTHING

● **Selecting colours** If you find a garment that fits and suits you, buy it in several colours.

● **Selecting underwear** Choose underwear that is not too tight or too loose. Avoid patterned items that may show under trousers or pale colours.

● **Embellishing garments** If you are on a limited budget, buy inexpensive clothes, and smarten them by changing the buttons or adding decorations.

● **Buying for others** Record the measurements of all your family members in a diary. Before buying a garment for someone, refer to the figures to check the correct size.

KEEPING OLD CLOTHES

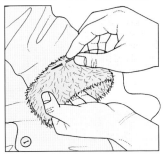

Rejuvenating coat sleeves
If the sleeves of a coat are short or frayed at the ends, but the rest still fits and is in good condition, sew a trim on to the cuffs to extend or smarten the sleeves. Attach the trim so that it extends beyond the end of each sleeve.

PLANNING PERSONAL GROOMING

It is important to set aside time every day to keep yourself clean and tidy. Create a daily care routine that you can carry out quickly even when you are busy in the morning or tired in the evening. Keep your toiletries within easy reach in the bathroom or bedroom.

ESSENTIAL TOILETRIES

You need only a basic selection of toiletries. The items shown here should be sufficient. Choose brands that suit your skin and do not irritate it.

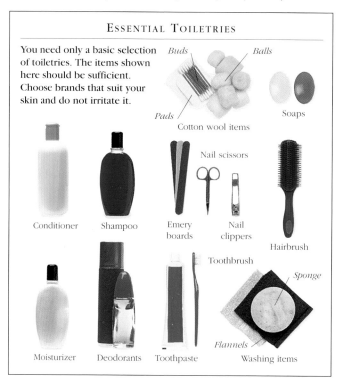

Buds

Balls

Pads

Cotton wool items

Soaps

Conditioner

Shampoo

Nail scissors

Emery boards

Nail clippers

Hairbrush

Toothbrush

Sponge

Moisturizer

Deodorants

Toothpaste

Flannels

Washing items

ARRANGING DAILY CARE

● **Keeping a portable kit** Make up a small toiletries kit to keep in your briefcase or handbag. Include basic items such as tissues, contact lens cleaners, toothbrush and toothpaste, and moisturizer.

● **Creating conditioner** If you have dry hair, beat one egg, and rub it into your hair. Leave for a few minutes, then rinse off with cold water.

● **Improvising dry shampoo** If you have no time to wash your hair, shake some talcum powder into your hand, and rub it into your scalp. Brush out the powder thoroughly.

● **Applying moisturizer** Use just enough to coat your skin. Excess moisturizer will not sink in so will not benefit you.

● **Refreshing your face** After cleaning, splash warm water on your face to refresh the skin.

USING LIPSTICK

● **Cleaning after use** Wipe lipstick with a tissue after every use to clean the surface and remove bacteria. Do this even if you use a lip brush.

Coat bristles of lip brush lightly with lipstick

Using up old lipstick

Make the best use of lipstick by removing the last traces with a lip brush. If the lipstick does not come away easily, stand the open lipstick container in a little hot water for a few minutes.

CARING FOR ITEMS

● **Maintaining hairbrushes** Pull loose hair out of hairbrush bristles with a comb.

● **Preserving soap** Store soap in a dish that lets it drain, so that it will not become mushy.

● **Cleaning flannels** Rinse flannels after every use to prevent soap deposits from building up on them. Launder flannels at least once a week.

● **Storing scents** Keep perfume bottles in a dark place. If scent is exposed to light, it will discolour and deteriorate.

● **Cleaning equipment** Wash hairbrushes, combs, and make-up applicators once a week in a gentle shampoo.

● **Storing nail varnish** Store nail varnish in a refrigerator to keep it runny for use.

MONEY-SAVING TIP

Making moisturizer

Mix 15 ml (1 tbsp) each of vegetable oil, coconut oil, and olive oil with 30 ml (2 tbsp) crushed strawberries. Put the mixture into a clean, screw-topped jar, and store it in a refrigerator. Use the moisturizer within 10 days.

TAKING TIME FOR RELAXATION

Allow some time every week for pampering yourself. Listen to music, read, or have a long bath. Ask other people in your household not to disturb you. For deep relaxation, try one of the methods listed in the chart below. Seek expert advice before trying these techniques.

RELAXATION METHODS

METHOD	TECHNIQUE	BENEFITS
Yoga	Uses sequences of movements and breathing techniques.	Gently stretches and tones muscles, and reduces anxiety.
Meditation	Involves focusing on a specific word or image for about 10 minutes.	Improves thought processes and reduces stress level.
Progressive relaxation	Involves tensing, then relaxing, each part of the body in turn.	Reduces mental and physical tension. If practised in bed, aids restful sleep.
Aromatherapy	Uses natural oils diluted in a base oil in a bath, or applied by massage.	Lessens stress. Used with expert advice, it can ease physical problems.
Massage	Involves relaxing muscles with types of touching and stroking.	Relieves stiff or tense muscles and comforts the mind.

MASSAGING TO REDUCE TENSION

● **Preparing for a massage**
When you massage yourself or someone else, use a warm, quiet, softly-lit room. Lie on a firm, padded surface such as a pile of blankets on the floor.

● **Using oil** To make your hands glide over the skin, use aromatherapy oil or a light cooking oil. Pour a tiny amount into one hand. Rub your hands to warm the oil before use.

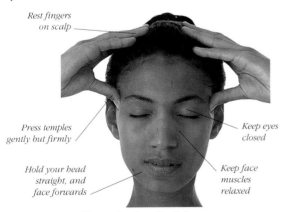

Rest fingers on scalp

Press temples gently but firmly

Hold your head straight, and face forwards

Keep eyes closed

Keep face muscles relaxed

Giving yourself a relaxing facial massage
To begin the massage, put your hands over your face, hold for a moment, then stroke outwards once. Using both hands, stroke the backs of your fingers up each cheek, from your mouth to your ear, 10 times. Stroke your forehead with your fingers, from your nose to your hairline, 10 times. Massage your temples by rubbing in small circles with your thumbs. To finish the massage, warm your eyelids with your palms, then put your hands over your face and stroke.

CALMING YOUR MIND

● **Taking exercise** Release tension in your body through activities such as swimming or walking. Exercise will improve the blood supply to your brain, helping you to clear your mind and lift your mood. It will also encourage restful sleep.

● **Breathing deeply** Sit or lie in a comfortable position. Take a deep breath, hold it for a few seconds, then breathe out. Let your abdomen as well as your chest move with your breath. Repeat for up to five minutes.

● **Using your thoughts** Sit or lie comfortably, then visualize a peaceful scene such as a sunlit beach. Imagine that you are there, sensing the light and warmth. Feel your body relax as your mind forms the image.

● **Listening to music** Play your favourite calming music. Wear headphones so that you can concentrate on the sound.

● **Popping bubble wrap** Dispel tension instantly by popping the bubbles in bubble wrap.

ORGANIZING CHILDCARE

WHETHER YOU LOOK AFTER YOUR CHILDREN YOURSELF or pay someone to do it, you will have to adapt your lifestyle so that the children's needs come first. Forward planning will enable you to make the most of your resources.

ESSENTIAL EQUIPMENT FOR A NEW-BORN BABY

The choice of baby equipment and clothes is considerable and can be bewildering. The items shown here comprise the basic kit that you will need to care for a new-born baby.

● **Assembling equipment** If you cannot afford to buy everything at once, buy essentials such as clothes, nappies, and a bed before the baby arrives, and gradually buy the rest later.

● **Ensuring safety** Make sure that you choose equipment and clothes that are non-flammable.

● **Finding dual-purpose items** Look for items that will suit the baby as it grows. For example, choose a pram that can be converted later into a buggy.

● **Sharing with others** Babies grow quickly, so their clothes may last only a few weeks. Buy second-hand garments from a local mother-and-baby group, and in return pass on anything that your baby has outgrown.

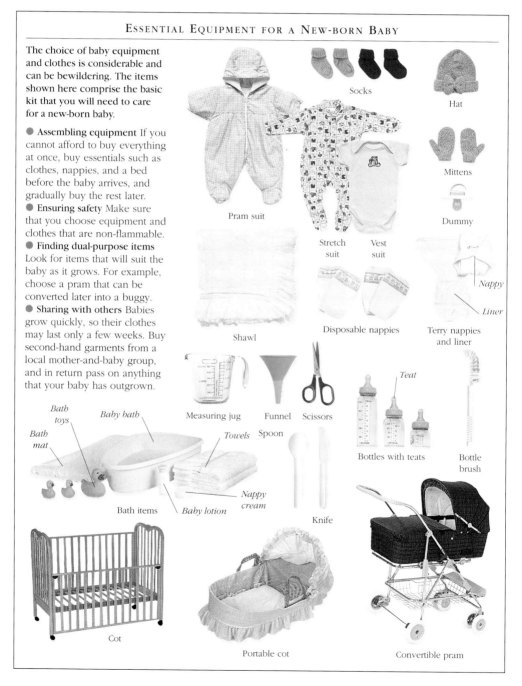

Socks

Hat

Mittens

Dummy

Pram suit

Stretch suit

Vest suit

Nappy

Liner

Disposable nappies

Terry nappies and liner

Shawl

Measuring jug

Funnel

Scissors

Teat

Bath toys

Baby bath

Bath mat

Towels Spoon

Bottles with teats

Bottle brush

Bath items

Baby lotion

Nappy cream

Knife

Cot

Portable cot

Convertible pram

ORGANIZING TIME WITH A BABY

Your child will be a baby for only a short time, so enjoy the experience – baby care need not consist solely of feeding, giving baths, and changing nappies. Babies like company, so spend time with yours, especially if you plan to start work outside the home after a few months.

SETTING UP A ROUTINE
● **Organizing daily activities** Establish a simple routine for feeds, nappy changing, sleep, and cuddles. This will minimize stress for you and the baby.
● **Checking body heat** Babies cannot regulate their body temperatures. Feel the back of the neck to ensure that a baby is not overly hot or cold.
● **Helping a baby to sleep** Do not let anyone over-excite a baby just before bedtime. An unsettled baby will not go to sleep – and neither will you.
● **Finding time to sleep** Fit your rest around your baby's sleep pattern, even if he or she tends to sleep during the day and be active at night. Use a baby monitor (see p. 84) to alert you if the baby wakes.

BATHING A BABY
● **Timing baths** Young babies need a full bath only every two or three days. Set aside sufficient time to allow for play as well as washing.

Drying a baby easily
Before you start bathing a baby, tuck a towel into the waistband of your clothes. Once you have finished, lift the baby on to your lap, and wrap the towel around it.

ORGANIZING FEEDS
● **Preparing equipment** When bottle-feeding, sterilize bottles before use according to the manufacturer's instructions. In addition, make sure that you regularly sterilize cleaning items such as bottle brushes.
● **Making feeds in batches** Prepare a whole day's formula feeds at once, and store them in a refrigerator. Reheat in a microwave oven or a pan of hot water. Check that the feed is the correct temperature by squeezing a few drops on to the back of your hand.
● **Introducing solid food** When you cook for adults, save plainly cooked vegetables to feed to a baby. Liquidize and freeze in meal-sized portions. Reheat when needed.

CATERING FOR CHILDREN'S NEEDS

As children grow, it is important to ensure that they feel safe in their environment, while gradually making them aware of any potential dangers – first in the home and then outdoors. Supply as much stimulation as they need, without encouraging over-excitement.

STIMULATING A BABY

Decorating a portable cot
Tuck colourful cards and pictures around the inside of a portable cot to give a baby something to look at. A new baby is not likely to pull them out. If the baby grabs the cards, remove them.

CARING FOR A TODDLER
● **Choosing clothes** Learning how to dress is a necessary skill that can also be fun for toddlers. Select clothes with simple fastenings such as poppers, touch-and-close tape, or large, colourful buttons.
● **Teaching through daily life** Let your child come with you while you do routine tasks around the house. Use the time to teach the child about his or her environment.
● **Coping with tantrums** The best way to deal with a small child in a temper is to leave the room. Tell the child why you are going, and return only when the tantrum is over.

STARTING SCHOOL

Marking possessions
Label every object that a child takes to school, including beaker and lunchbox. If a child cannot read, use blank labels in a bright colour so that the child will be able to identify the objects easily.

KEEPING CHILDREN SAFE INDOORS

The family home can be a dangerous place for children, but with some forethought you can prevent many accidents. Note the possible hazards in each room. Move harmful objects out of reach of children, and fit guards across areas such as the top and bottom of a stairway.

CHILDPROOF SAFETY EQUIPMENT

In most cases, you can make areas safe just by rearranging the objects in them. However, to protect small children, you will need safety items as well, such as the pieces shown on the right.

● **Using safety gates** Fit gates to the tops and bottoms of stairs. Make sure that the bars are vertical so that a child cannot climb up them. Check that the gates have childproof locks.
● **Making a cooker safe** Install a cooker guard so that children cannot touch hot rings. Use the back rings whenever possible, and turn pan handles away from the front of the cooker.
● **Testing a baby monitor** Check all parts regularly to see that they are working properly.
● **Fitting a door stop** Attach a stop to the top of a door so that a child cannot reach the stop.

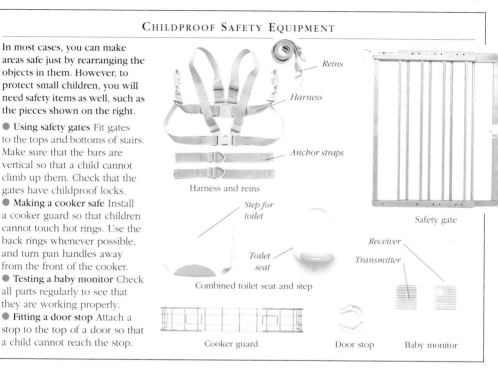

Reins

Harness

Anchor straps

Harness and reins

Step for toilet

Toilet seat

Combined toilet seat and step

Safety gate

Receiver

Transmitter

Cooker guard

Door stop

Baby monitor

BRIGHT IDEA

Using a box as a step
Keep an upturned box for a child to use as a step to reach a basin or toilet. Check that the box will bear the child's weight. Always supervise small children in the bathroom.

PREVENTING ACCIDENTS
● **Making a floor safe** Remove any loose rugs. Sand wooden flooring to remove splinters. Fit durable surfaces such as vinyl in areas used by children.
● **Preventing burns** Put guards in front of heaters and fires. Make sure that a child cannot knock the guards over.
● **Fitting safe flexes** Use coiled flexes on electrical appliances. These flexes take up little space, so are not likely to dangle within reach of a child.
● **Storing harmful items** Store items such as cleaning fluids and medicines in cupboards that a child cannot reach. When using the items, keep them away from children.
● **Using stairs safely** When carrying a child up or down stairs, hold on to a banister.

CREATING A SAFE HOME
● **Securing doors** Fit locks or high-level bolts to the doors of potentially hazardous rooms such as the kitchen. Keep the rooms locked when not in use.

Fit ball snugly on corner

Covering table corners
To protect each corner of a low table, make a dent in a ping-pong ball, then glue it to the table. The balls will make the corners visible, and will act as shields if a child falls against the table.

KEEPING CHILDREN SAFE OUTDOORS

Most children enjoy playing outdoors and going on journeys, but it can be difficult to keep them safe since the hazards are less predictable than those in the home. Accompany your children whenever they leave the home, until they have learned safety codes.

TAKING PRECAUTIONS

By following these simple tips, you can ensure that a child stays safe if he or she becomes separated from you.

● **Using telephones** Before going out, always check that your child knows the numbers of the emergency services, and has enough money for telephone calls.
● **Checking the surroundings** Teach a child to spot street names or shop names, and to give this information to the emergency services if you become separated.
● **Walking around** Tell a child to call the emergency services if he or she is lost.
● **Calling for help** Teach a child to carry a loud whistle and to blow it immediately when lost, in trouble, or being bothered by a stranger.

PREVENTING PROBLEMS

● **Arranging lifts** If your child is at someone else's house, carry the telephone number of the house so that you can telephone immediately if you will not be able to collect the child at the expected time.
● **Accepting lifts** Teach a child never to accept a lift from a stranger, and not even to take a lift with someone familiar, unless you have told the child about this in advance.
● **Using a code word** Agree on a special code word with your child so that, if you need another adult to collect them, the child will know that the person has been sent by you.
● **Protecting teenagers** When teenage children go out, ask them to leave an address and contact telephone number.

USING TRANSPORT

● **Taking a child in a car** Always put a baby or child in the back seat of a car, and never in the passenger seat of a car fitted with airbags. If a bag inflates, it could seriously harm the child's skull.
● **Using a carrycot in a car** Follow the manufacturer's instructions when securing a carrycot to a back seat. Keep the cover of the cot in place. This will prevent the baby from being thrown out of the cot if you have to brake suddenly.
● **Choosing a buggy** When buying a buggy, choose a type that has a high, padded seat, which will protect a child's head as well as its body. Test the brakes to make sure that they are effective.

MAKING PLAY SAFE

● **Adapting a garden** Remove or fence off any toxic plants in your garden. Do not let a child near any area that has been sprayed with weedkiller.

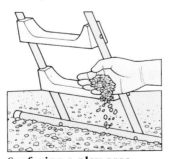

Surfacing a play area
If you have a swing or climbing frame in your garden, dig a shallow pit beneath it, and fill the pit with wood chippings. This will prevent children from being hurt if they slip or fall off.

ENSURING ROAD SAFETY

● **Crossing roads safely** When you cross roads with children, teach them to choose crossing places away from curves or parked cars. Tell them to look both ways and to wait until the road is clear before crossing.

Making children visible
Select a bright- or pale-coloured coat for a child. Stick or sew reflective shapes on to it. Ensure that the child wears it in poor light conditions, so that he or she is always visible to traffic.

SAFEGUARD TIP

Covering a drain
If you have an open drain outside your home, fix an old oven tray or cooling rack over the hole so that children cannot drop objects into it or trap their feet inside it.

SETTING UP A CHILDCARE ROUTINE

There are many types of carer for children, such as live-in carers, childminders (who work from their own homes), or babysitters for occasional help. Take time to choose the right carer – the most important thing is that you and your child are happy with the person.

EMPLOYING A LIVE-IN CARER

Set aside a few days for meeting prospective carers. Once you have made your choice, make a formal agreement with the carer.

● **Checking legal rights** To set fair pay and conditions, find out about carers' employment rights.
● **Agreeing hours** Discuss the hours that a carer will work, and which days they can have off. Make arrangements for weekends and holidays.

● **Defining duties** Write a list of childcare and household duties that you would like a carer to do. In return, ask what the carer is prepared or qualified to do. (For example, do not expect a nanny to do housework that is not directly linked to childcare.)
● **Discussing money** Decide on payment and who will deal with insurance and tax. Tell the carer if they are to pay costs such as their share of telephone bills.

● **Insuring your car** If the carer needs to use your car, include them on your insurance policy.
● **Allowing visitors** Say whether a carer may entertain guests. Tell the person if you object to visitors staying overnight.
● **Having a trial** Set a trial period of employment at the end of which you will both review the situation. Agree how much notice each side will give before ending the arrangement.

INTRODUCING A CARER

● **Testing a child's reaction** When you introduce a carer to a child, leave the child with the carer for a short time. When you return, see if the child is happy with the carer.
● **Briefing a child** Tell a child that they must do what a carer asks unless this is something very unusual or unpleasant.
● **Following up** After the carer's first day of work, ask the child what the carer did. You can then decide if the carer is right for the child.

CARER'S CHECKLIST

Give a carer details about a child, and safety information.

● **Personality** Details on behaviour and discipline.
● **Health** Information about allergies and other conditions.
● **Diet** What a child will eat.
● **Routines** When child is fed, bathed, and put to bed.
● **Telephone** Contact number for you in case of problems.
● **Emergencies** What to do in emergencies such as a fire.

USING A CHILDMINDER

● **Looking for a childminder** Ask friends with children the same age as yours whom they would recommend. Their advice is likely to be up-to-date and accurate.
● **Assessing a childminder** Visit a childminder while they are working to see how they look after other children. Find out how many children they care for at any one time.
● **Agreeing on care** Ask how a childminder feeds, disciplines, and cares for children, in case their views conflict with yours.
● **Discussing activities** Ask a childminder if they plan special activities for children, such as painting or visiting parks.
● **Dealing with illness** Make arrangements for looking after your child if the child is ill. A childminder will not usually look after sick children, and a child who feels unwell should not leave home.
● **Arranging informal care** If you regularly employ a friend or a relative as a childminder, agree on payment, hours, and expected duties, as you would with a professional carer.

USING A BABYSITTER

● **Employing a young person** Do not use babysitters under the age of 14, since they may not be able to cope in a crisis.
● **Giving advice** Advise a babysitter on how to cope if a child is ill or disobedient.
● **Showing essential items** Let a babysitter know where to find the first-aid kit and necessary items such as nappies.

BRIEFING A BABYSITTER

Looking after a baby
When leaving a baby with a babysitter, check that the person knows how to handle the baby. For example, when they pick up a baby, ensure that they support its head and body securely.

CATERING FOR SPECIAL NEEDS

I F YOU HAVE a condition such as arthritis or a physical disability, or if you care for someone in this situation, ask a doctor to suggest equipment to help with physical tasks. In addition, find ways in which home life can be adapted.

EQUIPMENT FOR A PERSON WITH SPECIAL PHYSICAL NEEDS

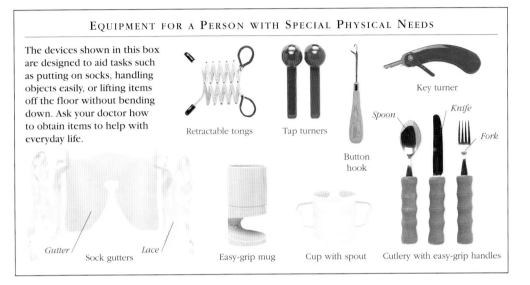

The devices shown in this box are designed to aid tasks such as putting on socks, handling objects easily, or lifting items off the floor without bending down. Ask your doctor how to obtain items to help with everyday life.

Retractable tongs

Tap turners

Button hook

Key turner

Spoon

Knife

Fork

Gutter

Sock gutters

Lace

Easy-grip mug

Cup with spout

Cutlery with easy-grip handles

PRESERVING INDEPENDENCE

There are several ways to cope with physical problems such as reduced mobility, vision, or memory. Try the tips given below to make common tasks easier, or to adapt household routines. Even a few of these steps can increase one's ability to manage everyday life.

OPENING CONTAINERS

Opening a jar
If a jar has a screw-top lid, put two or three thick elastic bands around the body and lid so that it will be easy to grip when you open it. Alternatively, put on rubber gloves before opening it.

TAKING EXERCISE

Keeping hands supple
To prevent stiffness in your hands, squeeze a large bulldog clip several times with each hand. Keep your fingers away from the open end of the clip. Do this exercise once or twice a day.

MANAGING DAILY LIFE
● **Choosing bedding** Select a duvet and a fitted sheet for ease of use. Check that you can open and close the fastenings on the duvet cover.
● **Prompting memory** Attach large labels to drawers and cupboards with a list of their contents to give an instant reminder when necessary.
● **Marking taps** Paint hot-water taps with red nail varnish to make them easily visible.
● **Buying an electric kettle** When buying a kettle, choose a cordless type for safety.
● **Monitoring heat** Keep easy-to-read thermometers in rooms that you use daily. The rooms should be at least 21°C (70°F).

MODIFYING A HOME

If you are elderly or have a disability, you may be able to have your home adapted so that you can lead an independent life. You can equip your home with purpose-built aids such as chair lifts for a staircase, and you can also make inexpensive items for use every day.

ADAPTING ITEMS

● **Retyping recipes** Have recipes retyped in large type to make them easy to use. If necessary, reduce quantities so that they suit one or two people. Store the adapted recipes in a ring binder.

● **Lengthening a shoe horn** Fix a stout bamboo cane securely to a standard shoe horn, so that you can use it without bending to reach your feet.

● **Adapting implements** Cut up an old bicycle inner tube, and slide lengths of it over the handles of tools or kitchen implements. Glue the lengths in place to make easy-grip surfaces for the handles.

● **Improvising a duster** If you have stiff hands, use a sock as a duster. Slip the sock over your hand, spray it with polish, and stroke surfaces clean.

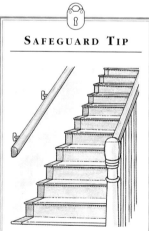

SAFEGUARD TIP

Modifying a staircase
Attach a second stair rail to the wall opposite an existing rail, so that anyone climbing or descending the staircase can steady themselves with both hands.

CREATING USEFUL ITEMS

● **Making a knee protector** Stick several layers of bubble wrap to a piece of board. This makes a comfortable surface to kneel on for gardening.

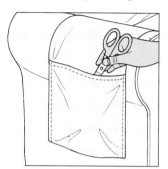

Sewing a chair pouch
Cut a length of narrow canvas. Fold up one end, and stitch along the outside edges. Sew curtain weights to the other end. Drape over the arm of a chair, and use to keep small items to hand.

CHOOSING EQUIPMENT

● **Aiding mobility** Fit handles to walls around a bath and a toilet, and in frequently used areas. Hold the handles to steady yourself while using a bathroom or walking around.

● **Buying kitchen appliances** Check that you can operate the controls of kitchen appliances. Choose types that have lights to show when they are on.

● **Using an electric blanket** An overblanket is safer than an underblanket. Choose one that can safely be left on all night. Never use an underblanket as an overblanket, or vice versa.

● **Using alarms** Install an alarm linked to a neighbour's house or a care centre. Alternatively, wear a personal alarm on a pendant so that you can attract instant help from passers-by.

ENSURING COMFORT

● **Altering layout** If you find it difficult to climb stairs but do not wish to install a chair lift, and you have a toilet on the ground floor, turn a downstairs room into a bedroom. Use top-floor rooms for storage.

● **Choosing new lighting** If you need to fit lights that are brighter than those that you already have, consider fitting halogen spotlights to brighten dim corners of rooms.

● **Using a kitchen easily** Keep an office chair with castors in a kitchen so that you can sit down while preparing food, and move around without standing up. Never stand or kneel on a chair with castors.

● **Showering in comfort** Install a sturdy plastic stool on a rubber suction mat to provide seating in a shower.

ENSURING SAFETY

● **Making floors safe** Check that floor surfaces have no uneven or broken patches. Avoid using loose rugs, or add non-slip backing (see p. 47).

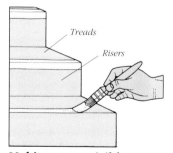

Treads

Risers

Making steps visible
Paint white strips along the edges of uncarpeted steps, using good-quality outdoor paint so that the markings will last. Paint both the treads (flat parts) and the risers (vertical parts).

ARRANGING MEDICAL CARE

BEFORE YOU EMBARK ON MEDICAL TREATMENT, find out what it involves and who will treat you. Explain your symptoms clearly, and state any other concerns that you may have, such as wishing to see a doctor of the same sex as yourself.

SEEING A DOCTOR

Unless it is an emergency, make medical appointments at least one week in advance, when the surgery is likely to have a range of times to offer you. Bear in mind that there may be a delay before you are able to see the doctor, and take something to occupy yourself.

PLANNING A VISIT

Make a list of points to raise with your doctor during your medical appointment.

- **Symptoms** Pain. Changes in temperature, bodily functions, eating and drinking habits, appearance, or energy levels.
- **Reactions and feelings** Allergies, reactions to drugs, stress or depression.
- **Requests** Prescription to be renewed or sick note needed.

UTILIZING TIME
- **Giving information** Record medical facts about yourself and your family in a health log (see p. 91). A doctor may ask you about family medical history, so take the log with you for instant reference.
- **Dressing for comfort** If you are likely to undergo a physical examination or have your blood pressure taken, wear clothing that you can easily adjust or remove.

TALKING TO A DOCTOR
- **Describing symptoms** Use plain language, rather than medical jargon. Mention all symptoms, not just those that you believe are relevant.
- **Letting a child talk** Let a child describe their symptoms before you add any details.
- **Concluding an appointment** Be sure that you understand a doctor's recommendations on treatment. Ask for extra information if available.

ORGANIZING HOME MEDICINE

Keep a basic medical kit in a safe place so that you can treat minor wounds and ailments yourself. Check the kit regularly, and replace items before they are completely used up. Throw away tablets or other medications that have passed their use-by dates.

KEEPING A HOME MEDICAL KIT

Store a medical kit in a cool, dark area to preserve the quality of the medicines. Make sure that everyone knows the location of the kit, but take care to keep it away from small children.

Sterile dressing
Safety pins
Antiseptic wipes
Scissors
Waterproof plaster
Packet containing triangular bandages
Antiseptic cream
Tweezers
Micropore tape
Crêpe bandage
Calamine lotion
Bandage with clip
Painkillers

KEEPING MEDICINES
- **Covering labels** Cover labels with clear adhesive tape to stop print from being rubbed off and to keep them legible.

Put tablets for one day in canister
Labels show days of week

Pre-packing tablets
If you take several tablets a day, put daily doses in black film canisters, which keep out air and light. Label the lids to show days of the week and contents.

VISITING A HOSPITAL

Try to prepare for a stay in hospital so that you will have all the necessary supplies with you. If you intend to visit someone who is in hospital, check the visiting times before you go, and take items that will make the person's stay pleasant, as well as necessities.

PREPARING TO STAY
● **Obtaining extra supplies**
Arrange for supplies of clean nightwear and flannels, and foods such as fruits, to be brought to you every few days.

Stocking a freezer
You may well feel too fatigued to cook when you return from hospital, so cook, label, and freeze meals in single portions before you go. Defrost and reheat them as required.

SUPPLIES TO PACK FOR A HOSPITAL STAY

You are unlikely to have much storage space in hospital, so pack only necessary items. However, days in hospital can seem long and tedious, so include items that will keep you occupied during your stay, such as a personal stereo and some music, a variety of reading matter, or materials for writing letters.

● **Taking medication** If you are on regular medication, take it with you and hand it to hospital staff for them to administer.

Earphones

Personal stereo   Medication   Moisturizer

Underwear

Slippers   Pyjamas   Book

CARING FOR A CHILD
● **Providing news** Ask family and friends to record cassettes telling a sick child what is going on at home and at school. This will reassure the child that he or she is not forgotten.
● **Taking reminders of home** Place photographs of family, pets, and friends on a child's bedside unit, and put a favourite cuddly toy in the bed.
● **Bringing extra meals** If a child is not eating hospital food, ask whether you may bring a few meals from home to encourage the child to eat.
● **Planning the trip home** Plan nice things for a sick child to do after returning home. However, do not discuss with a child when he or she might return until you know for sure, to avoid disappointment.

ORGANIZING GIFTS

Pack items in gift bag

Packing treats for a child
Fill a small bag with items such as a toy, a sketch pad, crayons, and pieces of fruit. Label the items with each day of a child's time in hospital. Tell the child to take out only one item each day.

VISITING A PATIENT
● **Arranging a visit** Call a patient's family before visiting to find out how the patient feels. Some people prefer to have no visitors for a few days after treatment, because they become tired easily.
● **Considering other visitors** If you are one of several visitors, try to coordinate your arrival and departure times so that you are not all there at once, and keep visits short.
● **Comforting a patient** Do not feel obliged to be cheerful all the time. Simply sitting quietly with a patient may be enough to comfort them.
● **Taking children** Young children can easily become bored when visiting a person in hospital. Take quiet activities to occupy them.

MAKING A FAMILY HEALTH LOG

Organize all the health information for each family member to make a log for quick reference. Update each person's data regularly. Keep the log in a ring binder, together with any other important medical information such as vaccination certificates and test results.

INFORMATION TO INCLUDE IN A FAMILY HEALTH LOG			
TYPE OF INFORMATION	**DETAILS TO RECORD**	**DATES AND TIMES TO REMEMBER**	**TREATMENTS TO FOLLOW**
Personal details	● **Physical data** Note each person's sex, birth date, height, and weight. ● **Blood group** Make a note of the blood group. ● **Allergies** List any food, drug, or object causing allergies, and the resulting symptoms.	● **Eye and hearing tests** Record the dates of the next appointments. ● **Medications** Note the dates for renewing any repeat presciptions. ● **Children's checks** Note the dates of checks on children's development.	● **Medications** Record the name and dosage of any regular medications. ● **Eyesight** Note the details of prescriptions for glasses or contact lenses. ● **Allergies** Note any preventative action to take for allergies.
Medical appointments	● **Symptoms** Make a list of any symptoms that you need to discuss with a doctor (see p. 89). ● **Causes** Make a note of external factors that may influence symptoms, such as poor air quality.	● **Appointments** Note the dates of forthcoming medical appointments. ● **Inoculations** Record the dates and types of inoculations for children. ● **Results** Note when any test results are due.	● **Medications** Note the dosage of recommended medications, and any other relevant details. ● **Routines** Note any changes suggested by a doctor, such as changes in diet or exercise habits.
Hospital visits	● **Information** Record the name and contact number of the hospital. ● **Reference** If a hospital assigns a reference number to a patient, write down this number.	● **Operations** Note the dates of operations, and specify what was done. ● **Emergencies** Record the dates and purposes of any emergency admissions to hospital.	● **Treatment** Record the details of treatment given at a hospital. ● **Time in hospital** If treatment involves a stay in hospital, note the duration of the stay.
Illnesses or injuries	● **Details** Write down the symptoms of illness or the signs of injury. Note the date when the problem first appeared. ● **Causes** Record the cause of an illness or injury, if known.	● **Tests** Note the nature of any tests carried out, and the dates when the results are due. ● **Return visits** Write down the dates of any further appointments for treatment.	● **Action** Ask medical staff for guidelines on coping with the illness or injury at home. ● **Side-effects** Record the details of any benefits or side-effects resulting from the treatment.
Dental checks	● **Information** List the details of problems to discuss with a dentist. ● **Children's teeth** Note when a child's milk teeth or adult teeth emerge. Keep records of any problems.	● **Appointments** Note the next appointments with a dentist or a dental hygienist. ● **Major events** Note the dates of any operations, or when dentures are due to be replaced.	● **Routines** Note any suggestions given by a dentist or hygienist, such as changes in daily care. ● **Treatments** Give the details of treatments such as operations or the fitting of braces.

PLANNING PETCARE

P ETS MAKE EXCELLENT COMPANIONS for single people. They are also good for children, who can learn useful life skills through caring for them. Whatever animal you choose, make sure that you can give it the attention that it needs.

KEEPING CATS AND DOGS

C ats are independent animals, requiring little more than regular feeding and a litter tray. However, they do need human attention if they are to be happy. Dogs need regular exercise and can become miserable if left alone, so do not have one if you are out all day.

ADAPTING YOUR HOME

Push cinnamon sticks firmly into soil

Discouraging digging
If a plant pot is within reach of a cat or dog, put cinnamon sticks or strips of lemon peel into the soil. Animals dislike the smell, so they will be unlikely to dig up the soil or chew the plants.

ORGANIZING CARE
● **Selecting carers** Before you buy an animal, agree who in the household will look after it. If you share tasks, draw up a rota so that people take turns in caring for a pet.
● **Setting rules** Take special care of a new animal, so that it feels secure in its new home. Do not be overly indulgent or encourage bad habits.
● **Planning a diet** Ask a pet's breeder or previous owner for guidelines on diet. Introduce any new foods gradually, so as not to upset the animal.

CALMING PETS

Using a ticking clock
If a new puppy cries at night, wrap a ticking clock in a soft towel, and put it in the puppy's bed. The quiet, regular noise is like the mother's heartbeat, and will comfort the animal.

LOOKING AFTER RODENTS

R odents, such as rabbits, hamsters, and mice, are easy to keep. However, these animals are often nervous, so handle them with care – otherwise they may bite. Some rodents can be let out of their cages to play for a time, but watch them to ensure that they do not escape.

BRIGHT IDEA

Providing toys
Use large marbles and plastic cotton reels as sturdy, inexpensive toys for small rodents such as guinea pigs, hamsters, and gerbils.

KEEPING MICE

Small bowl half-filled with vinegar

Neutralizing odours
Mice always smell, even if their cage is regularly cleaned. To absorb odours, put a bowl of vinegar by a cage with mice in it. Change the vinegar regularly.

CARING FOR RODENTS
● **Siting a hutch or cage** Put an outdoor cage in a place that is free from draughts and safe from predators. If a rodent lives indoors, try not to keep it in a bedroom, because rodents may be noisy at night.
● **Providing company** Before buying a rodent, find out whether the species prefers to live alone or with others. For example, hamsters are solitary, while rabbits need company.
● **Handling a rodent safely** Do not hold a rodent a long way off the ground, because it could be killed if it falls.

CARING FOR FISH, REPTILES, AND AMPHIBIANS

Fish, reptiles, and amphibians are fascinating pets. They are not as friendly as mammals but can be rewarding to observe. Monitor their health and environment to avoid problems. If you have children, check that your pets are not likely to pass on diseases such as salmonella.

KEEPING REPTILES

Very few pet reptiles are dangerous, but they all need special care. When buying a reptile, ask the breeder or shop for instructions on care.

● **Handling** If a reptile bites, wear rubber gloves when handling it. The animal will dislike the taste of the gloves, so it should not bite you.
● **Keeping groups** If you plan to keep several species of reptile together, check that none of them is likely to kill or injure other types.
● **Feeding** Ensure that you are able to feed the reptiles properly. For example, you may have to kill rodents or frogs for some snakes.

LOOKING AFTER FISH
● **Draining a tank** Fill a hose with water. Put one end in the tank, and the other in a bucket below it. The water will flow out of the tank by itself.

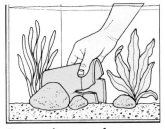

Decorating a tank
Fill a tank with features that will interest fish. Add natural objects such as water plants and a few large stones, and include some broken terracotta pots for the fish to hide in and explore.

USING A TERRARIUM
● **Choosing a tank** Make sure that a tank has a secure lid. Snakes, especially, are very good at escaping from tanks.
● **Creating an environment** Provide the right surroundings for an animal's lifestyle and habits. For example, provide a water area for bathing, sand for burrowing, or branches for tree-climbing animals.
● **Regulating temperature** Use a thermometer in a terrarium so that you can monitor the temperature. To give heat for basking, shine a desk lamp on to the terrarium.
● **Lining the floor** Choose a material, such as shredded paper, that is easy to clean and will not harbour parasites.

CHOOSING AND KEEPING BIRDS

Birds are intelligent, sociable creatures. They need company and attention as well as practical care. Keep them in pairs or groups if possible. Make sure that birds have room to move around their cage. Give them toys, and talk to them – even if they do not talk back.

BUYING BIRDS
● **Checking origin** Before you buy a bird, find out its country of origin and whether the species is bred in captivity. You can then avoid buying a bird that may have been illegally captured in the wild.
● **Determining life expectancy** Find out how long a bird is likely to live. Small birds may survive only a few years, but some parrot species may live as long as a human being.
● **Choosing a bird that will talk** If you wish to train a bird to talk, buy a young one about six weeks old. Keep the bird on its own, but give it a lot of attention so that it will listen to you and learn words easily.

KEEPING BIRDS
● **Checking air quality** Birds can suffer from breathing problems if exposed to dirty air. Never smoke cigarettes near them. Keep them away from strong smells such as burning fat or fresh paint.
● **Avoiding disease** Species imported from tropical areas may carry psittacosis (parrot fever), a disease that is fatal to humans. To avoid infection, wash your hands after handling a bird or cleaning a cage.
● **Positioning a cage** Place a bird cage on a sturdy stand, high enough for you to reach easily when you stand beside it. Position the cage away from direct light and draughts.

TRADITIONAL TIP

Prompting a bird to sing
If you want a bird to sing, position a small mirror in its cage so that the bird can see itself. It will think it is looking at another bird and will sing to its reflection.

MAINTAINING FAMILY TRANSPORT

Family vehicles can range from valuable cars to inexpensive, second-hand bicycles. Whatever types of vehicle you own, keep them in good condition and protect them from theft so that they will have long working lives.

USING MOTOR VEHICLES

Take care of motor vehicles so that they will be safe and reliable. Have them serviced regularly. Read the owner's manuals to learn how to maintain them correctly. When a vehicle runs well, make a note of its performance so that you can learn to spot any problems.

MAINTAINING CARS
● **Correcting problems** As soon as you notice a problem, arrange to have it repaired. Do not ignore it, even if the problem seems only minor.
● **Building up a tool set** When buying tools, start with only the items that you will need for basic car maintenance. Buy additional tools only if you are sure that you will use them regularly.
● **Cleaning interiors** If you or any regular passengers suffer from car sickness, spray the interior of your car with anti-static spray after cleaning. This will stop the accumulation of static electricity, which can make some people feel ill.

MAKING REGULAR CHECKS ON CARS	
INSPECTING A CAR	PREPARING TO DRIVE
Make the following checks to ensure that your car is in good condition and safe to drive.	Immediately before driving a car, always carry out the following safety checks.
● **Brakes** Test the brakes. Top up brake fluid if necessary. ● **Glass** Ensure that all mirrors and windows are clean. ● **Lights** Ensure that all lights work. Replace blown bulbs. ● **Tyres** Check that tread is not damaged or overly worn. ● **Oil** Check the oil level, and top up if necessary. ● **Radiator** Check water level. Top up if necessary. ● **Battery** Check fluid level. Add distilled water if necessary.	● **Doors** Check that all doors are securely closed. ● **Driving seat** Ensure that you are comfortable. Check that you can see all around and that you can reach controls. ● **Mirrors** Make sure that rear view and wing mirrors are all correctly adjusted. ● **Fuel** Check that you have enough fuel for the journey. ● **Seat belts** Make sure that you and any passengers are wearing seat belts.

LOADING MOTORCYCLES

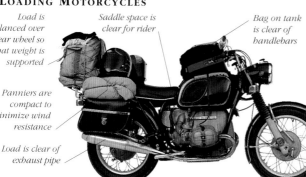

Load is balanced over rear wheel so that weight is supported

Saddle space is clear for rider

Bag on tank is clear of handlebars

Panniers are compact to minimize wind resistance

Load is clear of exhaust pipe

Tyres are well inflated to cope with extra load

Carrying luggage safely on a motorcycle
Load luggage on to a motorcycle so that it will not interfere with the flow of air around you while you are in motion. The load should be no wider than the rider, and should not overbalance the rear of the motorcycle. Ensure that the luggage does not hamper the wheels.

CHECKING MOTORCYCLES
● **Checking mechanical brakes** Look at the brake cables to see if they have stretched. If so, have them adjusted.
● **Checking hydraulic brakes** Examine the brakes to ensure that they are not leaking fluid.
● **Inspecting wheels** Regularly check the nuts and bolts on wheels to make sure that they are sufficiently tight.
● **Examining treads** Follow the tread pattern all around each tyre to ensure that the pattern is complete. If parts of it have worn away, replace the tyre.
● **Maintaining an engine** Have the engine serviced regularly so that it works efficiently.

MAINTAINING BICYCLES

Bicycles are a convenient, environmentally friendly form of transport. Bicycles need much less care than cars or motorcycles, but you must maintain them properly to keep them in peak running condition. Be sure to protect a bicycle from theft whenever you are not using it.

CHECKING BICYCLES FOR SAFETY

● **Testing brakes** As you ride, suddenly apply and release both brakes. They should grip the wheels instantly, allowing no further movement.

● **Checking a saddle** If you remove the saddle, check it once you have replaced it to ensure that it is secure. You should not be able to move it.

SAFEGUARD TIP

Marking a bicycle frame
Scratch the number and postal code of your home on one or two hidden areas such as the frame under the saddle and the back wheel rim. Photograph the identification, and note the parts of the bicycle shown.

Saddle is straight and secure

Brake cables are securely fixed to frame

Brake blocks are aligned with wheel rim

Tyre treads are in good condition

Chain is taut

Spokes are straight

Wheels are straight

Examining a bicycle

Ensure that a bicycle frame is aligned and undamaged. Check that the wheels are true, and that the spokes are straight. If the bicycle has mudguards, make sure that they fit correctly. Look for any cracks in the tyres, then check the inner tubes to see that they are in good condition. Make sure that the chain links are lubricated.

SECURING BICYCLES

● **Securing wheels** If you use a lock on a chain, thread the chain through both wheels as well as around the frame to make it difficult to remove. Alternatively, consider fitting your bicycle with two locks to secure both wheels from theft.

● **Removing parts** If your bicycle is fitted with quick-release mechanisms for removing the saddle and front wheel, practise using them to avoid having any difficulty at your destination.

● **Removing accessories** When you leave a bicycle unattended, remove any valuable accessories such as lights or panniers.

● **Decorating a frame** Paint colourful designs on a bicycle frame, or cover with strongly adhesive coloured stickers. This will make the bicycle conspicuous, so that it will be a less attractive target for thieves.

ESSENTIAL BICYCLE MAINTENANCE EQUIPMENT

The equipment shown below is necessary for general cleaning tasks and simple repairs. Refer to a bicycle manual to see if you will need any specialized tools for carrying out repairs.

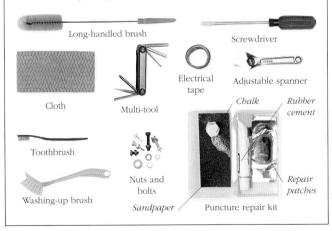

Long-handled brush

Screwdriver

Cloth

Electrical tape

Adjustable spanner

Multi-tool

Chalk

Rubber cement

Toothbrush

Nuts and bolts

Repair patches

Washing-up brush

Sandpaper

Puncture repair kit

PLANNING SPECIAL EVENTS

O RGANIZE FAMILY CELEBRATIONS METICULOUSLY so that they run smoothly, with no crises or sudden changes of plan. Carry out all the necessary tasks as far in advance as possible, so that you can relax and enjoy the occasion.

ORGANIZING A WEDDING

A llow plenty of time for planning so that you can be sure to have the arrangements that you would like. Venues, caterers, and florists are usually booked up a long time in advance, so you may need to make arrangements with them up to a year before the wedding date.

COORDINATING PLANS

- **Organizing tasks** Write out a countdown list that states the nature and time of each task to be done, so that all of the arrangements are made at the right time. Tick off tasks as you complete them.
- **Choosing guests** Make a provisional guest list with your partner. Allow roughly equal numbers of guests for each of your families.
- **Ordering clothes** If you are having clothes made, allow sufficient time for fittings.
- **Preparing maps** Draw simple maps showing how to reach the wedding venues. Include a map with each invitation.

ARRANGING A CEREMONY

- **Planning a religious service** Book the venue and celebrant well in advance. Check if there are other weddings on that day, and contact the families involved to ask if you can share flowers and decorations.
- **Choosing a venue** You can have a religious ceremony in places other than a church. For example, you may wish to use an historic house or the garden of your family home.
- **Planning a secular service** You can use an official form of ceremony or write a service yourself. Arrange to have an official witness or a registrar present to certify the marriage.

TRADITIONAL TIP

Making a gift for guests
Prepare small cloth bags of sugared almonds or pot-pourri as "favours" for the female guests at a wedding. Give out the favours after the wedding meal.

THINGS TO REMEMBER

Whatever your wedding plans, be sure to consider the following main elements.

- Participants.
- Marriage certificate.
- Guests.
- Ceremony venue.
- Reception venue.
- Catering.
- Accommodation for wedding couple and guests.
- Honeymoon: insurance, travel, and accommodation.
- Clothing, hair styling, make-up, and flowers.
- Transport.
- Still photography and video recording.
- Presents.

WORKING OUT EXPENSES

- **Planning a budget** Find out the cost of every element in advance, down to minor items such as stationery. Choose a range of options for each, and compare prices and quality.
- **Controlling food costs** If you intend to use a caterer, take care to keep track of the costs. Ask the caterer for a written estimate specifying what is included in the price.
- **Trimming costs** If you have a limited budget, look for ways in which to reduce costs. For example, ask family or friends to help with preparing food, grow your own plants for displays, or design and print stationery on a computer.

PLANNING A RECEPTION

- **Choosing a venue** Try to choose a reception venue that is not far from the ceremony venue, so that guests will not have to travel a long way.
- **Selecting food** Decide how formal the reception will be, so that you know whether to plan finger food, a buffet, or a full service with waiters.
- **Ordering drinks** Ask for more than you think you need. Drinks suppliers will usually take back unopened bottles.
- **Listing presents** Ask a friend or relative to mark the name of the giver on the label of each wedding present so that you will be able to write letters of thanks after the wedding.

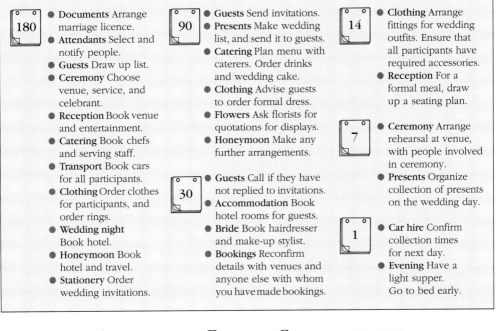

MAKING ADVANCE PREPARATIONS FOR A WEDDING

As soon as you have fixed a wedding date, start to book major elements such as the venue for the ceremony, and notify anyone whom you would like to assist with the wedding. The chart below gives numbers of days before a wedding and suggests arrangements to make at these times.

180
- **Documents** Arrange marriage licence.
- **Attendants** Select and notify people.
- **Guests** Draw up list.
- **Ceremony** Choose venue, service, and celebrant.
- **Reception** Book venue and entertainment.
- **Catering** Book chefs and serving staff.
- **Transport** Book cars for all participants.
- **Clothing** Order clothes for participants, and order rings.
- **Wedding night** Book hotel.
- **Honeymoon** Book hotel and travel.
- **Stationery** Order wedding invitations.

90
- **Guests** Send invitations.
- **Presents** Make wedding list, and send it to guests.
- **Catering** Plan menu with caterers. Order drinks and wedding cake.
- **Clothing** Advise guests to order formal dress.
- **Flowers** Ask florists for quotations for displays.
- **Honeymoon** Make any further arrangements.

30
- **Guests** Call if they have not replied to invitations.
- **Accommodation** Book hotel rooms for guests.
- **Bride** Book hairdresser and make-up stylist.
- **Bookings** Reconfirm details with venues and anyone else with whom you have made bookings.

14
- **Clothing** Arrange fittings for wedding outfits. Ensure that all participants have required accessories.
- **Reception** For a formal meal, draw up a seating plan.

7
- **Ceremony** Arrange rehearsal at venue, with people involved in ceremony.
- **Presents** Organize collection of presents on the wedding day.

1
- **Car hire** Confirm collection times for next day.
- **Evening** Have a light supper. Go to bed early.

ARRANGING FAMILY CELEBRATIONS

While family events such as anniversaries do not usually require as much work as a wedding, it is still important to organize them efficiently. Make a plan, and organize helpers. Provide foods and entertainment to suit all of the guests, bearing in mind different age groups.

ORGANIZING AN EVENT
- **Planning a formal event** For a formal occasion such as a baptism, make a detailed plan including guests to be invited, venue, food, and other details.
- **Involving children** If a child is to be the centre of a formal event, explain to him or her what the occasion entails. Involve the child's siblings as well – give them duties to do on the day, and put aside small presents for them so that they do not feel left out.
- **Celebrating achievements** Plan ahead so that if a child gains good exam results or wins a sporting event, you can surprise him or her with a simple celebration.

CREATING A THEME

Spread twigs so that you can see colour

Choosing a colour
For a special anniversary, choose decorations in an appropriate colour. For a golden wedding party, spray bare twigs gold, and arrange them in a vase to make an attractive display.

MAKING PREPARATIONS

If you are organizing an intimate family occasion, it is best to create a relaxed atmosphere where everyone can easily mingle and enjoy themselves, rather than to make complex plans.

- **Guests** If you are holding a family event at home, do not invite so many people that your home will be uncomfortably crowded.
- **Food** When doing your own cooking, make some dishes beforehand and freeze them. Buy some ready-made dishes as well, so that you do not need to spend a lot of time in the kitchen.

DEALING WITH CRISES

B Y KNOWING WHAT TO DO in a particular crisis, you can limit damage and find suitable professional help. Find out in advance how to deal with problems, since it can be difficult to think clearly in the midst of a tense situation.

HANDLING CRISIS SITUATIONS		
CRISIS	ACTION	PREVENTION
Assault	● **Contact police** Inform the police immediately. Do not wash yourself or change your clothes – your appearance may provide vital evidence. ● **Seek medical help** Have any injuries treated that day or the next morning. Ask someone to take you for treatment – you may be too shocked to go by yourself. ● **Make notes** Write down everything that you can remember about an attack. ● **Ask for support** Call a relative or friend for practical help and moral support. ● **Maintain confidence** Make yourself go out in public as soon as you can so that you will not lose your confidence.	● **Secure your car** Lock your car when you are inside it. Roll up windows before you stop at traffic lights. ● **Dress comfortably** If you are a woman, cover revealing clothing. Wear flat shoes so that you can walk comfortably. ● **Look confident** Check your route beforehand. Walk briskly. Be calmly aware of what is going on around you. ● **Shake off followers** If you suspect that someone is following you, walk away, cross the road, or go into a shop. ● **Plan in advance** Find your keys before you reach your house, so that you do not have to linger on the doorstep.
Theft/ mugging	● **Avoid violence** If a mugger becomes violent, hand over your money or bag immediately. If you resist and struggle with the person, you may be injured. ● **Contact police** Find a police officer as soon as possible. Ask them for a report on the crime for insurance purposes. ● **Contact your bank** Cancel any credit or debit cards, and let the bank know if your cheque book has been stolen. ● **Make notes** Try to write down as much as you can remember about the attacker's appearance. Note where you were attacked; the mugger may target other people in the same area.	● **Dress sensibly** Wear comfortable clothes, and dress in a way that will not attract attention. Avoid wearing a great deal of jewellery or other expensive items, such as a gold wristwatch. ● **Organize cash** If you will be visiting an area where muggers are known to operate, carry some loose cash in an inexpensive purse or wallet. If you are attacked, hand this over. ● **Protect valuables** If you are on holiday and have to carry valuable items such as a passport or travellers' cheques, conceal these items in a money belt or inside a hidden pocket.
Burglary	● **Repel burglar** If a burglar is still in your home, make a loud noise to scare them away. Do not confront them. ● **Contact police** Inform the police immediately. Do not disturb the scene of the crime until the police have finished examining it. Ask them to write a report for you to send to your insurers. ● **Contact your insurers** Telephone immediately. If nobody is there, leave a message stating the time of the burglary. ● **Change locks** If entry has been forced or you suspect that the burglar may have a key, change the locks immediately.	● **Replace locks** Change the locks as soon as you move into a new home, or if your keys are stolen. ● **Lock up securely** Lock windows and doors whenever you go out. If you feel vulnerable, lock outside doors even when you are in the house. ● **Make your home look occupied** Before going away, fit timers to light switches in heavily used rooms. If you go out for a short time, leave a radio or television on. ● **Hide valuables** Situate expensive or valued items so that opportunist burglars cannot see them through windows.

COPING WITH ACCIDENTS

First aid can save a life, or at least ensure that an injury does not become any worse. It is especially useful if you care for children or elderly people. Find out about first-aid courses from your local Red Cross or doctor, or ask your employer if they can provide first-aid training.

CHECKING FOR SERIOUS INJURY

If an injured person has any of the following symptoms, carry out emergency first aid immediately. Call for medical help as soon as possible.

- No sign of breathing.
- Absent or irregular pulse.
- Lost consciousness.
- Severe bleeding, with blood that spurts or continues to flow freely after five minutes.
- Shock.
- Difficulty in breathing.
- Severe abdominal pain.
- Fits or seizures.
- Blurred vision or seeing coloured haloes around lights.

CARING FOR CASUALTIES

- **Making a person comfortable** Keep a casualty warm with blankets. Do not use a direct source of heat such as a hot water bottle. Help them to sit or lie in the recommended position for their injury.
- **Coping with shock** Never let a casualty eat or drink. In particular, do not administer alcohol. It could react with drugs, and may be dangerous if an anaesthetic is needed.

> **WARNING!**
> Even if there is no visible injury, watch for signs such as pallor or confusion. They could indicate concussion, shock, or internal bleeding.

PADDING BROKEN LEGS

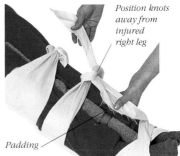

Position knots away from injured right leg

Padding

Bandage is tied in figure of eight to immobilize leg

Securing a child's lower leg
Bring the legs together, and put soft padding between them. Tie a narrow bandage around the feet. Tie broad ones at the knees and above the injury site. For an adult, tie another below the injury.

COPING WITH DEATH

The death of someone whom you know can be a shock, even when it is expected, and making the necessary arrangements can be a daunting task. If a family member has died, ask other relations to help you. Friends who are not emotionally involved may also be helpful.

REPORTING A DEATH

- **Confirming death** If a person dies at home, call out a doctor to confirm the death.

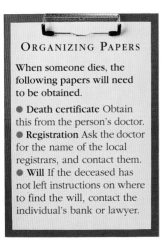

ORGANIZING PAPERS

When someone dies, the following papers will need to be obtained.

- **Death certificate** Obtain this from the person's doctor.
- **Registration** Ask the doctor for the name of the local registrars, and contact them.
- **Will** If the deceased has not left instructions on where to find the will, contact the individual's bank or lawyer.

MANAGING FEELINGS

- **Expressing grief** Allow yourself time to grieve. Do not let others force you to act "normally" until you are ready.
- **Seeing the body** If you wish, ask to view the body of the deceased, since this may help you to accept the death.

CARING FOR OTHERS

- **Providing emotional support** A bereaved person may feel disbelief, numbness, and guilt, as well as sadness. Keep them company, and let them talk.
- **Giving practical help** Offer to do tasks such as shopping and cooking. You could also take telephone calls and deal with enquiries from officials.

PLANNING A FUNERAL

If you feel unable to cope with making funeral arrangements by yourself, ask a friend to help.

- **Choosing a service** Ensure that you stipulate exactly the funeral arrangements that the deceased has requested or that you consider appropriate.
- **Organizing a gathering** You and other mourners may find it comforting to have a small gathering, or wake, after a funeral. Plan a simple event with refreshments. Either invite mourners back to your house, or reserve a private room in a quiet hotel.

PLANNING TRAVEL

QUICK REFERENCE

Preparing for
Travel, p. 101

Packing Efficiently, p. 104

Planning a
Journey, p. 108

Coping in All
Situations, p. 112

TRAVEL CAN BE ENJOYABLE *provided that you plan each trip well in advance, work out what you need to take, and confirm all booking arrangements at least 24 hours before departure. Secure your home so that it will be safe in your absence. Order any tablets or inoculations at least two weeks before travel. Prepare for any problems by taking a first-aid course and keeping belongings safe at all times.*

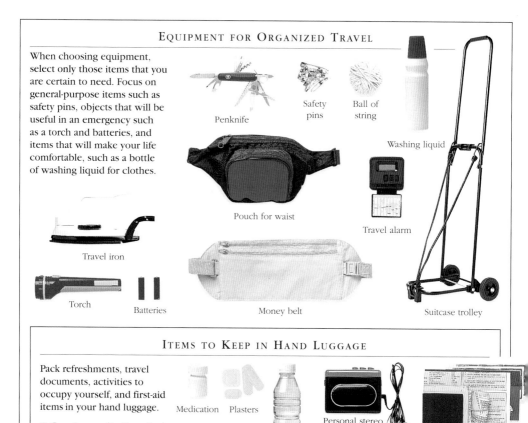

EQUIPMENT FOR ORGANIZED TRAVEL

When choosing equipment, select only those items that you are certain to need. Focus on general-purpose items such as safety pins, objects that will be useful in an emergency such as a torch and batteries, and items that will make your life comfortable, such as a bottle of washing liquid for clothes.

Penknife

Safety pins

Ball of string

Washing liquid

Pouch for waist

Travel alarm

Travel iron

Torch

Batteries

Money belt

Suitcase trolley

ITEMS TO KEEP IN HAND LUGGAGE

Pack refreshments, travel documents, activities to occupy yourself, and first-aid items in your hand luggage.

● **Carrying medications** Pack spare supplies in your main luggage. Then, if you lose your hand luggage, you will still have some medication.

Medication   Plasters

Personal stereo

Antiseptic wipes

Bottled water

Camera

Film

Travel documents

PREPARING FOR TRAVEL

START TRAVEL PREPARATIONS well before you leave. Make a list of what you are likely to need, then store the items in one place as you collect them. Tick the items off on the list as you gather them, and once again as you pack them.

ORGANIZING PAPERS

Order documents such as passports or visas up to three months before you travel. Check that you have the correct documents for each stage of a journey. Pack photocopies of important papers such as your travel insurance policy and records of booking arrangements.

PREPARING PASSPORTS
● **Checking expiry date** Make sure that your passport is valid and will not expire while you are on holiday.
● **Arranging visas** Allow plenty of time to apply for visas. If you have to visit an embassy in person, be prepared for a long wait.
● **Recording number** Note your passport number, and pack it separately from the passport. If you lose the passport, you can then give the number to the police and your embassy.

MAKING USE OF MAPS

Protecting a map
Cover the top side of a map with clear, adhesive film. The film will reinforce the paper so that it will not fall apart when you fold it repeatedly. It will also protect the surface from dirt and damp.

> ### ARRANGING INSURANCE
>
> Take out insurance for yourself and your luggage. Before buying a policy, check that it covers you for illness, injury, theft, and travel delays.
>
> ● **Exclusions** Check a policy for restriction clauses that may apply to you, such as clauses on travel during pregnancy.
> ● **Sport** If you are taking part in activities such as skiing and scuba diving, make sure that your policy does not exclude compensation for injury.

MANAGING MONEY

Work out how much money you plan to spend on travel, meals, accommodation, and souvenirs. Carry some extra cash to cover unforeseen expenses. If you will be travelling abroad, take a mixture of local currency and travellers' cheques, and a credit card as well.

ORGANIZING CASH
● **Ordering money** Order travellers' cheques and foreign currency from your bank at least a week before you need them. Banks often do not hold supplies of minor currencies, so allow time for them to order the money if necessary.
● **Carrying money** Carry local currency in a separate pocket or wallet from travellers' cheques and credit cards.
● **Using a safe** If you plan to stay in a hotel, find out if there is a safe. You can then keep money in the safe while you are there, and take out just what you need each day.

USING OTHER MONEY
● **Taking cards** Carry credit cards and debit cards with you even when you go abroad. You may be able to use them for drawing out local currency as well as for paying hotel bills and buying goods.
● **Cashing cheques** You will need to show identification when you cash travellers' cheques, so take your passport or driving licence with you.
● **Recording numbers** Note the number of each card, and of every travellers' cheque. Keep these numbers with you, but in a separate place from the cards and cheques.

STORING VALUABLES

Protecting from water
If you go to a beach, carry cash in a waterproof container hung around your neck. Put your car or room keys and watch into the container for safekeeping as well.

PLANNING DISEASE PREVENTION

At least three months before travelling, ask your doctor which immunizations you will need for the areas that you plan to visit. The chart below is a guide to the number of doses for immunizations, and will give you an idea of how many doses you will need before travel.

PLANNING INJECTIONS

● **Devising a schedule** If you need several injections, ask your doctor to help you plan a schedule for having injections, showing which can be done at the same time and allowing time to recover from each.

● **Choosing the best time** If possible, have injections done on a Friday so that you then have the weekend to recover from any side effects.

● **Selecting an injection site** An injection is likely to make the area around the injection site ache. Consider having an injection in your bottom or thigh instead of your arm so that you can still use your arm.

● **Checking cost** When assessing the budget for your holiday, ask your doctor or a specialized travel clinic in advance about the cost of injections. Incorporate this cost into your total budget.

COMMON IMMUNIZATIONS		
DISEASE	**DOSES**	**POSSIBLE EFFECTS**
Polio	Booster if due.	None with booster.
Hepatitis A	One.	Ache where injected.
Hepatitis B	Three.	Ache where injected, fever, rash.
Typhoid	Two.	Ache where injected, headache, nausea.
Yellow Fever	One.	Headache, mild fever.
Rabies	Two or three.	Ache where injected, muscle ache, headache, vomiting.
Malaria	Course of tablets.	Depends on type of tablets prescribed.
Cholera	One.	Ache where injected, fever, headache.
Tetanus	Booster if due.	Ache where injected.

LEAVING YOUR HOME

Ensure that your home will be secure while you are away. Ask a relative or friend to stay there, or ask neighbours to watch over it. Avoid leaving signs that you are away, such as piled-up post by a front door, so that burglars will not realize that your home is empty.

SECURING YOUR HOME

Take the following steps to ensure that your home will not be a target for burglars.

● **Valuables** Move expensive items so that they will not be seen through windows.

● **Alarm** Test your burglar alarm one week before you go, and remember to turn it on before leaving.

● **Luggage** Label luggage with your office address. Anyone who sees it will not be able to locate your empty home.

ARRANGING PROTECTION

● **Involving neighbours** Ask neighbours to watch over your home, and to call the police if they see anything unexpected. Return the favour when the neighbours are next away.

● **Ensuring daily checks** Ask a friend or neighbour to come in each day to collect post and draw the curtains.

● **Using time switches** Set lights in the bedroom, living room, and bathroom on time switches so that the house appears to be occupied.

PREVENTING ODOURS

Cleaning a refrigerator
If you will be away for more than a few days, empty the refrigerator, and freeze or dispose of the contents. Wash the interior, and set a bowl of bicarbonate of soda inside to absorb odours.

CARING FOR PETS AND PLANTS

Arrange care for pets and plants well before you go away. You can leave plants for quite a long period, as long as they have enough water. However, it is not fair to leave animals alone. Pets must be fed and given fresh water every day, and most animals need company.

LEAVING CATS & DOGS
● **Caring for cats** Never leave a cat to look after itself. It will suffer without regular care and company. Ask a friend to look after it, or take it to a cattery.
● **Choosing a kennel** Visit a kennel before you leave your dog there. Check that the animals look healthy and that their housing is clean. Watch the animals to see if they are happy with their handlers.

LEAVING OTHER PETS
● **Housing caged animals** Ask friends to keep caged animals in their home, or to come in and feed your animals every day. Let them handle your pets while you watch, so that they know how to treat them.
● **Caring for birds** Birds enjoy a routine, so when you leave a bird with someone, give the person instructions on times for feeding as well as on diet.

WATERING PLANTS

Watering automatically
Stand plants by a bowl of water. Cut a cloth into strips. Put one end of each strip in the bowl and the other in a plant pot. The strips will take up water for the plants.

PRESERVING MOISTURE
● **Sealing in a bag** Water a plant well. Put a plastic bag over it, and seal around the top of the pot. The bag will trap moisture for the plant.

TRAVELLING WITH PETS

Pack supplies for pets that will travel with you. Use a sturdy bag to keep a feeding bowl, water bowl, and brush, and extra items such as a toy or a lead. Put a rug on a car seat for the pet to sit on. Take paper towels and plastic bags to clear up any accidents.

| Travel bag | Water bowl | Feeding bowl | Toy | Brush |

MAKING FINAL PREPARATIONS

Write a list of final checks to make before you leave, and tick off tasks as you do them. Assemble comfortable clothes and shoes for the journey. Let a neighbour know when you will leave, and give them a contact address or telephone number in case of emergencies.

CLOSING UP A HOUSE
● **Loading a car** Put luggage in a car only when you are about to go. Do not leave it loaded where passers-by can see it, in case a burglar notices it.
● **Locating documents** Before you lock your home, check that you have all your travel papers in your hand luggage.
● **Checking your home** Make a final inspection of your home to check that you have not left any appliances switched on, and that you have locked all windows and doors.

ENSURING COMFORT

Shake bottle gently to release a few drops

Making scented wipes
Add a few drops of lavender oil to one or two moist flannels, then seal the flannels in plastic bags for keeping in your hand luggage. Use them to clean and refresh your face and hands.

PREPARING MEDICATION
● **Timing doses** If you are on medication that must be taken at a particular time and you will be travelling to a different time zone, discuss this in advance with your doctor.
● **Carrying contact numbers** Take your doctor's telephone number with you. If you lose any medication, you can then call the doctor for advice on obtaining new supplies.
● **Taking water** Take a bottle of water with you so that you can wash down tablets.

PACKING EFFICIENTLY

T HE SECRET OF PACKING LUGGAGE WELL is to know what to leave out. Consider the climate at your destination and the activities in which you will be participating, and take only the necessary minimum of supplies for your visit.

SUITCASES AND HAND LUGGAGE

Use good-quality luggage, which will be resistant to damage. Ensure that your luggage will be easy to identify in crowded places, and that it will be secure. Use a combination lock or a padlock to deter casual theft.

● **Choosing a suitcase** If you need a durable case, select a hard-sided variety. For a lighter case, opt for a soft-sided type.
● **Testing a suitcase with wheels** Ensure that the wheels on the suitcase run smoothly.
● **Choosing a rucksack** Match a rucksack to its function. If you will be carrying a small load, select a soft model without an internal frame. For a heavy load, use a rucksack with a frame.
● **Trying out a rucksack** Load a few heavy items into a rucksack and put it on before buying it to check that it is comfortable.
● **Using a shoulder bag** Fit a shoulder bag with a shoulder pad to prevent the strap from hurting your shoulder.
● **Using a sports bag** These are difficult to carry, so use them only for short journeys or in instances where you will not carry them for long distances.

Soft-sided suitcase

Suitcase with wheels

Rucksack with internal frame

Soft rucksack

Lockable shoulder bag

Sports holdall

Small shoulder bag

ORGANIZING PACKING

Arrange the contents of your luggage so that breakables will be protected on the journey. Keep the weight as low as possible to make sure that the luggage is comfortable to carry. Mark your baggage with your name and office address so that you can recover it if lost.

PROTECTING LUGGAGE

● **Keeping contents lists** List the contents of each piece of luggage so that you have a record if a piece is lost. Carry the list in your hand luggage.

Making luggage secure
For extra security, fasten a strong combination lock on to your luggage. Write down the combination number on a piece of paper, and keep the paper separately in your hand luggage.

MAKING USE OF SPACE

● **Filling small spaces** Roll stretchy garments such as swimsuits or cycle shorts, and tuck them into narrow spaces between pairs of shoes.

Packing inside shoes
To save space in your luggage, roll up small items of clothing such as underwear and pairs of socks, and tuck them inside shoes so that they take up the least possible space.

TIME-SAVING TIP

Marking luggage
Paint the corners of a suitcase with waterproof paint in a bright colour, so that you can find the case quickly on a luggage rack or an airport carousel. Alternatively, apply stickers, and paint over them with clear nail varnish so that they will not rub off.

DEVISING A PACKING SEQUENCE

When packing a suitcase or bag, note which areas will be at the bottom and top when the luggage is being carried. Put the heaviest objects at the bottom so that they will not squash clothes or other items. Never fill luggage so full that you have to struggle to close it, since this could strain the fastenings.

● **Distributing contents** When travelling with other people, put some of everyone's clothes in each suitcase. If a suitcase goes missing, nobody will have lost all their belongings.
● **Packing shoes** Lay shoes with their soles touching the sides of a suitcase so that they take up the least possible space.
● **Compressing garments** Pack jeans and sweaters before other clothes. The garments on top of them will compress them, creating some extra space in the suitcase.
● **Protecting clothes** Cover clothes with a towel to shield them from luggage fastenings.

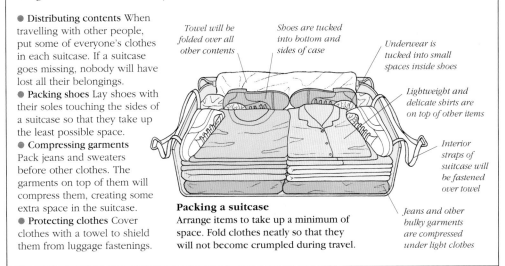

Towel will be folded over all other contents

Shoes are tucked into bottom and sides of case

Underwear is tucked into small spaces inside shoes

Lightweight and delicate shirts are on top of other items

Interior straps of suitcase will be fastened over towel

Jeans and other bulky garments are compressed under light clothes

Packing a suitcase
Arrange items to take up a minimum of space. Fold clothes neatly so that they will not become crumpled during travel.

PACKING FOR CHILDREN

Take only as much clothing as necessary so that you do not have more luggage than you can carry comfortably. If you are going abroad, pack enough toiletries and food to last for the entire holiday if you think that you will not be able to buy suitable brands at your destination.

BABY TRAVEL KIT

Choose comfortable clothes that are durable and versatile. Pack warm mittens and socks for long journeys, even if you are not going to a cold place. Babies, especially tired ones, can become chilled much more easily than adults. Keep a change of clothing and nappies, and one or two feeds, in your hand luggage.

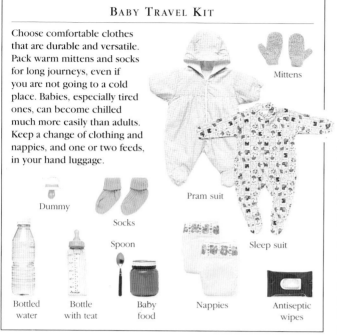

Mittens

Pram suit

Dummy

Socks

Spoon

Sleep suit

Bottled water

Bottle with teat

Baby food

Nappies

Antiseptic wipes

TAKING NECESSITIES

● **Selecting suitable clothes**
Pack suitable clothing for the climate and expected types of activity. Make sure that shoes fit comfortably, so that they will not become too tight if the child's feet swell.

● **Including swimming aids**
Take armbands or other floating aids for children who cannot swim, if they are going to be around water. It is wise to pack these items even for children who can swim, especially if they will be swimming in the sea.

● **Packing reminders of home**
Children may feel nervous when visiting a strange place and will appreciate having familiar objects around them. Pack a few of their favourite toys, or a security blanket.

CARRYING FOOD AND EQUIPMENT

As well as packing clothes, take items that will make life comfortable. Food and drink can ease long journeys and delays, particularly for young children. Include basic equipment such as items for laundering clothes, so that you can wear garments more than once.

PACKING REFRESHMENTS

● **Choosing snacks** Take fresh food such as sandwiches. Avoid salty foods, such as crisps, which will cause thirst.

● **Taking fresh fruits** Choose hard fruits, or items that can be peeled easily but will not be squashed, such as apples and oranges. Wash all fruits before you leave home.

● **Limiting drinks** To keep rest stops to a minimum, do not let children drink large amounts on a journey.

● **Packing cleaning items** Take paper towels and a damp cloth or wet wipes in a plastic bag for wiping sticky hands.

PREPARING FOOD

Airtight container

Ready-sliced vegetables

Packing fresh vegetables
Cut raw vegetables into sticks, or buy sliced vegetables, and pack them in an airtight container. If they may absorb smells from other foods that you plan to pack, wrap them separately in aluminium foil or cling film.

TAKING LAUNDRY ITEMS

Travel wash

String

Pegs

Making up a laundry kit
Take a laundry kit so that you can clean clothes while you are away. Pack a long piece of string and some clothes pegs to make a washing line. Pour some washing liquid into a small plastic bottle. Seal the kit in a plastic bag.

ESSENTIAL EQUIPMENT FOR DIFFERENT TYPES OF HOLIDAY

BEACH HOLIDAY

Ensure that you pack clothes and sun creams that will protect you from sunburn. Take additional items such as refreshments and seating. If possible, choose items that will be light and easy to carry, such as an inflatable bed or a mat that you can roll up.

- Antiseptic cream
- Insect repellent
- Sun-tan lotion
- After-sun lotion
- Beach towels
- Swimsuits
- Thin sweater
- Sun hat
- Sunglasses

- Trainers and cotton socks
- Cool box and freezer blocks
- Toys, such as a beach ball
- Sleeping mat
- Blankets
- Inflatable bed
- Beach bag

CAMPING HOLIDAY

Modern camping equipment is often compact and lightweight. Pack only items that you are sure to use. Use the best equipment that you can afford – it is likely to be well-made and durable.

- Tent, poles, and pegs
- Sleeping bag
- Sleeping mat
- Rucksack
- Cool box and freezer blocks
- Container of water
- Water purification tablets
- Torch and batteries
- Stove, fuel, and cooking pans
- Waterproof matches
- Cutlery and dishes

- Can opener
- Pocket knife
- Sweatbands
- Mosquito net
- Compass
- Maps

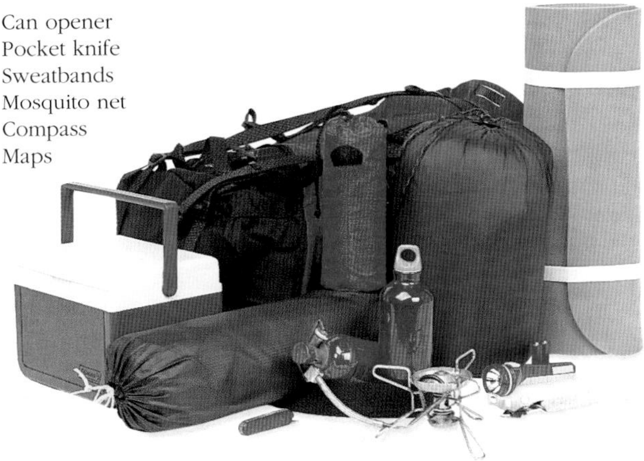

SKIING HOLIDAY

Skiing equipment is expensive, so consider hiring it rather than buying it, unless you intend to ski regularly. Take clothes and creams that will protect you from wind and bright sunlight as well as from the cold.

- Skis
- Ski bindings
- Ski boots
- Ski gloves
- Warm hat

- Weatherproof outer clothing
- Scarf
- Thick socks
- Goggles
- Ski pass holder
- Sun block

PLANNING A JOURNEY

BEFORE YOU BEGIN A JOURNEY, confirm all stages of the route in advance. Make sure that you have the means to make yourself comfortable while travelling. Prepare for problems such as delays so that you will not be bored or worried.

TRAVELLING BY AIR

Make preparations before flying to ensure that a journey will not be overly tiring or dull. Take refreshments, books, and activities to occupy yourself, and pack items such as an eye mask and a neck pillow so that you can make yourself comfortable during the flight.

AVOIDING JET LAG
● **Preparing for air travel** Do not drink alcohol for two days before flying to avoid becoming dehydrated. The day before a flight, eat only light meals to prevent yourself from feeling bloated or nauseous during the flight.
● **Altering your watch** When you board an aircraft, set your watch to the local time at the destination so that you can adjust to the new time zone.
● **Preventing dehydration** Drink water or fruit juice both while you are flying and just after the flight to avoid feeling dehydrated. Avoid caffeine and alcohol, which cause dehydration and disrupt sleep.

CARING FOR YOURSELF

Cotton wool pad soaked in diluted witch hazel

Eye mask

Making an eye mask
When you pack, prepare an eye mask to rejuvenate your eyes during the flight. Soak two cotton wool pads in diluted witch hazel. Cut slots in a fabric eye mask, and slip the pads into them. Store the mask in a plastic bag until needed.

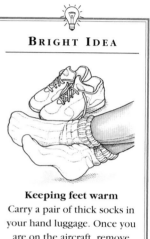

BRIGHT IDEA

Keeping feet warm
Carry a pair of thick socks in your hand luggage. Once you are on the aircraft, remove your shoes, and wear the socks to keep your feet warm and comfortable.

TRAVELLING BY TRAIN OR COACH

Book tickets well in advance, and reserve a seat so that you are sure to have a place. State whether you require a particular position, such as a seat in a non-smoking section or one with its back to the engine of a train. Allow plenty of time for travelling to the station.

THINGS TO REMEMBER

Bear in mind the following points to ensure that you have a stress-free trip.

● **Tickets** Keep your travel tickets handy to show to coach or rail staff at any time during your journey.
● **Luggage** When travelling by coach, ensure that all your luggage has been stowed in the vehicle before you board.

PLANNING AHEAD
● **Booking a ticket** Consider a range of times. If you travel at an off-peak time, or book well in advance, you could pay less than the usual price.
● **Making connections** Avoid changing aeroplanes, trains, or coaches more than necessary to lessen the chance of delay.
● **Reaching your destination** Contact the final station or airport to order a taxi or catch a bus to your destination.

TRAVELLING IN COMFORT
● **Making yourself comfortable** Remove and store your coat. Put your hand luggage in a place that will be easy for you to reach during the journey.
● **Taking exercise** From time to time, stand up, and take a walk if there is room to do so.
● **Avoiding travel sickness** If you are prone to sickness on trains, sit with your back to the engine. Take plastic bags in case you are sick.

TRAVELLING BY CAR

Before undertaking a long journey by car, have your car serviced. Check that your insurance policy covers everyone who might drive the car. Pack supplies for the journey as well as the destination. If you wear glasses to drive, take a spare pair in case of breakage.

EQUIPPING A CAR BEFORE TRAVEL

Take spare fuel and other supplies for your car. Keep refreshments and essential telephone numbers in case of delays or breakdowns.

● **Packing for your car** Carry a can of petrol, a can of oil, and some distilled water. Take sets of spare bulbs for lights – even if you cannot fit them, you can ask someone at a garage to do this for you.
● **Gathering information** Put maps and the manual for the car in the glove compartment. Keep telephone numbers for a car breakdown service and for your destination.
● **Keeping an emergency kit** Put basic first aid items, sick bags, a torch, and money for telephones or toll roads into a plastic box. Keep the box underneath a front seat.

PLOTTING A ROUTE
● **Selecting road types** Decide whether you wish to travel on a motorway or via quiet roads. If travelling on a motorway, check whether you will have to pay a toll at any point.
● **Using a route plan** Write a list of the roads that you will take and cities or towns through which you will pass on a journey. Attach the list by the dashboard so that it is easy to find. If you think that you may have taken a wrong turning, stop the car at a safe place, and check the list.
● **Driving in remote areas** If you are travelling by road in an unfamiliar area, it is often worth buying a local map at the nearest town you pass through. This will show small roads and local routes that may not be shown on a more general, small-scale map.

KEEPING A CAR TIDY
● **Collecting litter** Keep empty plastic bags in the car. Use them to collect rubbish while you are travelling. Throw them away at the end of a journey.

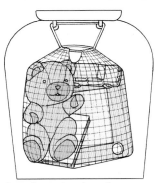

Stowing toys in a bag
Put toys and games for children into a string bag. Pull one of the bag's handles through to one side. Slip this enlarged handle over the headrest of a front seat so that the bag hangs behind the seat.

LOADING A CAR ROOF RACK

Stack luggage carefully on a roof rack to minimize wind resistance, and distribute the items evenly to spread the weight over the roof area. A full roof rack will increase the stress on a car's body, so drive more slowly than you would normally, taking care not to come to a sudden halt or accelerate quickly.

● **Securing luggage** Intertwine four long bungee cords so that they overlap in the middle of their lengths. Fix the free ends of the cords to the corners and sides of a roof rack to hold luggage securely.

Arranging luggage
Lay items flat so that they will not disrupt airflow over a car roof. Load heavy luggage first so that it will not crush lightweight pieces.

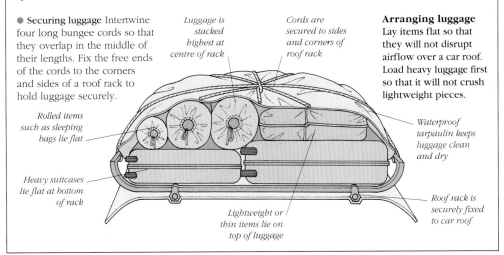

Luggage is stacked highest at centre of rack

Cords are secured to sides and corners of roof rack

Rolled items such as sleeping bags lie flat

Waterproof tarpaulin keeps luggage clean and dry

Heavy suitcases lie flat at bottom of rack

Lightweight or thin items lie on top of luggage

Roof rack is securely fixed to car roof

MAKING JOURNEYS BY BOAT

Travelling by sea can be relaxing, but this is dependent on the weather conditions. Pack something to occupy yourself, such as a book, game, or magazine, in case you are delayed. Even if you are not usually seasick, include treatments in case of rough weather.

AVOIDING NAUSEA
● **Eating and drinking** Avoid alcohol, and eat only light food while travelling. If you know that you will feel sick, do not eat during a voyage.
● **Focusing your attention** To avoid nausea, find a quiet place to sit, such as near a window, where you will have access to fresh air. Try not to look at the moving water. Instead, concentrate on the horizon so that your brain can orient itself.
● **Taking remedies** When you buy a seasickness remedy, ask if it will make you drowsy or affect skills such as driving. Do not drink alcohol after you have taken any treatment.

PREVENTING SICKNESS
● **Limiting nausea** Avoid toilets and other areas where people have been sick, until the areas are cleaned. The smell may aggravate your own nausea.

Fix magnet to inside of band

Making a pressure band
Glue a small, round magnet to a sports wristband, and put it on. The magnet will press the acupressure points between the central wrist tendons, three fingers' width below each hand.

PASSING THE TIME
● **Going on deck** Take a jacket or sweater to wear on deck, since open stretches of water can be cool even on sunny days. Carry binoculars so that you can see wildlife.
● **Reading in comfort** When reading, look up from your book or glance out of the window every few minutes so that you do not make yourself feel ill by staring at the print.
● **Taking exercise** On long trips, use a swimming pool or gym if there is one. If the weather is good, walk or jog around the deck. Exposure to fresh air will wake you up and add variety to your journey.

ORGANIZING A GROUP HOLIDAY

Group holidays can be enjoyable provided that you like your fellow travellers and you are all prepared to reach compromises. Discuss all important practical matters, such as accommodation and journey plans, before you go to avoid confusion during the holiday.

PLANNING A TRIP

Meet your travel companions to look at brochures, discuss budgets, and agree on dates. Draw up a rough itinerary.

● **Agreeing plans** See that everyone is happy with the degree of comfort. If the holiday will include physical activity, check that everyone is fit enough to cope and is insured in case of accidents.
● **Setting a budget** Find out in advance about the costs of accommodation and transport. Allocate a generous sum of money for meals.
● **Anticipating extra costs** Take out insurance to cover extra expenses in case anyone drops out and you cannot find a substitute.

PLANNING AHEAD
● **Plotting movements** If the group is to split up while travelling, arrange in advance a time and place where you will all meet. Agree a time beyond which the other group members will summon help if someone does not appear.

AVOIDING TROUBLE
● **Keeping possessions safe** Ask a friend to guard your luggage if you have to leave it. If you have communal goods or money, take turns to look after the items each day.
● **Protecting people** When travelling in a dangerous area, stay in a tight group. If you are walking, position any children and vulnerable adults at the centre of your group.

AGREEING DETAILS
● **Avoiding arguments** Before you set off, discuss any matter that may cause friction within the group. For example, if the standard of accommodation for the group varies, check that everyone is happy with this, or agree to swap rooms part-way through the holiday.
● **Planning meals** Agree whether you are all going to eat together or whether people would prefer to make their own eating arrangements. Agree on how everyone will pay when eating out.
● **Catering for yourselves** If the accommodation is self-catering, set up a communal kitty for goods such as coffee, tea, milk, and bread, which everyone in the group will probably use.

TRAVELLING WITH CHILDREN

Make a journey as easy as possible for the children and yourself by plotting the route carefully in advance. Before you go, explain to the children how long or complex the journey may be. Promise them a treat when you arrive, such as a picnic or a visit to a beach or cinema.

ORGANIZING A TRIP
● **Arranging breaks** Allow for frequent rest stops so that children can go to the toilet and stretch their legs. If you will be travelling by car, mark locations of inns or service stations on a map. If travelling by coach or train, break your journey at one or two stations.
● **Managing long car journeys** For long journeys, let children travel in sleeping bags, or book the family into a bed and breakfast stop overnight.
● **Starting early** Provided that it is light, set off early in the morning. This will increase the chance that children will sleep for part of the journey.

PROVIDING AMUSEMENTS
● **Choosing toys** Take plenty of little things for children to do. If they take a book or computer game, explain that they should not stare at it for a long time because this may make them feel sick. See that toys do not make loud noises that can distract the driver.

Filling a toy case
Give a child a small case for items such as toys, crayons, and books, and allow the child to do his or her own packing. Choose a case with rigid sides that make good surfaces to lean on for drawing.

PREPARING DRINKS

Push straw through cross-shaped cut

Modifying a beaker
Adapt a plastic beaker with a lid for each child. Cut a hole in each lid so that you can fit a plastic straw into it. Take the beakers on journeys, along with bottles of drink and a packet of straws.

MANAGING A JOURNEY
● **Charting progress** Keep children up to date with your progress by telling them what will happen at the next stop. Give them a simple map, and let them mark on it the distance that you have covered and the places that you have visited.
● **Avoiding boredom** Keep some extra toys hidden in a bag, so that if you are delayed or children have finished with the toys that they have there is something else for them to do.
● **Stopping overnight** Book a family room in the place you are staying so that young children will not be alone in a strange place. If this is not possible, ensure that each adult shares with different children.
● **Ending a trip** Before you reach your destination, plan a short, pleasurable activity, such as a walk, that the children will enjoy when you arrive. Try not to do anything that will over-excite tired children.

ARRANGING HELP
● **Planning children's activities** Find out in advance if your destination has a crèche or provides activities for older children. If it does, children can be entertained by other people and enjoy themselves while you have a break.
● **Taking a helper with you** Ask a reliable teenage babysitter or local student whether he or she would like a free holiday, and perhaps the chance to improve a foreign language, in return for a few hours of childcare every day. Agree hours and duties beforehand, and allow the person to have a number of the evenings off.

TRAVELLING ON FOOT

Never let children out of your sight. Explain to them that they must not wander away from you in case they run into trouble or have an accident.

● **Identifying children** Dress children in bright clothes and hats so that you can see if they become separated from you. For small children, write a label with your surname and details such as your hotel and its telephone number. Fix this to their clothes with a safety pin.
● **Staying close** Keep toddlers on reins, especially in areas with crowds or heavy traffic. Accompany small children to the toilet, even if they can usually manage on their own.
● **Supervising sports** Stay with children while they are involved in sports and other activities. Even if they can be trusted on their own at home, they may have problems in a strange place.

COPING IN ALL SITUATIONS

F IND OUT AS MUCH AS YOU CAN about any unfamiliar area that you plan to visit. Be aware of possible physical dangers such as poisonous animals, and social problems such as mugging. Observe laws and recommendations on clothing.

DEALING WITH HEAT

T ake care when visiting an area with a hot climate. Avoid going out in the intense heat of midday, and do not sunbathe if your shadow is shorter than you are. Take a siesta between midday and four o'clock, or stay in the shade. Drink plenty of water to prevent dehydration.

PREVENTING SUNBURN

● **Protecting your head** Wear a wide-brimmed hat that has holes around the crown so that heat and perspiration can evaporate from your head.
● **Applying sunblock** Use a sunblock as recommended on all exposed flesh, including earlobes and, if sunbathing, the soles of your feet.
● **Sunbathing safely** Slowly increase the time that you spend in the sun. Remember that you can tan gently while you are in the shade.
● **Swimming in safety** If you have sensitive skin, swim in a T-shirt to keep your back from burning through the water.

PROTECTING SKIN

Sew fabric to inside of cap

Adapting a baseball cap
Sew a clean handkerchief or scarf to the back of a baseball cap so that the fabric covers the back of your neck. This will prevent your neck from being exposed to sunlight and burned.

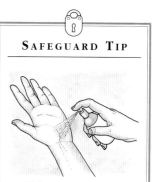

SAFEGUARD TIP

Using a water spray
Clean a pump-action spray bottle, and fill it with water. Carry the bottle of water with you to the beach, and mist areas such as your wrists and palms to cool yourself.

MAKING A SUNSHIELD FOR A CAR

To protect the interior of a car from direct sunlight, make this sunshield. Keep the sunshield in your car, and secure it inside the windscreen whenever you park in the sun for any length of time.

Adhesive tape

Paper covers cardboard

1 Trim a piece of cardboard to fit the windscreen. Cut the cardboard vertically into equal parts. Cover each with adhesive paper for protection. Lay them down with small gaps between them. Join with adhesive tape.

2 To store the sunshield, fold it in a zigzag. When you need the sunshield, open it, and tuck it between the windscreen and the steering wheel. Use the fold-down sunvisors in the car to hold the sunshield in place.

AVOIDING DEHYDRATION

● **Quenching thirst** Drink plenty of water at regular intervals and with meals. If you intend to be outdoors for several hours, take several bottles of water with you.
● **Drinking pure water** If the local water is unsafe, only drink sealed bottled water.
● **Drinking herbal tea** Coffee and tea can dehydrate you, so choose herbal teas as a thirst-quenching alternative. You can buy mint tea and other flavours in many countries. Boil bottled water for the tea.
● **Avoiding alcohol** Never have a strong alcoholic drink while you are out in the sun, because it will dehydrate you.

DEALING WITH COLD

Travelling in cold countries can be enjoyable and invigorating if you prepare adequately for the likely weather conditions. As with hot climates, find out about the area in advance. Pack weatherproof clothes, and take enough food and fuel to keep you comfortable.

PRESERVING BODY HEAT

● **Covering your head** You will lose most of your body heat from your head, so wear a warm hat. Select a style with flaps that cover your ears.

● **Protecting your skin** Avoid extremes of heat and cold. As far as possible, keep your skin covered, warm, and dry. To prevent cold perspiration from chilling your body, choose clothes that draw perspiration away from the skin.

● **Carrying spare clothes** Carry a spare pair of trousers, a sweater, socks, and a set of underwear in a sealed plastic bag. You can then change your clothes if they get wet, and so avoid becoming chilled.

AVOIDING HYPOTHERMIA

● **Taking extra protection** Carry a silver "space blanket" (available from travel shops), which is compact and light to carry. This preserves body heat by trapping it and reflecting it back to the skin.

● **Having drinks** Keep warm by taking hot drinks regularly. Avoid alcohol: although it gives a temporary illusion of warmth, it actually dilates the blood vessels and increases heat loss from the body.

● **Staying active** Walk around briskly, or at least keep your body moving, when you are out in the cold. The exercise will keep you warm and stop you from falling asleep.

DRIVING IN SNOW

Tuck mat under tyre

Providing extra grip
If a car is stuck in snow, use rubber mats from the footwells of the car to give extra grip. Tuck the mats under the tyres. If there are only two mats, put them under the wheels that provide traction for the car.

DRESSING FOR COLD CLIMATES

To protect your body from cold, wear layers of thin clothing. The layers will trap heat, and can be removed or added as necessary. Choose thin underclothes that totally cover your body and draw perspiration away from your skin. Select outer garments that are roomy enough to fit several layers underneath. Outer clothes must be weatherproof and resistant to tearing.

● **Buying outer clothes** Choose garments that will keep out wind as well as damp, since strong winds can make air feel even colder than it actually is.

● **Hiring equipment** If you do not plan to do a great deal of travelling in cold weather, hire the appropriate clothing.

● **Selecting boots** Try on new boots with two pairs of thick socks. The heat and tightness simulates the effect of walking a long distance, which will cause your feet to swell.

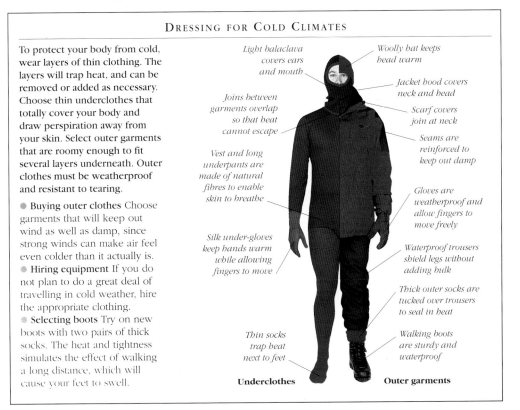

Light balaclava covers ears and mouth

Woolly hat keeps head warm

Jacket hood covers neck and head

Scarf covers join at neck

Joins between garments overlap so that heat cannot escape

Seams are reinforced to keep out damp

Vest and long underpants are made of natural fibres to enable skin to breathe

Gloves are weatherproof and allow fingers to move freely

Silk under-gloves keep hands warm while allowing fingers to move

Waterproof trousers shield legs without adding bulk

Thick outer socks are tucked over trousers to seal in heat

Thin socks trap heat next to feet

Walking boots are sturdy and waterproof

Underclothes

Outer garments

VISITING REMOTE AREAS

Travelling to remote places can give you the chance to see dramatic landscapes and meet fascinating people. Before you travel, find out as much as possible about likely hazards, and assemble a pack of medical supplies so that you can focus on enjoying your trip.

MAKING A MOSQUITO NET

Use 5 m (16½ ft) of netting to make a basic mosquito net. Weight the edges of the fabric with beads so that the mosquito net will stay in place when you use it.

*String runs
under fold*

Making a hanging arrangement for a mosquito net
Fold the length of net in half lengthways. Make holes on the fold 1 m (39 in) from each end. Thread a 4-m (13-ft) length of string through the holes, knotting the string at the holes to secure it in the net.

ENSURING SAFETY

● **Distributing an itinerary** Make copies of your itinerary for your family, and for your country's embassy if you plan to go abroad. State on the itinerary when you will return, so that if you are not back by then people will look for you.
● **Leaving travel details** When you intend to move on from a place, or to do something hazardous such as climbing a mountain, let local people know where you are going. This will help them to find you if problems arise.
● **Using a guide** If you plan to travel through unknown territory, consider hiring a local guide to accompany you.

ASSEMBLING A MEDICAL PACK

In remote places, you will need to have your own medical supplies. Buy a pack of sterilized medical equipment from a good chemist or assemble your own in a waterproof bag. Carry this with you at all times. Take it with you if you have to go to hospital so that staff can treat you with your own equipment.

Latex gloves

Waterproof pack

Water-purifying tablets

Waterproof plasters

Thermometer in case

Tubular support bandage

Antiseptic ointment

Anti-diarrhoea tablets

Oral rehydration mixture

Travel-sickness tablets

Sterile wound dressings

Scissors

Safety pins

Micropore tape

Compact medical pack for travel

Crêpe bandage

AVOIDING HEALTH PROBLEMS

Your body will take time to become used to a foreign environment. Allow yourself a few days to acclimatize before participating in strenuous activities. Wear comfortable clothes and shoes. Choose food and drink carefully to minimize the likelihood of illness.

SAFEGUARD TIP

Disinfecting hands
Carry a pack of antiseptic baby wipes with you, and use them to wipe your hands before you prepare food or have a meal. Buy a handbag-size pack if the usual size is too bulky to carry.

AVOIDING ILLNESS

● **Relieving diarrhoea** Carry anti-diarrhoea tablets with you at all times, and take them if you start to feel unwell.
● **Preventing infection** Do not put your fingers in your mouth when visiting areas in which the hygiene is poor, because you may transfer harmful bacteria to your mouth. If you have children with you, tell them not to suck their fingers.
● **Swimming safely** Never swim in areas of dirty and polluted water, especially around effluent pipes in the sea, and avoid stagnant water, which may be infested with bacteria. Swim only in pools that are regularly chlorinated.

EATING & DRINKING

● **Avoiding ice** Do not have ice cubes in drinks, because the ice may be made from tap water. Instead, ask for drinks to be chilled in their containers.
● **Choosing raw foods** Do not eat fresh fruits or vegetables unless you are able to peel them and wash them yourself with purified water.
● **Choosing meat** Avoid meat unless you are sure that it has been cooked adequately.
● **Eating fish** Avoid shellfish, because it may have been caught in contaminated water.
● **Eating desserts** Avoid ice-cream, because it may be made from unpasteurized cream or unwashed fruits.

GUARDING AGAINST ANIMALS & INSECTS

● **Avoiding wild animals** If you are on a safari, do not attempt to confront any wild animals. Do not leave your vehicle or your group unless the guide says that it is safe to do so.
● **Preventing infection** Do not stroke dogs or cats. They could pass on infection or parasites.
● **Repelling insects** Carry a can of insect repellent with you. Apply every few hours.

KEEPING FOOD SAFE

● **Preparing food** Before you prepare a meal, purify water for washing fresh foods. Keep ingredients covered until you need them. Cook food thoroughly to destroy bacteria.

SAFETY

Ensure that you will be fit enough to cope with the conditions in remote areas. Do not take risks. Carry extra clothes, food, and first-aid items in case you are lost or delayed anywhere.

● **Avoiding health risks** Do not travel if you are unwell. You could make an illness worse and hamper other people.
● **Improving fitness** If you plan to do strenuous activities such as mountain-climbing, take regular exercise before you travel. You should be fit enough to manage even if you have never tried the activity before.

● **Dressing sensibly** Wear comfortable shoes in order to prevent sprains or blisters.
● **Treating blisters** Carry large sticking plasters and antiseptic wipes with you to cover blisters.
● **Protecting feet** Wear socks if you are walking in rocky terrain to stop your feet from chafing.
● **Boosting energy** Take food for regular meals to maintain your blood sugar level. Take glucose tablets with you as well.
● **Scheduling rests** Plan several rests per day, especially if you are walking. This will prevent fatigue, which could cause you to make hazardous mistakes.

Protecting fresh foods
To protect food from animals on the ground, put it on a plate and tie it in a piece of cloth. Hang the cloth from a tree branch so that animals cannot reach it.

PREVENTING CRISES

Crises can occur during even a carefully planned holiday. You can save yourself a lot of trouble if you anticipate any emergencies that may arise. For example, make sure that you will not run out of water, and take sensible measures to prevent problems such as theft.

PREVENTING THEFT

● **Finding police** Find out the telephone number of the local police station as soon as you arrive in a new place. This will allow you to contact the police quickly if you have anything stolen. Remember to obtain a written report for insurance purposes.

● **Buying travellers' cheques** When you buy travellers' cheques, make sure that the company issuing them will replace any that are stolen. If cheques are stolen, quote the reference numbers (see p. 101) to the company so that they can stop the cheques.

● **Carrying cash** Divide cash into several bundles, and keep them in different pockets or bags to prevent all your cash from being stolen at once.

● **Carrying a bag** Carry a shoulder bag or handbag with the strap across your body to deter thieves from snatching it.

PROTECTING VALUABLES

● **Concealing jewellery** It is best to keep valuable jewellery in a safe or other secure place. If you have to carry it around, wear it under your clothes so that it cannot be seen.

Taking items into a shower
Keep money, jewellery, credit cards, and your wristwatch with you at all times. When you take a shower, put these items into a waterproof bag, and hang the bag from the shower head.

COLLECTING WATER

● **Asking local people** Learn the word for water in the language of your host country. Make a note of the word in case you have to ask someone for help in finding clean water.

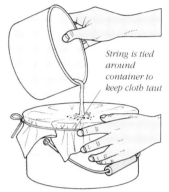

String is tied around container to keep cloth taut

Filtering water
To remove debris from fresh water, cover a container with a cloth such as a handkerchief, secure the cloth with string, and pour the water through it. Boil the water before use to sterilize it.

AVOIDING TROUBLE

● **Checking before travel** If you plan to visit a country where there is political unrest, contact your embassy or consulate and ask for advice on whether to go and what precautions to take.

● **Taking contact numbers** If you are going abroad, take the number of your country's embassy in case of trouble.

● **Keeping away from conflict** Avoid war or unrest if at all possible. If you are caught up in trouble, keep indoors until you can leave the area.

● **Dressing sensibly** Respect the clothing code of your host country, especially when visiting religious sites.

PREVENTING PROBLEMS WHILE CAMPING

Camping in a wilderness area can be an exciting experience. There are dangers, but you can often avoid serious problems if you take care to plan ahead.

● **Choosing a site** If you do not want to stay on an officially approved camp site, ask local residents where you may camp. As well as being polite, this will alert other people to your location in case you run into trouble or go missing.

● **Marking safe paths** Tie guide ropes to trees to mark a path from your tent to the latrine. This will stop you from losing your way if you have to leave the tent during the night.

● **Making a fire** Choose an area well clear of vegetation. If there is no suitable place, dig a fire pit. Keep a bucket of water or sand nearby in case the fire starts to blaze out of control.

● **Using lanterns** For light inside a tent, use a large torch or a battery-powered lantern. Never use a gas lamp. Apart from the fire risk, the flame will use up oxygen and may produce toxic gases such as carbon monoxide.

● **Making alarms** Put empty cans around the edge of the camp. If people or animals approach in the night, they will knock the cans, and the noise will warn you of their presence. Take the cans with you when you leave.

TREATING ILLNESS AND INJURY

Before you go on a holiday, make yourself familiar with first-aid techniques. Enrol on a course with your local branch of the Red Cross, and carry a first-aid manual with you at all times. If you are worried about an injury or health problem, seek professional medical help.

TREATING WOUNDS

● **Cleaning an animal bite** Wash a minor bite with water and soap. Hold it under running water for at least five minutes to rinse away bacteria, and seek medical attention.
● **Stopping bleeding** Wash a minor bleeding wound as described above, and cover with a sterile pad. Raise the area above the level of the heart to slow bleeding. Cover larger wounds with a sterile pad, apply a firm pressure, and seek medical attention.

WARNING!
Rabies can be fatal. Have an inoculation before you travel, and avoid wild or feral animals. If you are bitten, seek medical care immediately.

SOOTHING SUNBURN

● **Reducing temperature** Take small sips of cold water. This will reduce body heat and cause the skin to cool.
● **Easing pain** Sponge the burned area with cold water, then apply calamine lotion or witch hazel to soothe the skin.

Use fingers to apply yoghurt

Applying yoghurt
Cover any sunburned areas with a thick layer of natural yoghurt to cool the skin and relieve pain. Lie on towels, or sit in an empty bath, so that the yoghurt will not drip on to floors or furniture.

COUNTERACTING VENOM

● **Treating a snake bite** Do not try to suck out snake venom. Wash a snake bite with water and soap, and bandage it. Hold the bite below the level of the heart to keep the venom from spreading through the body.
● **Removing a sting** Using tweezers, grasp a sting near the point at which it enters the skin. Do not pull from the top in case you squeeze venom out of the poison sac. Cool the area with a cold compress or a can of cold drink, and apply antiseptic cream.
● **Dealing with allergies** If a person who is allergic to wasp and bee venom is stung, take them to hospital immediately. Severe reactions can develop within a matter of minutes, and can often be fatal.

COPING WITH INJURY

● **Grouping together** Travel in a group of three. If one person is hurt, another can stay with them while the third finds help.
● **Supporting a broken limb** Cushion a broken limb with rolled-up clothes to protect it from shocks during a journey.

Improvising a sling
To make a sling, raise the injured arm to a comfortable level, and fold a sweater around it. Tie the sleeves behind the neck. Using safety pins, fasten the end of the sweater around the elbow.

TRADITIONAL TIP

Soothing a jellyfish sting
If you plan to go into the sea, and you know that there may be venomous jellyfish in the water, take some vinegar with you in a small bottle. If you are stung, drip the vinegar over the inflamed area to neutralize the venom.

TREATING HEAT STROKE

● **Finding a cool place** Move a heat stroke victim into a cool, dark room. Fan the victim to move cool air over the body. Do not put the victim in a cold room, or switch on cold air conditioning, because a sudden change in temperature could cause severe shock.
● **Releasing heat** Clothes trap heat around the body. Strip a heat stroke victim completely, or at least to their underwear, so that the excess body heat can disperse quickly.
● **Reducing skin temperature** Sponge a heat stroke victim with tepid water, and leave to dry. The evaporating water will cool the skin.
● **Seeking help** Seek medical aid for victims of heat stroke, especially if they are confused or lose consciousness.

Moving Home

Quick Reference

Preparing to Move, p. 119

Sorting and Packing, p. 120

Carrying Out a Move, p. 125

Moving In, p. 127

Sharing Your Home, p. 129

MOVING INTO A NEW HOME *can be a daunting prospect. Once you have chosen a new home, plan every stage of the move so that you will have sufficient time to finish all of the preparations. Be sure to allow enough money to cover removal work, cleaning, and buying new possessions. If you are buying a home, have the structure checked properly by professionals.*

MAKING PREPARATIONS IN THE DAYS BEFORE A MOVE

Once you have finalized your plans to move home, allow several weeks to make preparations so that you will not be swamped with work as the moving day approaches. The countdown chart below gives specific numbers of days before a moving day, and suggests arrangements to make at these times.

35
- **Making inventory** Write an inventory to show every item that you intend to move.
- **Inspecting new home** Ask the occupiers to show you the locations of stopcocks, meters, the water tank, and water heaters.
- **Checking appliances** Find out if any appliances will be left in your new home.

30
- **Making floor plans** Measure rooms in your new home. Make floor plans to show where your furniture will go.
- **Ordering furnishings** Order furnishings to be delivered to your new home.
- **Storing** If you need to put any items into storage, contact a storage firm.

21
- **Insuring items** Arrange to have all your possessions insured during the move.
- **Packing** Start to pack up little-used rooms, unless a removal firm will be carrying out the packing for you.
- **Emptying a freezer** Begin to utilize or dispose of existing freezer contents.

14
- **Changing address** Notify organizations and personal contacts of your new address.
- **Booking removal firm** If using a removal firm, book a date and time with them.
- **Caring for pets** Arrange to leave pets in kennels, or with friends, during the move.
- **Servicing appliances** Arrange to have any appliances in your new home serviced.

7
- **Organizing child care** Arrange to have small children cared for during the move.
- **Briefing a removal firm** Send a copy of your inventory to the removal firm. Brief them on any items that need special care.
- **Laundering** Start to launder clothes and bedding so that they are ready to pack.

4
- **Packing** Start to pack up living areas, unless a removal firm will be carrying out the packing for you. Leave your curtains up to ensure privacy.
- **Packing appliances** Find the instruction manuals for any appliances so that you can see how to pack them properly.

2
- **Checking removal times** Confirm all details with the removal firm or with anyone else who will be helping you.
- **Confirming plans** Confirm that your new home will be ready for the move.
- **Packing appliances** Pack up all appliances except for essential items.

1
- **Packing essential items** Pack a box of food and household supplies to keep to hand during the move (see p. 125).
- **Moving house plants** Water plants well. Pack in boxes for transport (see p. 123).
- **Cleaning appliances** Empty and clean the refrigerator and freezer.
- **Moving pets** Take pets to kennels.

PREPARING TO MOVE

MAKE LISTS OF PREPARATIONS TO CARRY OUT in your existing home before a move, and of people to inform of a move. Make these lists several weeks in advance. If you need family or friends to help, ask them in good time.

MAKING ARRANGEMENTS

Organize necessary tasks such as repairs and removals well before the moving day. Reconfirm your arrangements a couple of days before you move, in case there are any last-minute changes of plan. Notify family, friends, and official bodies of your change of address.

PLANNING AHEAD
● **Selecting a day** Arrange to move in the middle of a week when the roads will be quiet, rather than at a weekend or on a public holiday.
● **Planning repair work** If there are major repairs to be done in your new home, try to arrange it so that the work happens before you move in.
● **Having meters read** Arrange to have the gas and electricity meters read at both homes on the day of the move.
● **Servicing vehicles** If you will be moving a long way, arrange to have your car serviced well before the day of the move.

WHOM TO NOTIFY BEFORE A MOVE	
FINANCIAL BODIES	**UTILITY COMPANIES**
Contact at least two weeks before a move. ● Banks. ● Tax office. ● Insurance companies.	Arrange services for your new home two weeks in advance. ● Gas and electricity suppliers. ● Water supplier. ● Telephone companies.
LOCAL BODIES	**PERSONAL CONTACTS**
Notify schools immediately. Contact other bodies at least two weeks in advance. ● Schools. ● Local council office. ● Postal service.	Tell family and friends, and any other personal contacts, at least one week in advance. ● Doctor and dentist. ● Employer. ● Family and friends.

ORGANIZING YOURSELF AND OTHERS

Whether you use a removal firm or ask friends to help you, make the necessary arrangements well before a move. Ensure that anyone driving a removal vehicle has directions for finding your new home. Reconfirm the plans a couple of days beforehand.

MOVING ITEMS YOURSELF

Move all fragile and valuable objects yourself. If you are using a car, do not leave it unattended during the move.

● **Jewellery** Lock it into the glove compartment of a car.
● **Audio equipment** Fit boxes securely into a car boot.
● **Money** Carry small supplies of cash in a bag and in the pockets of your clothes.
● **Documents** Carry important papers in a bag or a briefcase.

USING A REMOVAL FIRM
● **Selecting a firm** Ask several firms for estimates. Check the type of vehicles they use, and what their insurance covers.
● **Assessing costs** A removal firm may send an estimator to assess the cost of a move. Show the estimator everything to be moved so that he or she can work out a fair price.
● **Checking travel plans** If removal vehicles are to make an overnight stop, ask where they will park, and insist that someone guards each one.

MANAGING HELPERS
● **Organizing a team** Enlist at least two strong people to cope with large items, and two more to handle boxes.
● **Protecting possessions** Draw up a rota of people to travel with removal vehicles and people to stay in each home. By doing this you will ensure that your belongings will never be left unattended.
● **Taking out insurance** Arrange extra insurance cover in case any of your helpers injures themselves during a move.

SORTING AND PACKING

A FEW WEEKS BEFORE A MOVE, make a plan for packing the contents of each room, and collect packing materials. As you pack, dispose of clutter, and label boxes so that you can put them in the appropriate rooms in your new home.

LISTING AND INSURING POSSESSIONS

Before starting to pack, make an inventory of your possessions, including any appliances or fixtures that you will take with you. Keep this list for reference. When you pack up each room, use it to note which items have been packed and which have been thrown or given away.

MAKING AN INVENTORY
● **Working in pairs** Ask someone to help you make an inventory. Have one person calling out the names of items while the other logs them.
● **Recording reference** Make a note of the names and model numbers of appliances.
● **Listing sets of items** For items in groups, such as cutlery or crockery, note how many are in the group and whether there are any missing.
● **Keeping an inventory** Put a completed inventory in an accessible place so that you can refer to it during a move.

INSURING OBJECTS
● **Insuring possessions** Check that your insurance policy covers your possessions while they are in transit, especially during overnight stops.
● **Making visual records** Take photographs of all valuable objects in case you need them for an insurance claim.
● **Recording damage** If an item is damaged before you pack it, photograph the damaged part. If the item suffers further damage during the move, you will have proof of what was done in transit and what had already been done.

TIME-SAVING TIP

Recording an inventory
Walk around each room with a hand-held tape recorder, and record the name of every object in the room. Make a copy of the tape for reference.

CLEANING ITEMS BEFORE A MOVE

Moving is a dusty business, so clean only very dirty objects before you pack them. Remove accumulated dirt from appliances such as a cooker or vacuum cleaner. Clean your old home to make it pleasant and welcoming for the next occupants when they move in.

LEAVING ITEMS UNCLEANED

Do not clean the following items before moving, since they are likely to gather dust in the course of a move.

● Crockery.
● Glassware.
● Cutlery.
● Mirrors.
● Pictures.
● Books.
● Pots and pans.
● Vases.
● Ornaments.
● Wooden furniture.

REMOVING DIRT

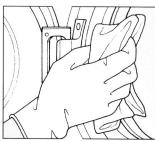

Wiping kitchen appliances
Clean appliances with a solution of 60 ml (2 fl oz) dishwashing liquid in 4.5 litres (1 gallon) of very hot water. Wipe areas such as door seals with a dry cloth.

REMOVING DUST

Cleaning a lampshade
Dust a fabric lampshade by using heavy-duty adhesive tape. Wrap a loop of tape around your hand sticky side out, then dab the shade with the tape to pick up the dust.

PACKING MATERIALS AND CONTAINERS

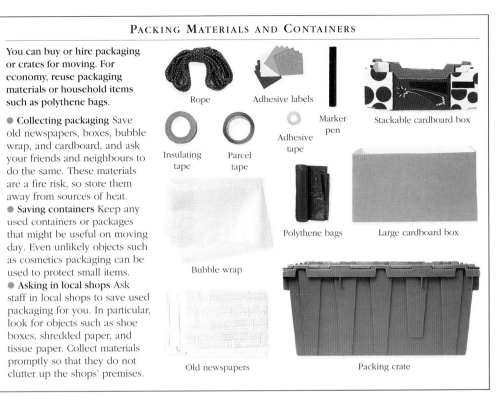

You can buy or hire packaging or crates for moving. For economy, reuse packaging materials or household items such as polythene bags.

- **Collecting packaging** Save old newspapers, boxes, bubble wrap, and cardboard, and ask your friends and neighbours to do the same. These materials are a fire risk, so store them away from sources of heat.
- **Saving containers** Keep any used containers or packages that might be useful on moving day. Even unlikely objects such as cosmetics packaging can be used to protect small items.
- **Asking in local shops** Ask staff in local shops to save used packaging for you. In particular, look for objects such as shoe boxes, shredded paper, and tissue paper. Collect materials promptly so that they do not clutter up the shops' premises.

Rope   Adhesive labels   Marker pen   Stackable cardboard box

Insulating tape   Parcel tape   Adhesive tape

Polythene bags   Large cardboard box

Bubble wrap

Old newspapers   Packing crate

PACKING FRAGILE AND VALUABLE ITEMS

Allow plenty of time for packing fragile or valuable items such as china and audio equipment. Pad the objects so that they do not move around in their containers. If possible, carry the objects with you when you move, rather than putting them in a removal van.

PACKING FRAGILE ITEMS
- **Protecting computers** If possible, put a computer in its original packaging. Packaging for computers is often made to measure, and will hold items securely during a move. If you have not kept the packaging, ask a local shop for similar material.
- **Protecting fragile items** To protect fragile items such as small glass ornaments, wrap them in cotton wool before covering them with newspaper.
- **Padding fragile items** Wrap fragile items in newspaper, then cover in bubble wrap. Put the items in a sturdy box, and pad them well around the sides to make sure that they are held securely in place.

WRAPPING VALUABLES
- **Packing jewellery** Wrap pieces of jewellery in rolls of cotton wool to protect them.

Protecting ornaments
Wrap ornaments in cleaning cloths, then pack them into plastic food containers with lids. Tuck extra padding around the items to hold them securely.

PACKING CROCKERY
- **Using mugs** Put a wrapped item such as a glass inside a mug to protect both items.

Bubble wrap is laid on each plate

Padding plates
Cut circles of bubble wrap the same size as your plates. Sandwich bubble wrap between the plates as you stack them so that they do not chip each other.

PACKING FURNITURE

Before packing furniture, prepare it so that it will be easy to carry and safe from damage. If possible, dismantle it or remove parts such as drawers. Shield corners and surfaces. Secure any loose parts with masking tape, which can be peeled off without damaging most surfaces.

PACKING STORAGE UNITS
● **Preparing cupboards** Secure cupboard doors with masking tape so that the doors will not swing open when moved.

Wrapping a drawer
Leave drawers full. Slide them into polythene bags, and fasten the bags tightly around them to keep the contents clean. Label the bags to show the contents.

PACKING TABLES
● **Securing legs** To pack loose table legs, wrap the legs in newspaper, then tape them to the underside of the table top.

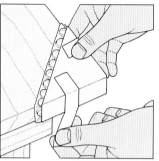

Padding a table corner
To shield the corners of a table, wrap in bubble wrap, then cover with corners cut from cardboard boxes. Secure with tape, avoiding surfaces that could be marked.

PACKING OTHER ITEMS
● **Stowing book cases** Remove any loose shelves from a book case. Stack the shelves in the bottom of the case, or tape them to the back.
● **Wrapping mirrors** Put a mirror in several polythene bags, or wrap it in polythene sheeting. If the mirror shatters during the move, the shards of glass will not escape.
● **Using cupboard space** Fill space in empty cupboards with soft, bulky objects such as bedding, sleeping bags, and table linen.
● **Protecting appliances** Put sheets of cardboard around an appliance such as a cooker so that its surface will not be damaged if it knocks against other objects during a move.

PACKING CLOTHES

When you pack clothes before moving, the main priorities are to keep them clean and ensure that none are lost. Put garments in polythene bags or suitcases, or keep them in their wardrobe or drawers. If you need extra packaging, use clothes to wrap other items.

PREPARING CLOTHES
● **Cleaning garments** Dry clean or launder dirty clothes before packing. However, do not iron them, in case they are creased during the move.
● **Keeping items in a wardrobe** You can transport clothes in their wardrobe if this will not make the wardrobe too heavy to be lifted. Cover the clothes with polythene bags to keep them clean. Lock the wardrobe doors, or tape them shut.
● **Preparing shoes** Put shoe trees inside shoes, or stuff the shoes with newspaper, so that they will keep their shape. Put each pair of shoes in a plastic bag to keep the outsides clean.

WRAPPING & PACKING
● **Rolling up clothes** Roll up garments such as T-shirts so that they will take up as little space as possible.

Securing items on hangers
Group hangers holding clothes, and join the tops with tape. Pull polythene bags up over the clothes to keep them together.

BRIGHT IDEA

Packing in underwear
Wrap bedroom ornaments in underwear to protect them and keep them clean. Put them in containers, and keep with other bedroom items so that they will be in the correct place when you unpack.

PACKING AND MOVING AWKWARD ITEMS

Some items may be difficult to pack because they are an awkward shape, are large and bulky, or because they have sharp surfaces that could make them dangerous to handle. Gather enough materials to pack the objects safely and to secure them inside removal vehicles.

PACKING HOUSE PLANTS

Stretch polythene over stakes

Stakes are higher than tallest plant

Box holds plants securely

Stake is pushed into soil

Grouping plants
Stand plants on a layer of newspaper in a sturdy box. Push a thin, wooden stake into each pot. Stretch clear polythene sheeting over the top, and tape it to the box to seal in warmth and moisture for the plants.

PACKING RUGS
● **Rolling in sheets** To stop the top of a rug from being dirtied by the underside, use a dust sheet. Lay the sheet on top of the rug, then roll up the rug.

PREPARING EQUIPMENT
● **Packing a turntable** To protect the needle of a turntable, pad it with a piece of foam. Secure the arm to the base by attaching it with masking tape at 5-cm (2-in) intervals along the arm.
● **Packing up a computer** To keep loose parts of a computer such as a mouse and leads together, put these parts in a padded paper bag. Tape the bag to the top of the monitor or the body of the computer.
● **Carrying electrical items** Allow plenty of space in a car to fit delicate electrical items such as televisions or audio equipment. Secure these items inside the car so that they will not move around while you are driving.

WRAPPING PAINT CANS
● **Sealing safely** If possible, get rid of flammable paint before moving. If you do take it with you, seal can lids with tape, then tie the cans in plastic bags.

SHIFTING HEAVY ITEMS
● **Moving books** Do not fill boxes with books, otherwise they will be too heavy to lift. Half-fill each box with books, and put lighter objects on top.
● **Improvising rollers** As you pack, put aside wheeled items such as skateboards or roller skates. You can then use these items to help move heavy boxes or pieces of furniture.
● **Moving large items** To shift a large object easily, lay it on a piece of polythene sheeting, and fix the sheeting to the sides of the object. You can then slide it across a floor without harming the object or the floor.
● **Shifting furniture** To move a heavy chair or sofa, turn it on to its back or side, and slide it across the floor.

PACKING TOOLS

Split length of garden hose

Safeguarding a saw blade
Cut a piece of garden hose lengthways. Slide it over the teeth of a saw to prevent damage to objects or people.

● **Packing a lawnmower** Wrap newspaper around exposed lawnmower blades. Cover the body with polythene bags. Wrap old blankets around the machine, then cover with more bags to protect the blankets.

MOVING LARGE ITEMS
● **Using a roof rack** Buy or borrow a roof rack and bungee cords for transporting large items such as bicycles.

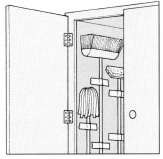

Packing mops and brooms
Secure objects such as mops and brooms inside a wardrobe with strong adhesive tape. Attach the handles at each end and in the middle to hold them firmly.

CLEARING YOUR OLD HOME

Once you have completed the bulk of your packing, make a plan for clearing each room. Work out an order for loading items into vehicles. Make a note of supplies for use on the moving day, and of items that you will need once you have moved into your new home.

FINISHING PACKING
● **Buying labels** Buy packets of adhesive labels for your possessions, and for the doors of rooms in your new home.

Piece is cut to fit box exactly

Using leftover materials
If you have any leftover boxes, cut them into pieces, and use the pieces to reinforce other boxes. Put pieces in the base and around the inside of a box.

COLLECTING OBJECTS
● **Grouping boxes** Put packed boxes in a room that you do not use daily. Position them so that they will not obstruct access. Keep them out of sight of potential burglars.
● **Collecting essentials** Pack boxes of household equipment for use in your new home. Discard worn-out or nearly empty items. Put aside a few items for use during the move.
● **Gathering stray items** Search down the backs of chairs and sofas, and underneath pieces of furniture, to find any stray items such as socks or coins.
● **Finding keys** Collect and label door and window keys to give to the new occupants.

PREPARING FOR LOADING
● **Dealing with furniture** To save effort, leave furniture in place until you are ready to load it into a removal vehicle.
● **Gathering equipment** Collect ropes and bungee cords for securing items inside vehicles, and coverings to protect the floors in your new home.
● **Collecting work wear** Keep old clothes, strong gloves, and sturdy shoes for helpers to wear on the day of the move.
● **Using covers** Keep a few pieces of plastic sheeting handy to cover objects in case it rains on the moving day.
● **Leaving objects behind** Put labels on any items that are to remain in your old home.

USING A LABELLING SYSTEM

To enable you to organize your new home quickly, plan in advance where you will put your possessions. Make a floor plan showing all the rooms, and work out a labelling system to show which containers and pieces of furniture are to go into each room of your home.

LABELLING OBJECTS
● **Keeping labels visible** Attach labels where they will be clearly seen on objects at all times. For example, fix them to the fronts of furniture, or to the tops and sides of boxes.
● **Tying on labels** Use tie-on labels for any objects that might be damaged by an adhesive label, such as pieces of antique furniture.
● **Protecting labels** Cover labels on your belongings with clear adhesive tape so that they will not become wet if it rains on the day of the move.
● **Keeping spare supplies** Put aside several extra labels of each colour for the day of the move, in case you need to add or replace labels on any items.

COLOUR CODING ROOM CONTENTS

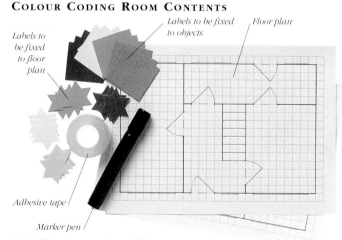

Labels to be fixed to floor plan

Labels to be fixed to objects

Floor plan

Adhesive tape

Marker pen

Labelling items for different rooms
Draw a floor plan of your new home (see p. 11). Write the name of each room on the plan. Stick labels of different colours to the rooms, and attach labels of the relevant colours to items that will go in the rooms. Keep the plan handy for reference on the day of the move.

CARRYING OUT A MOVE

O N THE DAY OF A MOVE, have a good breakfast to give you energy for work. Brief helpers on moving items and loading vehicles. Ensure that children or pets accompanying you will be safe and well cared for during the day.

LOADING A VEHICLE

N ever overload a vehicle, otherwise you may damage the chassis. Make several trips or use several vehicles if you have a lot to move.

If you hire a vehicle, check the maximum load that it will carry. Carry essential items with you in a car so that they are easily accessible.

ARRANGING CONTENTS

● **Loading heavy items** Put heavy items around the edges of a vehicle. Space them out to spread their weight evenly.
● **Adding boxes** Fit boxes securely in the spaces between heavy items. Put padding, such as old blankets, around boxes so that they will not move.
● **Checking visibility** When loading a car, check at regular intervals to see that the load does not block the view in the rear-view mirror. Leave a clear space so that you can use the mirror and drive safely.

SECURING LARGE ITEMS

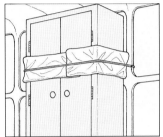

Fixing an item to a vehicle
Fix a large item to the inside of a vehicle with bungee cord or rope. Lay the cord or rope over an old blanket so that it does not chafe the surfaces of the item.

LOADING EFFICIENTLY

Make sure that you can shift heavy objects smoothly, so that you do not damage the objects or cause anyone to be injured.

Lifting safely
Buy or borrow a packing-case carrier to move heavy items safely.

ITEMS TO KEEP TO HAND ON MOVING DAY

HOUSEHOLD ITEMS AND FOOD		CLOTHES, BEDDING, AND TOILETRIES	
● Toilet paper.	● Can opener.	● One change of	● Shampoo.
● Cleaning items.	● Picnic items	clothes per person.	● Hairbrush.
● Lubricating oil.	(see p. 64).	● Towels.	● Deodorant.
● Basic tools such as an	● Teaspoons.	● One set of bedding	● Toothbrushes and
adjustable spanner.	● Kitchen knives.	per person.	toothpaste.
● Parcel tape.	● Paper towels.	● Moisturizer.	● Home medical kit for
● Safety pins.	● Tea and coffee.	● Soap.	first aid (see p. 89).
● Vacuum flask.	● Food for meals.		
● Light bulbs.			
● Torch.			
● Fuses.			
● Kettle.			

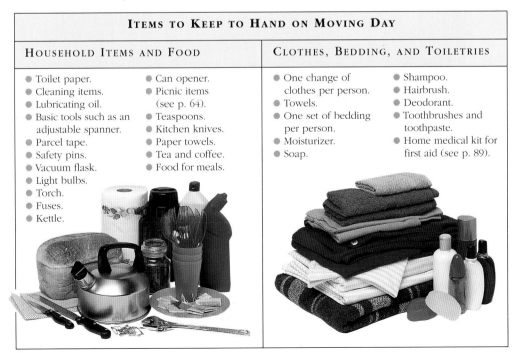

SUPERVISING CHILDREN DURING A MOVE

Small children may obstruct workers or may be injured during a move, so it is best to ask a relative or a friend to look after children until the new home is ready for them. If you must have children with you, keep them safe and make them feel involved in the event.

CARING FOR CHILDREN

● **Travelling between homes** If you have to make several trips between homes, always check where the children are before you go, so that no child will be left alone in an empty house.

● **Making a long journey** Stop at intervals so that everyone can stretch their legs, go to the toilet, and perhaps have something to eat. Do not leave your vehicle unattended.

● **Preparing a quiet room** Clear a space in a room away from removal work, so that children can watch television or keep themselves occupied with quiet activities.

INVOLVING CHILDREN IN A MOVE

Even young children can be given useful tasks to do, and may enjoy feeling that they are part of the activities. However, they will become tired sooner than adults, so allow time and space for them to rest.

● **Preparing children** Tell the children how exciting it will be to move home, so that they view the move positively.

● **Organizing bedrooms** Move furniture into the children's bedrooms as soon as possible. Encourage the children to unpack their own belongings.

● **Delegating tasks** Ask older children to start jobs such as cleaning cupboards, unpacking items such as crockery and cutlery, and washing items before putting them away. Make sure that the children will not be in the way of removers.

● **Guarding pets** If you have brought pets with you, ask a child to put them in a quiet room and stay with them so that they do not escape.

● **Having breaks** Whenever the removers have a break, ask the children to come and share refreshments and company.

LOOKING AFTER PETS DURING A MOVE

Once you have brought pets to your new home, make them feel settled as soon as you can. Give them food and water, and take them for a run or provide fresh litter for them. Keep pets well away from the removal work so that they will not be worried by the commotion.

TRANSPORTING FISH

● **Taking water** Before packing a tank, put some of the water into vacuum flasks. Use it to keep the fish at the correct temperature during the move.

Secure polystyrene with insulating tape

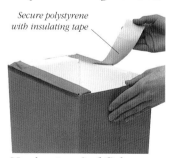

Moving tropical fish
To maintain tropical fish at the correct temperature, insulate a sturdy box with polystyrene. Put the fish into a polythene bag with water from the tank. Seal the bag, and place it in the box.

MOVING CATS & DOGS

● **Using kennels** Consider putting cats and dogs into kennels until your new home is organized, to keep them from being upset by a move.

● **Taking refreshments** When transporting a cat or dog with you, carry food and water, bowls, and a litter tray (for cats). Take rest stops so that the animal can have a little fresh air or exercise.

● **Moving in** On arriving at your new home, shut a cat or dog in a room with food, water, and a litter tray if needed. Put a "do not disturb" sign on the door to prevent further agitation of the animal.

● **Keeping indoors** Confine pets to your home or garden for a few days to let them settle in to their new territory.

MOVING OTHER PETS

● **Travelling with rodents** Ask your vet if you may borrow a purpose-built pet carrier for rodents. Secure the carrier in a car using a seat belt, and make sure that someone sits beside it to look after the animals.

Using a hutch
If you do not have a pet carrier, adapt a hutch for travel. Fix a flap of old carpet over the front to keep out draughts. Cut some more carpet to fit the floor so that the pet will not slip around.

MOVING IN

O NCE YOU HAVE BROUGHT ALL YOUR POSSESSIONS to your new home, make some initial checks before unpacking. By working to a system, you can quickly make your home habitable and pinpoint any existing or potential problems.

ORGANIZING A NEW HOME

B efore you start to unpack, check the power supplies and structure of the property to make sure that there are no problems. If the previous occupants promised to leave you any appliances or fittings, check that these are in place. See that all areas are clean and safe.

MAKING A CHECKLIST

Check the following items to test the efficiency of all household items and systems.

- Door and window locks.
- Windows.
- Electricity.
- Boiler and radiators.
- Cooker.
- Stopcock and taps.
- Drains.
- Telephone.
- Kitchen appliances.

CHECKING SYSTEMS

- **Testing hot water** Run the hot tap of a bath for a few minutes, then run the shower. Check that the water is hot and the water pressure is adequate.
- **Assessing water quality** Turn on the taps to see if the water is clear. If it is coloured, leave the taps running for a few minutes. If the water does not become clear, call a plumber or contact the water board.
- **Looking for leaks** To check for leaks in water pipes, open taps up to their full extent.
- **Testing electric circuits** Carry a small lamp, and plug it into all the sockets in each room to see if the circuits are working.
- **Trying a cooker** Boil a small pan of water on each ring in turn to ensure that they all work. Turn on the oven and grill to see if they work.

FINDING PROBLEM AREAS

- **Assessing rooms** Look around the bare rooms. Make a note of problems such as scuffed walls or damp areas so that you can treat them before you settle into the property.
- **Testing floors** Walk across any bare floorboards to find out if they creak or sag. Avoid placing items on these areas, and repair before carpeting.
- **Checking insulation** Make a note of areas where insulation could be improved, such as gaps around a window or door.

PREPARING ROOMS

- **Airing rooms** If your new home has been empty for longer than a few days, the air may be stale. Open the windows for a while, then close them, and put on the heating if necessary. This will also give you an opportunity to check that the radiators work.
- **Cleaning quickly** Make sure that surfaces are clean before positioning furniture on them. Dust paintwork, vacuum clean carpets, and wash kitchen and bathroom floors.
- **Hanging curtains** Use a damp cloth to wipe curtain rails and clean windows before you hang curtains.
- **Airing furnishings** If pillows, cushions, or mattresses have been transported in plastic covers, unwrap them, and leave them to air before use.

MAKING A HOME SAFE

- **Masking danger spots** Cover unsafe areas, such as weak flooring or exposed wires, to make them safe until you can have them properly repaired.
- **Blocking windows** Position furniture in front of windows where children could fall out. When possible, replace the furniture with window guards.
- **Inspecting a garden** Check the garden for any poisonous plants. Do not let children or pets out until you have moved or destroyed such plants.

SAFEGUARD TIP

Repairing a leaking tap
If the body of a tap leaks, the packing inside may be worn. To replace it, remove the tap handle and the topmost nut on the spindle. If the packing consists of string, scrape it out. Coat a new length of string with petroleum jelly, then wind it into the space. Push it in with a screwdriver.

UNLOADING POSSESSIONS SAFELY

Using your room plan (see p. 124), place each object in the desired position in the correct room before unloading the next. To keep people and possessions safe, make sure that you and your helpers do not risk injury, and never leave a removal vehicle unattended.

ANTICIPATING ACCIDENTS
● **Shielding hands** Provide strong gloves for helpers to prevent cuts and blisters. Supply hand cream so that people can keep their hands from becoming dry.
● **Moving furniture upstairs** To move a large piece of furniture upstairs, first lay it on its back on the stairs. Have one or two people pushing it from below, and another person above the object to steady it.
● **Taking breaks** Make sure that everyone takes regular breaks for rest, and provide refreshments to help people maintain energy levels.

ORGANIZING VEHICLES
● **Reserving parking** Talk to your new neighbours before a move. Ask them to keep the road in front of your home clear for removal vehicles.
● **Parking safely** Before you unload a vehicle, have it parked as close as possible to the entrance of your home. As well as minimizing the distance for carrying objects, this will enable you to watch the vehicle from a window.
● **Standing guard** Ask a helper to stay with an open vehicle at all times, either unloading objects from the interior or standing guard beside it.

PLANNING A SYSTEM FOR UNLOADING

Prepare rooms before starting work. Unload items in a logical order to save yourself work once the move is over.

● **Preparing floors** Cover floors with newspapers to protect them from damage while you are unloading.
● **Labelling rooms** Label each door as shown on your floor plan. Display the plan by the front door for reference.
● **Moving possessions** Unload large pieces of furniture first, so that you can position them correctly at the outset.

UNPACKING POSSESSIONS

At first, unpack only furniture and items that you need immediately. Leave objects such as books, ornaments, and linens until you have finished organizing furniture and storage areas. Take time to decide where to put these items so that you can store them in a suitable way.

UNPACKING EFFICIENTLY
● **Cleaning spaces** Clean storage spaces before filling them. Dust and wash shelves and the insides of cupboards. Allow washed areas to dry completely before use.
● **Checking objects** As you unpack, check items for damage, and carry out any necessary cleaning.
● **Dusting books** Brush books with a clean feather duster to remove any dust before putting them on bookshelves.
● **Washing ornaments** Wash ornaments carefully in a bowl of warm, soapy water, and dry them thoroughly using a clean tea towel.
● **Unpacking kitchen items** As you unpack equipment in a kitchen, position it nearest to the areas where it will be used.

RECYCLING MATERIALS
● **Saving polythene bags** Once you have unpacked items from polythene bags, fold the bags and keep them in a cupboard for reuse in dustbins.

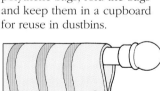

Improvising a curtain
If you have used any blankets for wrapping items, take them off the items and fasten them over a curtain rail with safety pins. This will give you some privacy until you can unpack your curtains.

MONEY-SAVING TIP

Using up packaging
If you have used newspapers as packing material during a move, save clean newspapers and use them to buff windows after washing. Make sure that the windows are damp when you buff them, otherwise the newspaper may scratch the glass.

SHARING YOUR HOME

Letting space in your home is a good way to make money if you are on a tight budget. As well as sharing costs, a flatmate or lodger also provides company. Choose people with care to ensure that they will be friendly and reliable.

FINDING A FLATMATE OR LODGER

Flatmates are equal partners in the home with you, sharing expenses on an equally divided basis, while lodgers are your tenants and will pay rent and an agreed proportion of the bills to you. Whichever arrangement you choose, set it out in writing and give a copy to all parties.

CHOOSING A FLATMATE OR LODGER

Interview anyone who seems suitable. Discuss practical matters before the person moves in.

● **Advertising effectively** Before placing an advertisement in a magazine or newspaper, read a few issues to form an idea of the intended readers. This will enable you to judge if you are likely to attract a suitable person through that publication.

● **Interviewing candidates** Ask whether the person smokes. Find out if they have a steady partner or a busy social life. Ask for character references.
● **Giving notice** State the period of notice required if anyone wishes to end the arrangement.
● **Taking legal advice** Employ a lawyer to look at any agreement you draw up to make sure that nobody is at a disadvantage.

SETTING HOUSE RULES
● **Accommodating visitors**
Find out in advance whether a lodger or flatmate intends to have a guest staying for a long time. Arrange for visitors to contribute to the rent if they stay longer than a few days.
● **Drawing up a bath rota** If you share a bathroom, draw up a rota for bathing to avoid disagreements at busy times. Give priority to those who go out first in the morning.

ESTABLISHING A HOUSEHOLD SYSTEM

Life in shared premises will run smoothly if everyone in the household agrees on how to allocate space and divide household chores. If you are new to a shared home, work out practical matters as soon as you have moved in so that you develop good habits from the start.

ALLOCATING SPACE

Sharing shelves
If shelves and cupboard space are shared, group each person's belongings in lids from large, sturdy cardboard boxes. Write each person's name clearly on the front edge of each lid.

DIVIDING TASKS
● **Organizing meals** Decide whether everyone will cook separately or for each other. If you all cook for yourselves, draw up a rota for using the cooker. If you eat together, take it in turns to cook.
● **Cleaning common areas** Plan a rota for cleaning all shared areas, such as the kitchen.
● **Tidying quickly** Ask people to wipe the bath and basin after every use, and to wipe kitchen surfaces when they have finished cooking.
● **Washing up** Ask everyone in the household to do their own washing up. If you have shared a meal, nominate someone to wash up.

SHARING EXPENSES
● **Keeping a kitty** Have a kitty for buying household items. Agree an amount for each person to pay in every week.
● **Keeping an expenses file** Keep copies of bills in a file for reference. Put receipts for household goods with the bills so that you can monitor the costs for budgeting purposes.
● **Paying bills** Divide energy bills equally between all members of the household.
● **Logging telephone use** Log telephone calls in a book. Note the name, date, time, and duration. List the area code to help in working out the cost. Check telephone bills against the entries in the book.

CONVERSION CHARTS

 THERE ARE A NUMBER OF DIFFERENT MEASUREMENT SYSTEMS *in use around the world. The conversion charts on the following pages show some of the most common types of shoe and clothing sizes, as well as metric and imperial systems for length, weight, and other measures. Use them to convert measurements easily from one form to another.*

SHOE AND CLOTHING SIZES

 Shoe and clothing sizes vary between makes, so use the following conversions as a rough guide to adult sizes. Manufacturers may classify children's sizes by age or height, but children may not fit these categories, so always carry a child's measurements (see opposite).

SHOE SIZES

FOOT LENGTH	UK	EUROPE	US (MEN)	US (WOMEN)
24.2 cm	3½	36	4	5
24.6 cm	4	36	4½	5½
25.0 cm	4½	37	5	6
25.4 cm	5	38	5½	6½
25.8 cm	5½	38	6	7
26.2 cm	6	39	6½	7½
26.7 cm	6½	40	7	8
27.1 cm	7	40	7½	8½
27.5 cm	7½	41	8	9
27.9 cm	8	42	8½	9½
28.4 cm	8½	42	9	10
28.8 cm	9	43	9½	10½
29.2 cm	9½	43	10	11
29.6 cm	10	44	10½	11½
30.1 cm	10½	45	11	12
30.5 cm	11	45	11½	12½
30.9 cm	11½	46	12	13
31.3 cm	12	47	12½	13½

SHIRT COLLAR SIZES

EUROPE	UK/US
36 cm	14 in
37 cm	14½ in
38 cm	15 in
40 cm	15½ in
41 cm	16 in
42 cm	16½ in
43 cm	17 in
44 cm	17½ in

MEN'S SUIT SIZES

CM	EUROPE	UK/US
81	42	32
86	44	34
91	46	36
97	48	38
102	50	40
107	52	42
112	54	44

WOMEN'S CLOTHING SIZES

UK	EUROPE	US
10	38	8
12	40	10
14	42	12
16	44	14
18	47	16
20	50	18
22	52	20

TAKING BODY MEASUREMENTS FOR CLOTHING

Keep accurate measurements for yourself and other family members, and use them as reference when buying or making clothes. When taking a person's measurements, ensure that they are standing straight.

When you go shopping to buy clothes for yourself or your family, carry the measurements with you. Revise children's measurements regularly, and always have their shoe sizes tested by professional fitters.

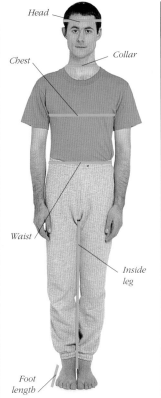

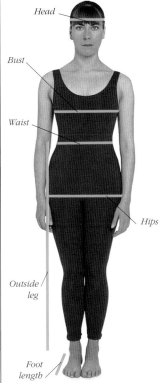

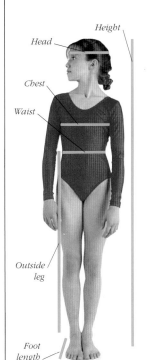

MAN'S MEASUREMENTS

- **Head** Measure horizontally around the head, level with the middle of the forehead.
- **Collar** Measure around the fullest part of the neck.
- **Chest** Measure around the fullest part of the chest, keeping the tape measure straight across the back.
- **Waist** Tie a piece of string around the waist, and let it settle into the natural waistline. Measure around this marker with a tape measure.
- **Inside leg** Measure vertically down the inside of the leg, from the crotch to the ankle bone.
- **Foot length** Measure along the sole of the foot, from the big toe to the heel.

WOMAN'S MEASUREMENTS

- **Head** Measure horizontally around the head, level with the middle of the forehead.
- **Bust** Measure around the fullest part of the chest, keeping the tape measure straight across the back.
- **Waist** Tie a piece of string around the waist, and let it settle into the natural waistline. Measure around this with a tape measure.
- **Hips** Measure around the fullest part of the hips and buttocks, keeping the tape measure straight.
- **Outside leg** Tie string around the waist to find the natural waistline. Measure the outside leg from the string to the ankle bone.
- **Foot length** Measure along the sole of the foot, from the big toe to the heel.

CHILD'S MEASUREMENTS

- **Height** Stand the child against a wall. Mark the wall by the top of the child's head, and measure from this mark to the floor.
- **Head** Measure horizontally around the head, level with the middle of the forehead.
- **Chest** Measure the fullest part of the chest, keeping the tape measure straight across the back.
- **Waist** Measure around the waist, keeping the tape measure level with the navel.
- **Outside leg** Use string to mark the natural waistline. Measure the outside leg from the string to the ankle bone.
- **Foot length** Measure along the sole of the foot, from the big toe to the heel.

WEIGHTS AND MEASURES

The charts below give conversions for metric and imperial measures. The central columns show the number of units to be converted. For example, to convert 7 miles to kilometres, let 7 stand for miles, then find the number beside 7 in the kilometres column (11.27). To multiply by 10, move the decimal point one place right. For numbers not shown, add the chart figures together. For example, to convert 14 inches to centimetres, add the figures for 10 inches and for 4 inches: 25.40 + 10.16 = 35.56. The dashes indicate where there is no exact conversion.

KILOMETRES AND MILES		
KM	NUMBER	MILES
1.61	1	0.62
3.22	2	1.24
4.83	3	1.86
6.44	4	2.49
8.05	5	3.11
9.66	6	3.73
11.27	7	4.35
12.88	8	4.97
14.48	9	5.59
16.09	10	6.21
32.19	20	12.43
48.28	30	18.64
64.37	40	24.86
80.47	50	31.07
160.93	100	62.14
402.34	250	155.34
804.67	500	310.69
1,609.34	1,000	621.37

CENTIMETRES AND INCHES		
CM	NUMBER	IN
0.64	0.25	⅛
1.27	0.5	¼
1.91	0.75	⁵⁄₁₆
2.54	1	⅜
5.08	2	¾
7.62	3	1¼
10.16	4	1½
12.70	5	2
15.24	6	2⅜
17.78	7	2¾
20.32	8	3⅛
22.86	9	3½
25.40	10	4
50.80	20	8
76.20	30	12
101.60	40	16
127.00	50	19½
254.00	100	39⅜

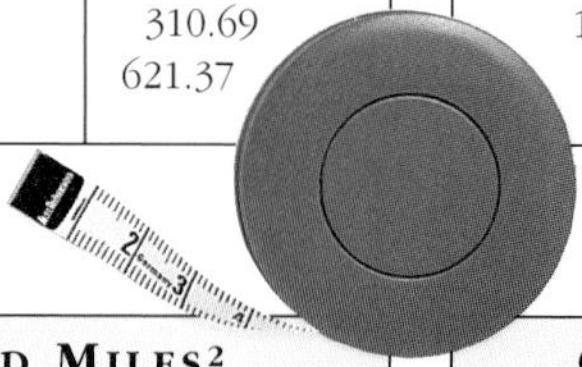

KILOMETRES^2 AND MILES^2		
KM^2	NUMBER	MILES^2
2.59	1	0.39
5.18	2	0.77
7.77	3	1.16
10.36	4	1.54
12.95	5	1.93
15.54	6	2.32
18.13	7	2.70
20.72	8	3.09
23.31	9	3.48
25.90	10	3.86
51.80	20	7.72
77.70	30	11.58
103.60	40	15.44
129.50	50	19.31
259.00	100	38.61
647.50	250	96.53
1,294.99	500	193.05
2,589.99	1,000	386.10

CENTIMETRES^2 AND INCHES^2		
CM^2	NUMBER	IN^2
1.61	0.25	0.04
3.23	0.5	0.08
4.84	0.75	0.12
6.45	1	0.16
12.90	2	0.31
19.36	3	0.47
25.81	4	0.62
32.26	5	0.78
38.71	6	0.93
45.16	7	1.09
51.61	8	1.24
58.06	9	1.40
64.52	10	1.55
129.03	20	3.10
193.55	30	4.65
258.06	40	6.20
322.58	50	7.75
645.16	100	15.50

CENTIMETRES³ AND INCHES³

CM³	NUMBER	IN³
16.39	1	0.06
32.77	2	0.12
49.16	3	0.18
65.55	4	0.24
81.94	5	0.31
98.32	6	0.37
114.71	7	0.43
131.10	8	0.49
147.48	9	0.55
163.87	10	0.61
819.35	50	3.05
1,638.71	100	6.10
16,387.06	1,000	61.02

LITRES AND GALLONS

LITRES	NUMBER	GALLONS
4.55	1	0.22
9.09	2	0.44
13.64	3	0.66
18.18	4	0.88
22.73	5	1.10
27.28	6	1.32
31.82	7	1.54
36.37	8	1.76
40.91	9	1.98
45.46	10	2.20
227.30	50	11.00
454.60	100	22.00
4,546.00	1,000	220.00

KILOGRAMS AND POUNDS

KG	NUMBER	LB
0.45	1	2.21
0.91	2	4.41
1.36	3	6.61
1.81	4	8.82
2.27	5	11.02
2.72	6	13.23
3.18	7	15.43
3.63	8	17.64
4.08	9	19.84
4.54	10	22.05
22.68	50	110.23
45.36	100	220.46
453.59	1,000	2,204.62

MILLILITRES AND FLUID OUNCES

ML	NUMBER	FL OZ
30	1	—
57	2	1/16
85	3	—
114	4	1/8
142	5	
170	6	3/16
199	7	—
227	8	1/4
256	9	—
284	10	5/16
852	30	1
1,420	50	1 1/2
2,840	100	3 1/8

GRAMS AND OUNCES

GRAMS	NUMBER	OUNCES
28.35	1	—
56.70	2	1/16
85.05	3	—
113.40	4	1/8
141.75	5	3/16
170.10	6	—
198.45	7	1/4
226.80	8	—
255.15	9	5/16
283.50	10	3/8
425.24	15	1/2
566.99	20	3/4
850.49	30	1
1,417.48	50	2
2,834.95	100	4

°CENTIGRADE AND °FAHRENHEIT

°C	NUMBER	°F
−23.3	−10	14
−20.6	−5	23
−17.8	0	32
−15.0	5	41
−12.2	10	50
−9.4	15	59
−6.7	20	68
−1.1	30	86
4.4	40	104
10.0	50	122
15.6	60	140
21.1	70	158
26.7	80	176
32.2	90	194
37.8	100	212

INDEX

A

accessories, grouping, 79
accidents, coping with, 99
accidents, preventing:
  with children, 84–85
  with filing cabinets, 69
  in home, 47
address, changing, 118, 119
air travel, preparing for, 108
airing:
  beds, 29
  laundry, 36
  new home, 127
alarms:
  making when camping, 116
  installing, 88
  see also burglar alarms
alcohol, avoiding, 112, 113
  during travel, 108, 110
aluminium foil:
  oven-cooking in, 61
  wrapping food in,
    57, 58, 106
animals:
  avoiding on holiday, 115
  treating bites, 117
  see also pets
answerphones, using, 46
appliances:
  buying for special needs, 88
  keeping manuals, 34, 118
  maintaining, 44, 45, 49
  moving, 118, 122
appointments:
  confirming business, 71
  making medical, 89
aprons, making pockets, 29
aromatherapy, practising, 81
assaults, coping with, 98
audio equipment:
  moving, 119, 123
  protecting, 16, 47

B

babies:
  collecting equipment for, 82
  feeding, 83
  packing travel kit for, 106
  planning time with, 83

baby monitors, using, 83, 84
babysitters, briefing, 86
bananas, preserving, 57
banks:
  cancelling credit cards, 98
  checking statements, 77
  depositing documents, 69, 77
  keeping records, 76, 77
baptisms, organizing, 97
barbecues, cooking on, 65
baseball caps, adapting, 112
basins:
  checking, 44
  storing under, 14
  using steps for children, 84
bathing:
  drawing up rotas, 129
  planning for babies, 83
bathrooms, 10, 14
  children using, 84
  cleaning, 29, 32
baths:
  cleaning, 29, 129
  fitting handles above, 88
  fixing shelves by, 14
beach holiday, taking
  equipment, 107
beakers, 65
  adapting, 111
bedding:
  buying for special needs, 87
  storing, 26
bed-heads, making, 15
bedrooms, 10
  cleaning, 30, 32
  planning, 15
  saving space, 15
beds:
  airing, 29, 30
  buying, 15
  changing, 30
  providing extra, 15
  storing under, 22
  using table in, 15
bedside lights, positioning, 15
bedside tables, creating, 15
bicycles:
  maintaining, 95
  preventing theft, 95
  storing, 23

bills, dividing, 129
birds, pet:
  buying and keeping, 93
  leaving with others, 103
biscuit mixture, freezing, 58
blades, protecting, 21, 27
blankets, storing, 26
blenders, using, 49
blinds:
  cleaning, 31
  maintaining, 43
blisters, treating, 115
boat, travelling by, 110
book cases, moving, 122
book-keeping, 77
books:
  dusting, 128
  making into mini-safes, 47
  packing, 123
  storing, 25, 67
bookshelves:
  cleaning, 34
  preventing mildew on, 25
boots, trying on, 113
bottles:
  baby's, sterilizing, 83
  corking, 49
  opening, 87
  storing, 21
bottling soft fruits, 56
boxes:
  fitting wheels on, 22
  preparing for moving, 124
  storing files in, 76
  using as steps, 84
bread:
  defrosting, 49
  part-cooking, 61
breadcrumbs, making, 49
breakfast table, laying, 27, 62
brush carrier, making, 30
brushes, household, 29, 30
bubble wrap, 120
  making kneeling board, 88
  using for relaxation, 81
  wrapping items, 26, 121
budgeting, 77
  for holidays, 102, 110
  in shared home, 129
  for weddings, 96

buggies, choosing, 85
bulk buying, 68
burglar alarms, 46
    checking, 45
    setting before travel, 102
burglaries, coping with, 98
business cards, filing, 77

C

cakes, storing, 54
calculators, using in shops, 53
camp beds, keeping, 15
camping:
    preventing problems, 116
    taking equipment, 107
can openers, using electric, 49
cans:
    checking for safety, 54
    storing, 54, 55
    using to hide jewellery, 24
cars, 94
    checking, 94
    insuring, 86
    keeping data for, 76
    keeping emergency kit
        in, 109
    loading, 103, 125
    loading roof rack, 109, 123
    maintaining, 94
    making sunshield for, 112
    protecting children in, 85
    securing against assault, 98
    servicing, 119
    travelling by, 109, 111
carers:
    finding for children, 86
    finding for pets, 92, 103
carpets:
    deodorizing, 34
    insulating, 11
    removing dents from, 16
    shampooing, 31
carpet tiles, using, 41
carrycots, using in car, 85
carving knives, using
        electric, 49
cash:
    avoiding theft, 98
    moving home, 119
    preparing for travel, 101, 116
    storing, 69
casseroles, 59
cats:
    caring for, 92
    leaving with others, 103
    moving, 126

ceilings:
    cleaning, 34
    hanging items from, 12, 22
celebrations, planning, 97
celery, drying, 56
central heating, checking, 45
cereals, storing, 55
chair pouches, making, 88
chandeliers, washing, 31
chemicals:
    avoiding ill effects, 37, 68
    storing safely, 84
    using in garden, 65
childcare, 86
    and moving home, 118
    organizing on holiday, 111
childminders, finding, 86
children, 9, 82–86
    holding parties for, 63
    involving in tasks, 33, 53
    keeping safe, 84–85
    and moving home, 126
    packing for, 106
    planning celebrations for, 97
    sharing a bedroom, 19
    and shopping, 52, 53
    taking to doctor, 89
    travelling with, 111
    visiting in hospital, 90
china, dusting, 30
chocolate, freezing, 58
chopping boards, 50
    choosing, 48
    cleaning, 51
cleaning, 29–34
    cleaning office items, 68
    creating family roster, 33
    dividing tasks, 129
    doing monthly tasks, 30
    doing occasional tasks, 31
    doing weekly tasks, 30
    making log, 9, 34
    when moving home,
        120, 127
    organizing full clean, 31
    organizing help with, 33
    planning quick clean, 32
    setting up daily routine, 29
    working efficiently, 29
cleaning equipment, 28
    cleaning after use, 29
    collecting before move, 124
    making up kits, 9, 27
    packing for journeys, 106
    renewing, 52
    storing, 12, 29, 68

clothes:
    assembling for babies, 82
    buying, 79
    choosing basics, 79
    choosing for toddlers, 83
    colour-coordinating, 79
    dressing for cold
        climates, 113
    dressing for medical
        appointments, 89
    dressing for safety, 98, 116
    dressing for shopping, 52
    embellishing, 79
    ordering for weddings,
        96, 97
    organizing for next day, 79
    packing for journeys, 106
    packing for a move, 122
    storing, 19, 21, 26
clothes lines, fitting
        indoors, 36
coach travel, planning, 108
coat hangers:
    colour-coding, 19
    labelling, 79
    securing items on, 122
coats:
    altering sleeves, 79
    attaching reflective
        shapes to, 85
    hanging, 17, 79
coffee percolators, using, 49
colanders, choosing, 48
cold climates, coping with, 113
collars, laundering, 35, 36
colour-coding:
    coat hangers, 19
    files, 76
    room contents, 124, 128
    taps, 87
communicating, 74
compact disc racks, making, 23
complaints, making written, 74
computers:
    filing on, 76
    keeping clean, 68
    packing, 121, 123
    protecting, 69
    tidying disks for, 76
condiments, storing, 55
containers:
    making for hanging files, 76
    saving for a move, 121
    taking for shopping, 53
    using for food storage, 49
    using for frozen foods, 58

cooked foods:
 freezing, 58
 refrigerating, 57
cookers:
 ensuring child safety, 84
 testing, 127
cooking, *see* preparing food
cooking tins, grouping, 12
cookware:
 choosing, 48
 storing, 50–51
correspondence:
 including in work log, 73
 organizing, 74
corridors, planning, 17
credit cards:
 cancelling, 98
 destroying, 77
 photocopying, 69
 recording data from, 77
 travelling with, 101
crises, 98–99
 handling on holiday, 116
crockery:
 organizing, 12
 packing, 121
 washing up, 32
cup hooks:
 fitting in cupboards, 13
 hanging necklaces on, 24
cupboards, 18
 arranging food in, 55
 cleaning, 31
 packing, 122
 sharing space in, 129
 using in kitchens, 13, 18
curriculum vitae, setting out information, 75
curtains:
 cleaning, 31
 hanging, 127
 improvising, 128
 maintaining, 43
cushions, using in bed, 15
cutlery, draining, 50

D

damp, preventing, 44
data:
 preserving, 76
 protecting, 69, 77
 storing, 77
death, coping with, 99
decorating, 37–42
 choosing equipment, 37
 estimating quantities, 39

making log, 9, 38
planning, 37
preparing for, 39–40
scheduling, 41
deep breathing, 81
dehydration:
 avoiding during air travel, 108
 preventing in heat, 112
delegating, 73
delicate fabrics, laundering, 35, 36
dental records, including in family health log, 91
desks, using in offices, 66, 67
 tidying drawers, 8, 68
desk lamps, using, 70
desk tidies, making, 68
diarrhoea, avoiding, 115
dining areas, planning, 10, 16
dining chairs, stacking, 16
dining tables, making, 16
dinner parties, planning, 62
disease:
 avoiding psittacosis, 93
 planning immunization schedules, 102
dishwashers, using, 32
doctors:
 obtaining death certificates from, 99
 visiting, 89
documents:
 arranging for travel, 101, 103
 arranging for weddings, 97
 carrying during a move, 119
 depositing in banks, 69, 77
 laying out information in, 75
 organizing for deceased, 99
 protecting, 69
 storing copies of, 77
dogs:
 caring for, 92
 leaving with others, 103
 moving, 126
doors:
 checking, 45
 cleaning, 31
 cupboard, utilizing, 13
 fitting door stop, 84
 fitting shelves over, 22
 freeing, 43
 glass, making safe, 47
 kitchen, using, 55
 locking, 84
 making secure, 46

oiling metal parts, 43
protecting handles, 40
using door chains, 46
wardrobe, utilizing, 19
double glazing, 11
down pipes, checking, 44, 45
drainage racks, using for vegetables, 50
draining boards, protecting from rust, 50
drains:
 checking, 45
 covering, 85
 keeping clear, 44
 unblocking, 44
draughts, blocking out, 11
drawers, 21
 lining, 21
 making dividers, 21
 making safety stops, 21
 standing in wardrobe, 15
 using as work surfaces, 13
 waxing runners, 21
 wrapping for a move, 122
dresses, *see* clothes
dress rails, using, 17
dressing-tables, lighting, 15
dried foods, storing, 49, 54
drinks:
 buying for weddings, 96, 97
 cooling in wheelbarrow, 65
 hot, whisking, 49
 packing for picnics, 64
 packing for travel, 106, 111
 storing, 55
 taking in cold climates, 113
 taking in hot climates, 112
drinks cabinets, creating, 16
driving, in snow, 113
dry shampoo, improvising, 80
drying:
 babies, 83
 celery, 56
 herbs, 56
 laundry, 36
dusting, 30, 32
 china, 30
 keyboards, 68
 lampshades, 120
 light bulbs, 30
 mouse mats, 68
 using old socks, 88
duvets, cleaning, 35
duvet covers:
 choosing, 87
 fitting, 30

E

earrings, tidying, 24
electric blankets, using, 88
electrics:
    checking, 44, 45
    cleaning fittings, 30
    siting in home offices, 66
    testing in new home, 127
    using in bathrooms, 14
    using in garages and
      sheds, 22
    using in hobby rooms, 17
    using time switches, 98, 102
    see also appliances
engagements, including in
    work log, 73
entertaining, *see* parties
entertainment, planning for
    children, 63
equipment, choosing for:
    babies, 82
    car, 109
    child safety, 84
    cleaning, 28
    decorating, 37
    holidays, 107
    home offices, 68
    laundering clothes, 28
    maintaining bicycle, 95
    maintaining home, 43
    moving home, 121
    personal grooming, 80
    preparing food, 48
    special needs, 87
    travel, 100
everyday items, organizing, 27
exercising, 70, 81
    hands, 87
    on journey, 108, 110
eye masks, making, 108
eyes, relaxing, 70

F

fabrics, softening, 35
face:
    massaging, 81
    refreshing, 80
    relaxing, 70
family roster, creating, 33
fancy dress, choosing, 64
fax machine, siting, 69
faxes:
    filing, 74
    writing, 74
festive lights, packing, 26

filing, 76
    boxes, making, 76
    business cards, 77
filing cabinets, 66
    protecting, 69
filing trays, 67
film, storing, 24
finances, managing, 77
    in shared home, 129
fires:
    checking equipment for, 45
    making while camping, 116
    using guards, 84
fire escapes:
    indicating, 47
    keeping clear, 17
fireplaces, putting
    cupboards in, 18
first aid, 99, 117
    maintaining kit, 43
fish (food):
    freezing, 58
    microwaving, 61
    refrigerating, 57
    storing, 59
fish (pets), 93
    transporting, 126
flannels, laundering, 80
flatmates, finding, 129
flexes:
    checking, 44, 69
    choosing for safety, 84
    tidying, 17
floor plans, using, 11, 118, 124
floorboards, treating, 41
flooring:
    choosing for safety, 84, 88
    estimating quantities, 39
    fitting in bathroom, 14, 47
    preparing to lay, 41
floors:
    checking, 45
    cleaning, 32, 34
    protecting, 37, 40, 128
    testing, 127
floppy disks, arranging, 76, 77
flour, storing, 55
flowers:
    arranging in advance, 62
    ordering for wedding, 97
food:
    chilling, 57–59
    choosing containers, 49
    choosing on holiday, 115
    freezing, 58, 60
    keeping essential items, 54

keeping supplies for
    emergencies, 55
making for parties, 63, 64
ordering for weddings, 97
organizing in shared
    home, 129
packing for journeys, 106
planning for family
    celebrations, 97
planning for pets, 92
preserving, 56
protecting from animals, 115
refrigerating, 57
shopping for, 52
storing 54–55
using economically, 60
food mixers, using, 49
food poisoning, avoiding, 61
food processors, using, 49
foreign currency, ordering, 101
fragile objects:
    cleaning, 30
    moving home, 119
    packing, 121
    positioning, 27
freezers:
    defrosting, 59
    emptying, 118
    maintaining, 59
    stocking, 59, 90
    storing food in, 59
frozen foods, transporting, 52
fruits:
    bottling, 56
    buying, 53
    choosing for cooking, 60
    freezing, 58
    making into lantern, 64
    packing for journey, 106
    selecting on holiday, 115
    storing, 54, 55
    straining, 56
fruit drinks, making in
    advance, 64
funerals, organizing, 99
furniture, 37, 38
    cleaning, 31
    maintaining, 43
    moving upstairs, 128
    packing, 122, 124
    positioning, 11
    protecting, 37
    putting in new home, 118
    showing on floor plans, 11
    siting in home offices, 66
futons, using, 15

G

games, planning for
    parties, 63
garages, storing in, 22
gardens:
    making safe, 85, 127
    preparing for parties, 65
gateaux, slicing, 49
glasses:
    decorating, 63
    packing, 121
    storing, 26
    washing, 30, 32
glaze, disposing of, 42
gloves:
    protecting hands
      during move, 128
    using rubber, 28, 32
grains, storing, 55
grief, coping with, 99
gripper strips, laying, 41
grooming, organizing, 80
group holidays, planning, 110
grout, cleaning, 50
guests:
    entertaining, 62–63
    inviting to wedding, 96, 97
gutters, checking, 44, 45

H

hair conditioner, creating, 80
hairbrushes, cleaning, 80
hallways, planning, 17
halogen spotlights, using, 88
hand luggage:
    collecting items for, 100
    using, 104, 108
handles:
    door, protecting, 40
    fitting on walls, 88
hand-washing, 35
hanging files, 66
    making containers for, 76
hanging frames, 12
hanging rails, using, 51
hard drives, organizing, 76
hats:
    choosing for cold, 113
    choosing for sun, 112
    storing, 26
health:
    making log, 91
    protecting on holiday, 115
heat, dealing with, 112
heat stroke, treating, 117

help:
    finding for children's
      parties, 63
    having in bereavement, 99
    having from children,
      32, 33, 53
    organizing domestic, 33
    organizing for move, 119
herbal tea, taking, 112
herbs:
    drying, 56
    freezing, 58
    storing dried, 54, 55
hobby rooms, planning, 17
holidays:
    occupying children, 111
    planning for groups, 110
    selecting equipment, 107
    see also travel
home:
    making safe, 47, 84, 127
    organizing help in, 33
    safeguarding before travel,
      102, 103
    sharing, 129
home maintenance, 43–45
    choosing equipment, 43
    inspecting new home, 119
    making checks, 44
    making log, 9, 45
home offices, 66–70
    creating under stairs, 17
    equipping, 68
    making comfortable, 70
    planning, 66
    protecting equipment, 69
    setting up, 67
hoses, tidying, 25
hospitals:
    staying in, 90, 91
    visiting patients, 90
house rules, setting, 129
household organizer,
    making, 8, 78
household, running, 78–99
house plants:
    discouraging pets from
      damaging, 92
    keeping in home
      offices, 70
    packing for move, 9, 123
    watering while away, 103
humidity:
    protecting books, 25
    protecting cakes, 54
    protecting tools, 27

hutches:
    moving, 126
    siting, 92
hygiene, ensuring in house 29
hypothermia, avoiding, 113

I

ice-cream:
    choosing on holiday, 115
    storing, 59
    wrapping, 58
ice cubes:
    avoiding on holiday, 115
    cooling drinks outdoors, 65
    cooling food, 57
identification:
    checking callers, 46
    keeping for computer, 69
    marking valuable items, 47
illnesses:
    recording in log, 91
    treating on holiday, 117
immunizations:
    recording in log, 91
    for travel, 102
infections, avoiding, 115
information, arranging in
    documents, 75
injuries, dealing with, 99, 117
insects:
    repellent, using, 65, 115
    stings, treating, 117
insulation:
    checking, 127
    fitting, 11
insuring:
    against burglaries, 98
    audio equipment, 23
    cars, 86
    cleaners, 33
    jewellery, 24
    keeping records, 77
    for moving home, 118, 119
    for travel, 101
inventories, making,
    118, 120
invoices, setting out, 75
ironing, 36

J

jars:
    handling, 56
    opening, 87
    sterilizing, 56
jellyfish stings, treating, 117
jet lag, avoiding, 108

jewellery:
  moving, 119
  packing, 121
  storing, 19, 24
  travelling, 116
journeys, *see* travel

K

kennels, leaving pets in, 103, 126
kettles, choosing, 87
keyboards, cleaning, 68
keys, hanging, 46
kitchens:
  cleaning, 29, 32
  filling niches in, 22
  organizing in new home, 128
  planning, 10, 12–13
  using cupboards, 13, 18
kitchen utensils, 48
  storing 51
  using for special needs, 88
knee protectors, making, 88
knife blocks, using, 51
knife rolls, making, 8, 51

L

labelling:
  child's possessions, 83
  coat hangers, 79
  drawers, 21
  files, 76
  first-aid kit, 43
  floppy disks, 76
  frozen foods, 58, 59
  herbs, 56
  linen cupboards, 18
  luggage, 102
  medicine bottles, 89
  for moving, 118, 124, 128
  pre-printing labels, 72
  preserves, 56
  as reminders, 87
  shelves, 20, 76
  video tapes, 23
ladders, securing, 23
lampshades, dusting, 120
lanterns:
  choosing for camping, 116
  making from fruits, 64
lap-top computers, protecting, 69
laundry, organizing, 35–36
  assembling holiday kit, 106
  choosing equipment, 28

hanging out, 33
preparing for a move, 118, 122
preparing for storage, 31
lawnmowers, packing, 123
lawyers:
  depositing data with, 77
  taking legal advice, 129
laying out:
  rooms, *see* room layout
  text, 74
leather bags, storing, 36
leftovers, using, 60
legs, padding fractures, 99
leisure time, scheduling, 70
letters:
  drafting, 74
  setting out, 74, 75
  storing, 76
  writing to complain, 74
lids, tidying, 50
lifting, 29, 125
light bulbs:
  dusting, 30
  using daylight bulbs, 66
lighting:
  bedroom, 15
  home office, 66, 70
  outdoor, 65
  for special needs, 88
  using time switches, 98, 102
linen cupboards, tidying, 18
lipsticks, using up, 80
lists, making:
  of freezer contents, 59
  for insurance, 23
  of luggage contents, 105
  of tasks for move, 119, 120
  for shopping, 52
  of wedding presents, 96, 97
  of wedding tasks, 96
litter, collecting in car, 109
live-in childcare, finding, 86
living areas, planning, 10, 16
  laying out, 11
locks, 46
  adding to luggage, 105
  changing, 98
  lubricating, 43
  preventing burglary, 98
  using on filing cabinet, 69
lodgers, finding, 129
lofts, checking, 45
logs, making:
  for cleaning, 9, 34
  for decorating, 9, 38

for dinner parties, 62
for family health, 9, 91
for maintaining home, 9, 45
for telephone calls, 129
for work, 9, 73
loose covers, cleaning, 31
luggage:
  checking on journeys, 108
  choosing, 104
  labelling, 102
  loading in cars, 103
  loading on motorcycles, 94
  loading on roof racks, 109
  making secure, 105
  marking, 105
  packing, 100, 105–106
lunch, having at work, 70

M

magazine racks, using, 16
maps:
  buying on car journeys, 109
  giving to wedding guests, 96
  protecting, 101
massaging face, 81
mattresses:
  cleaning, 30
  turning, 30
  using as spare beds, 15
meat:
  avoiding part-cooked, 61
  choosing on holiday, 115
  freezing, 58
  refrigerating, 57
medical care, 89–91
  seeking after assaults, 98
medical packs, 114
  taking to doctor, 89
medications:
  protecting labels, 89
  storing, 84
  taking to hospital, 90
  taking for travel, 100, 103
medicine kit, keeping in home, 89
meditation, practising, 81
meetings, planning, 71, 73
memo boards, making, 67
memory, aiding, 87
menu planning:
  for dinner parties, 62
  for economy, 60
messages, taking, 74
metal:
  cleaning, 30
  storing, 27, 30

meters, having read, 118, 119
microwaves:
    cooking in, 61
    sterilizing jars in, 56
    wall-mounting, 13
mildew, preventing, 25
mince, cooking in bulk, 60
mirrors:
    siting in bedrooms, 19
    wrapping for move, 122
mixing bowls, grouping, 12
mobile telephones,
        keeping, 69
moisturizer:
    applying, 80
    making, 80
morale, boosting, 70
mosquito nets, making, 114
moths, deterring, 26
motorcycles:
    checking, 94
    positioning luggage, 94
mould, inhibiting growth
    of, 54
mouse mats, cleaning, 68
moving home, 118–129
    caring for children
        and pets, 126
    carrying essentials, 125
    moving into new home, 127
    preparing for, 118–119
    sorting and packing, 120–124
    using floor plan, 11, 124
muesli, mixing, 49
mugging, dealing with, 98
music, listening to, 70, 81

N
nail varnish:
    keeping, 80
    marking taps with, 87
necklaces, storing, 24
neighbours, briefing before
    travel, 102
newspapers, using, 120
    as carpet underlay, 11
    to clean windows, 128
    to protect floor, 37, 128
    to wrap fragile items, 121
nylon tights, washing, 35

O
odours:
    controlling in oven, 61
    dispelling in refrigerator,
        57, 102
neutralizing for mice, 92
removing from food
    processor, 49
offices, see home offices
oil:
    flavouring, 56
    storing olive, 55
    using for massage, 81
ornaments:
    packing, 121, 122
    positioning, 27
    washing, 128
ovens, using efficiently, 61

P
packaging materials, 120
packing:
    for holiday, 105–107
    for a move, 118, 121–124
paint brushes:
    cleaning and drying, 42
    storing, 42
paint cans:
    packing, 123
    storing, 42
paint pads, storing, 42
paint rollers, cleaning, 42
paint stripper, applying, 40
painting:
    estimating quantities, 39
    lining containers, 40
    preparing for, 40
    protecting yourself, 40
    scheduling, 41
paintwork, cleaning, 31, 34
pan scourers, keeping, 50
pancakes, pre-cooking, 60
paper, recycling, 68
parties, 62–65
    arranging for teenagers, 63
    devising themed, 64
    dinner, planning, 62
    hanging coats during, 17
    organizing for children, 63
    outdoor, planning, 65
passports, preparing, 101
pasta, storing, 55
pastry:
    freezing, 60
    part-cooking, 61
personal alarms, using, 88
personal care,
    organizing, 79–81
pets, 9
    arranging holiday care, 103
    cleaning food dishes, 29
keeping data on, 76
moving home with, 118, 126
planning care for, 92–93
storing canned food, 54
travelling with, 103
photographs, sorting, 24
picnics, 64
    taking equipment, 23
pie charts, making, 72
pin boards, making, 67
pipes:
    checking, 45
    fixing leaks, 44
    insulating, 44
pizzas, making for children, 63
plan chests, storing in, 21, 66
planners, using in offices, 67
planning:
    cleaning, 34
    dinner parties, 62
    family celebrations, 97
    funerals, 99
    moving home, 118–119
    personal grooming, 80
    shopping, 52
    telephone use, 74
    time with babies, 83
    travel, 100–117
    weddings, 96–97
    work, 71
plants:
    dealing with poisonous,
        65, 127
    deterring burglars, 46
plaster, repairing, 39
plates, packing, 121
play areas, surfacing, 85
play-houses, making, 63
plumbing, 14
    preventing emergencies, 44
police, contacting, 98
    during holiday, 116
portable cribs, using, 82, 83
potatoes:
    baking, 61
    roasting, 61
    storing, 54
poultry:
    storing, 57, 59
    wrapping, 58
pre-cooking food, 60
preparing food, 48–65
    barbecuing, 65
    choosing equipment, 48–49
    making in bulk, 60
    planning, 60

pre-printing:
    invoice forms, 75
    labels, 72
preserving and chilling
    food, 56–59
pressure bands, making, 110
progressive relaxation,
    practising, 81
puppet theatres, making, 63
puppies, soothing, 92

R

radiators:
    fixing shelf over, 11
    maintaining, 44, 45
receipts, filing, 77
recesses, storing in, 18, 19
recipes:
    making book holders for, 13
    putting inside cupboard
        doors, 13
    typing, 88
records, keeping, 76–77
    of clothes sizes, 79
recycling:
    containers, 49
    paper, 68
    polythene bags, 128
reference numbers:
    marking on possessions, 47
    using on documents, 75
refrigerators, 57
    cleaning, 102
    storing food in, 54, 57
relaxing, 81
    eyes, at work, 70
remote areas:
    driving in, 109
    visiting, 114–115
removal firms, using,
    118–120
repairing, 31, 45
    cars, 94
    clothes, before storing, 26
repetitive strain injury,
    avoiding, 70
reptiles, keeping, 93
rice, storing, 55
ring posts, making, 24
rodents, caring for, 92
    moving home with, 126
rollers, improvising, 123
roofs:
    checking, 44, 45
    insulating, 11
roof racks, loading, 109, 123

room layout, planning, 10
    for bathrooms, 14
    for home offices, 66, 67
    for kitchens, 12
    for living areas, 11
rooms:
    adapting, 88
    assessing, 127
    clearing, 124
    dividing, 20
    planning, 11–17
route planning, 109
routines, setting up, 8
    for babies, 83
    for childcare, 86
RSI, see repetitive strain injury
rucksacks, choosing, 104
rugs:
    packing, 123
    securing, 47, 88

S

safes, 69, 77, 101
    making mini, 24, 47
safety, ensuring:
    at home, 47, 84, 127
    before driving, 94
    for children, 84–85, 111
    for swimming, 106
    in remote areas, 114
safety deposit boxes, using, 77
safety gates, fitting, 84
safety goggles, using, 37
samples, collecting, 37, 38
saucepans, 48
    hot, protecting worktop, 50
    stacking, 12, 50
sauces, whisking, 49
savings, organizing, 77
saws, shielding teeth of, 123
scalds, preventing, 47
scent, storing, 80
scheduling, 8–9, 41, 71, 118
seals, checking:
    on freezer, 59
    on preserving jars, 49
seasickness, relieving, 110
seating:
    planning for dinner
        parties, 62
    providing in bathrooms, 14
    taking on picnics, 64
    using in showers, 88
security:
    arranging in home,
        46–47, 102

arranging for parties, 63
    ensuring personal, 98
    marking property, 47, 95
    protecting data, 77
    protecting luggage, 105
    protecting office items, 69
shared home, organizing 129
sharp objects:
    disposing of, 47
    storing, 21
sheet music, keeping, 25
shellfish, avoiding, 115
shelves, 20, 22
    adapting, 13
    building, 20
    cleaning, 31
    fitting in cupboards, 13
    fitting above doors, 22
    fitting in hallway, 17
    fitting in home offices, 67
    fitting above radiator, 11
    fitting above sink, 13
    labelling, 20, 76
    sharing, 129
    using glass, 22
    using space under, 67
    using to divide rooms, 20
shock, coping with, 99
shoe horns, adapting, 88
shoes:
    choosing for travel, 106, 115
    packing, 105
    storing, 19
shopping:
    buying clothes, 79
    buying household
        goods, 52–53
    packing goods, 53
    preparing for, 52
shopping lists, compiling, 52
    making holders for, 52
shoulder bags, choosing, 104
showers:
    checking, 45
    guarding valuables in, 116
    providing seating in, 88
silk, ironing, 36
sinks, cleaning, 34
skiing holiday, taking
    equipment for, 107
sleep, ensuring for baby, 83
sleeping bags, 23
    packing for moving, 122
small objects:
    packing, 124
    storing, 20, 21

smoke detectors, 47
  checking, 44
snake bites, treating, 117
snow, driving in, 113
soap, storing, 80
socks:
  packing for air travel, 108
  using as dusters, 88
  washing, 35
  wearing on holiday, 115
sofa-beds, using, 15
soft toys, tidying, 15
sorbets, making, 58
space blankets, carrying, 113
spare rooms, storing in 19
speakers, making stands
  for, 16
special events, planning,
  96–97
special needs, catering for,
  87–88
spices, storing, 55, 59
sports bags, choosing, 104
sports equipment, storing:
  on hallway shelves, 17
  in laundry baskets, 23
  seasonally, 26
sports, supervising, 111
spring cleaning, 31
spring onions, keeping, 54
stairs:
  carrying children on, 84
  fitting extra rails by, 88
  moving furniture up, 128
stationery:
  buying for offices, 67, 68
  organizing for weddings, 97
steam irons, cleaning, 36
steps, marking edges, 88
sterilizing:
  baby bottles, 83
  glass jars, 56
stock, making, 60
stopcocks, checking, 44, 45
  in new home, 118
storage containers, using, 49
storage spaces, cleaning, 128
storing, 18–27
  in bathrooms, 14
  in bedrooms, 15, 22
  books and papers, 25
  bulky items, 23
  in cupboards, 18
  data, 77
  in drawers, 21
  food, 54–55

frequently used items, 27
  in garages and sheds, 22
  in hobby rooms, 17
  in home offices, 66
  jewellery 24
  in kitchens, 12–13, 50
  in living rooms, 16
  long-term, 26
  while moving home, 118
  photographs and films, 24
  rarely used objects, 26
  on shelves, 20
  tools, 25, 27
  video tapes and music, 23
  in wardrobes, 19
strangers:
  dealing with, 46, 69, 74
  protecting children from, 85
stress, relieving, 70
structure, checking, 44
suitcases:
  choosing, 104
  marking, 105
  packing, 105, 111
  storing in, 26
sunburn:
  avoiding, 112
  soothing, 117
sunshield, making for car, 112
supermarket trolley, using, 53
surfacing:
  bathroom, 14
  play area, 85
swimming:
  avoiding sunburn, 112
  ensuring child safety, 111
  packing safety items, 106

T

table:
  covering corners, 84
  dining, improvising, 16
  laying in advance, 27, 62
  packing, 122
  using in bedroom, 15
tablets, pre-packing, 89
tantrums, coping with, 83
tape recorder, using, 120
taps:
  checking, 45
  fixing leaks, 127
  marking, 87
  stopping drips, 44
tasks:
  organizing in shared
    home, 129

prioritizing, 73
scheduling, 8, 27, 71, 96
timing, 31
teenagers:
  arranging parties, 63
  ensuring outdoor safety, 85
telephones:
  cleaning, 68
  keeping log, 129
  planning calls, 74
  positioning, 66
  protecting, 69
  staying on hold, 74
  using answerphones, 46
  using in emergencies, 85
temperature:
  of air, 70, 87
  of baby, monitoring, 83
  of body, reducing, 117
templates, making, 41
tension, relieving, 81
terrarium, keeping, 93
theft, preventing, 98
  on holiday, 116
tickets, booking for travel, 108
tidying up, 16, 29
  arranging help with, 32
  doing in shared home, 129
tiling, 41
  estimating quantities, 39
  washing tools, 42
time, managing, 8, 71–73
time switches, using, 98, 102
timetables, carrying, 108
toasters, cleaning, 49
toddlers, caring for, 83
toilets:
  checking, 44
  cleaning, 29
  fixing handles by, 88
  providing child steps, 84
  storing behind, 14
toiletries:
  choosing essentials, 80
  renewing, 27, 52
  storing, 14
tomato purée, making, 60
tools:
  adapting, 88
  hanging, 22, 27
  keeping for bicycles, 95
  keeping for cars, 94
  locking away, 65
  packing, 123
  storing, 25
  see also equipment

toothbrushes, cleaning
    with, 50, 51
towel rails, fixing inside
    wardrobe, 19
toys:
    choosing for pets, 92
    cleaning, 30
    keeping in bathrooms, 14
    keeping in living rooms, 16
    packing for travel, 109, 111
    soft, storing, 15
train, travelling by, 108
train sets, covering, 17
transport:
    arranging for weddings, 97
    ensuring safety, 85
    maintaining, 94–95
    see also travel, vehicles
travel, planning, 100–117
    arranging documents,
        101, 103
    with children, 106, 111
    choosing equipment, 100
    in cold climates, 113
    in groups, 110
    in hot climates, 112
    leaving pets and plants, 103
    making final checks, 103
    organizing money, 101
    packing, 104–107
    protecting health,
        102, 115, 117
    in remote areas, 114
    securing home before,
        102, 103
    taking emergency action, 116
    working and, 71
travel sickness, relieving, 108
    in car, 94
    seasickness, 110
travellers' cheques
    cashing, 101
    losing, 116
trivets, using, 50
trolleys, using in offices, 67
tubes, hanging, 42
tumble dryers, using, 36
typewriters, cleaning, 68

U

umbrella holders, making, 17
underlay, improvising, 11
underwear, 79
    packing for travel, 105
    wrapping ornaments in, 122
unpacking, 128

V

vacuum cleaning, mattress, 30
valuables:
    hiding under clothes, 98
    packing, 121
    protecting, 24, 47, 101
    safeguarding in home, 102
    see also jewellery
vegetable racks, 54
    using as filing trays, 67
    using to store items in
        hobby rooms, 17
    using to store toys in
        bathrooms, 14
vegetables:
    buying, 53
    choosing on holiday, 115
    freezing, 58
    making baby food with, 83
    packing for journeys, 106
    peeling, 50
    storing, 54, 55
    using imperfect, 60
vegetarian diets, 60
vehicles:
    loading, 125
    unloading, 128
    see also cars, motorcycles
ventilating rooms, 11, 17, 68
vessels:
    choosing, 48
    storing, 50
video tapes, storing, 23
visas, arranging, 101
visualization, practising, 81

WY

wall-mounting:
    microwaves, 13
    office equipment, 67
wallpaper, repairing, 43
wallpapering, 41
    estimating quantities, 39
    preparing for, 39
    scheduling, 41
    stripping, 39
    wiping tools, 42
walls, checking, 44, 45
wardrobes, 19
    arranging, 79
    moving, 122
    putting drawers in, 15
washing machines, using, 35
washing up, 32
    in shared home, 129

waste bins:
    cleaning, 29
    fixing in cupboard, 13
water, purifying, 116
water sprays, using, 112
water system, checking, 44, 45
    in new home, 127
water tanks, 118
    checking, 44
    insulating, 11
wedding anniversaries:
    choosing decorations for, 97
weddings, planning, 96–97
    countdown, 97
wheelbarrows:
    storing, 25
    using to hold drinks, 65
whisks, using hand, 49
wills, locating, 77, 99
windows:
    checking, 45
    cleaning, 34, 128
    fitting glass shelves, 22
    oiling metal parts, 43
    painting, 40
    securing, 46
    washing, 31
wine, saving, 59
wine racks, improvising, 22
wipes:
    making scented, 103
    using antiseptic, 115
woks, cleaning, 50
wood cleaner, making, 31
wooden utensils, caring for, 51
work:
    allocating time, 72
    communicating, 74–75
    keeping records, 76–77
    making pie charts, 72
    managing time, 71–73
    setting up a home
        office, 66–70
    structuring, 66–77
work log, making, 9, 73
work surfaces:
    organizing in home
        offices, 66, 67
    using in kitchens,
        13, 29, 50
workshops:
    adding work surfaces, 22
    tidying, 25
yoga, practising, 81
yoghurt, using to treat
    sunburn, 117

ACKNOWLEDGMENTS

AUTHOR'S ACKNOWLEDGMENTS

I should like to dedicate this book to my sister Vanessa who is
the most organized person I know. And, as always, I should like
to say thank you to my husband Michael Taylor who has put up
with a very unorganized household during the writing of this book.
Thanks also to my editor Katie John who has been consistently
more organized than I in keeping this book on track, and also to
art editor Ellen Woodward whose ideas have been very helpful.
I am also grateful for behind-the-scenes input from DK management
in the form of Krystyna Mayer, Stephanie Jackson, Nigel Duffield, and
Jayne Jones. The support given by the team has made my task very
much easier than it might otherwise have been.

PUBLISHER'S ACKNOWLEDGMENTS

Dorling Kindersley would like to thank the following:

Consultancy Age Concern England (special needs), and Kidscape
(child safety). The first aid information was validated by
the British Red Cross on 12 May 1997.

Prop loan Homecare Equipment Hire (equipment for
special needs); Moss Bros Group Plc (shoes);
Mothercare (baby clothing and equipment); and the
Youth Hostel Association (equipment for travel and skiing).

Editorial and design assistance Jude Garlick, Sasha Heseltine,
and Emma Lawson for editorial assistance; Austin Barlow
and Rachel Symons for design assistance; Dr Sue Davidson for
checking immunizations chart and health log; Chris Bernstein
for the index; and Debbi Scholes for proofreading.

Artworks by Kuo Kang Chen and Halli Marie Verrinder,
apart from an additional artwork
by Simone End on page 19.

Models by Peter Griffiths.

Photographs by Andy Crawford and Steve Gorton.
Photographic assistant Gary Ombler.
Hand models Ade Bakare; Michelle Culham; Andy Faithful; Mun Fong;
Carl Gough; Nicola Hampel; Darren Hill; and Sara Watkins.